North Oxford

NORTH OXFORD

Tanis Hinchcliffe

1992
Yale University Press
New Haven & London

Frontispiece is a detail of plate 15, Bird's-eye view of Norham Manor, watercolour attributed to William Wilkinson, *c* 1860 (Bodleian Library)

Designed by Mary Carruthers
Set in Linotron Bembo by Excel Typesetters Co., Hong Kong
Printed and bound by Kwong Fat Offset Printing Co. Ltd, Hong Kong

Library of Congress Cataloging-in Publication Data

Hinchcliffe, Tanis, 1944–
　　North Oxford / Tanis Hinchcliffe.
　　　p.　cm.
　　Includes bibliographical references and index.
　　ISBN 0-300-05184-0 (cloth)
　　　1. Suburban homes—England—Oxford.　2. Architecture, Victorian—
　England—Oxford.　3. Oxford (England)—Buildings, structures, etc.
　I. Title.
MA7572.H56　1992　　　　　　　　　　　　　　　　91-51109
　942.5′74′009733—dc20　　　　　　　　　　　　　　　CIP

To the memory of my parents, Cecil Irving and Mary Ellen Hinchcliffe

CONTENTS

PICTURE CREDITS

The author and publisher are very grateful to the following for their help in providing illustrations:

The Bodleian Library, Oxford   15, frontispiece and jacket (MS Top, Gon. A. 22), 25 (Det. C541)
The British Library, London   35, 37–9, 42–5
Barry Capper   3, 10, 12, 16–19, 21–3, 26, 28–9, 32–3, 41, 46–8, 51, 53–7, 59, 61–3, 68, 70–3, 75–81, 83–6, 88, 90–6, 99
Local Studies Library, Oxford Central Library   1, 4, 6, 9, 20, 24, 34, 36, 40, 66, 87, 98
Geoffrey Randell   2, 13, 50, 52, 58, 67, 69, 74, 82
St John's College Muniments   5 (Studio Edmark) 7, 11, 14, 27, 49 (Studio Edmark), 64–5, 97 (Studio Edmark)

Other illustrations are in the author's collection.

PREFACE

IN THE EARLY decades of this century no epithet was bad enough for the suburb which was seen to encroach upon the countryside and drain away the vitality of the town. In Britain it took the wave of redevelopment after World War II to bring about the realisation that suburbs were vulnerable, especially those Victorian suburbs close to town centres. Too often these were regarded simply as places on the way to somewhere else and their street patterns were destroyed by the new roads built to serve the increase in traffic. At this point, the value of the suburbs began to be appreciated anew, and appreciation led to curiosity about their origins.

Serious interest in the suburb started with the large London estates and Sir John Summerson's work on Georgian London must be recognised as the pioneering study. This line of investigation has been ably continued by Donald J. Olsen in his study of the Bloomsbury estates and the Eton estate on the fringes of central London. Olsen has also worked on suburbs outside London, and David Cannadine has made a significant contribution by looking at the aristocratic estates in provincial towns.

Most suburban development during the nineteenth century took place on modest pockets of land and was undertaken by small-time developers and builders. All this remained obscure until H.J. Dyos led the way in his work on Camberwell which illuminated the building process at the opposite end of the market from the big estates. His story concerned the entrepreneurs who risked their own security to produce the suburbs which gave respectability to the middle classes. This fascination with the process of the production of the suburbs by the small builders has been chronicled for other parts of London in the recent volumes of *The Survey of London*. While not abandoning its commitment to the history of public buildings, *The Survey* has taken suburban development seriously in areas such as Notting Hill and South Kensington.

The study of the suburb in Britain has been enriched by the work which has appeared in America, such as Sam Bass Warner's *Streetcar Suburb*, now considered a classic analysis of nineteenth-century Boston. But American work has been conducted in the context of a theoretical debate about the social implications of the suburb. Historical studies now being undertaken seek to deal with the cultural meaning of the suburb and its didactic role. Both Gwendolyn Wright and John R. Stilgoe have extended what constitutes suburban history beyond the building process to questions about the significance of what was built, an approach still new in this country.

Most suburbs remain anonymous to all except those who live there, but a few have come to wider notice, thanks largely to the associations linked to the lives of past residents. Hampstead and Bedford Park in London, Clifton in Bristol, and Edgbaston in Birmingham are well known, and aspects of their histories have been written. North Oxford, because it has been the home of generations of very articulate academic families, has acquired a certain notoriety both in Britain and in America, but, despite being described by Cannadine as 'the most quintessentially Victorian of all England's suburbs', its history has not been written. The story of North Oxford is also the story of St John's College Oxford, the owners of the land on which the suburb was built, and it is through the initiative of the Fellows of the College that this history has been undertaken and through their support it has been completed.

In writing this book I have followed those historians mentioned above, and the many others who have laid down the agenda for urban history over recent years. I have sought to set the story of North Oxford within the context of the social and economic life of Oxford, but I have also tried to show how it related to contemporary developments in architecture and urban design. The physical fabric of North Oxford still bears witness to its origins and its development, but I hope I have never lost sight of the people who were responsible for its building and for its subsequent history. I have observed them when they were constrained by external circumstances and when they could act freely, and I have seen how their freedom made them vulnerable to financial and social ruin. I have watched them encumbered by tradition and yet expected to break the bonds to create a new mode of living in accordance with the model of middle-class family life emerging at the time. The contradictions inherent in the development of North Oxford have been at times a puzzle and at times a joy, sentiments I hope my readers will share.

I wish to thank the President and Fellows of St John's College Oxford for making this project possible by supporting me financially in my work for three and a half years. I also thank them for giving me free access to their well-ordered muniments on which much of this work is based. While working at St John's I have been greatly helped by Angela Williams, the assistant librarian, and by the College secretary, Mrs Thornton and her staff. I would also like to thank Dr Anthony Boyce for his help with my faltering moves towards devising a computer data base.

No research would be possible without the assistance of the libraries, and I wish to thank especially Malcolm Graham and his staff at the Local Studies Library, Oxford Central Library. I have also found helpful the staff of the Bodleian, particularly Colin Harris in the Modern Manuscripts Room, and I wish to thank the staffs of the London and British Libraries. As always I am indebted to the library of the Royal Institute of British Architects and I am grateful to Lynne Walker and the Library Group for giving me the opportunity of trying out some of my ideas on them.

I am greatly indebted to Christina and Howard Colvin, Dr Ross McKibbin, and Dr Malcolm Vale, who read my chapters as they were produced and saved me from many mistakes. Those errors which remain are, of course, my own responsibility. I have had discussions with many whose knowledge of North Oxford was greater than mine, and among those I would like to mention especially Ronald Barnes, Christina Colvin, Peter Howell, Harry Kidd, Andrew Saint, David Sturdy, Ann Spokes Symonds, Pamela and Ronald Symonds, and members of the Victorian Group of the Oxford Architectural and Historical Association. I have also enjoyed the hospitality in Oxford of Ann Laurence, Dorothy Rowe, Jeanne Sheehy, and Malcolm and Juliet Vale.

I am grateful to Barry Capper for his care in taking many of the photographs, and to Geoffrey Randell for his skill in redrawing the plans. And I would like to thank John Nicoll and Mary Carruthers at Yale University Press for their expert transformation of the manuscript into the book.

I would also like to acknowledge early debts to John Newman of the Courtauld Institute who, against his better judgment, encouraged my embarkation on the study of suburbs, and to Robert Thorne, without whose interest I may never have proceeded this far.

Finally, I would like to thank my husband, Richard Hill. It is traditional to say that without the help of one's spouse the work would never have been completed. I have come to realise the truth lying behind those words.

CHAPTER I
St John's College and its Property

NORTH OXFORD DOES not describe a vague geographical location in the northern region of the City of Oxford, but a specific area of residential suburb stretching from St Giles's Church in the south almost to Summertown in the north. Some would also include Summertown, but for the purpose of this study the boundary is taken to be the northern extent of the land formerly owned by St John's College. North Oxford displays those characteristics associated with the low density, nineteenth-century suburb and enjoyed by the middle classes in the second half of the century. The houses are for the most part large, detached or semi-detached villas, set in generous gardens, now well grown (Plate 1). The streets are broad and are so arranged that except for the two main roads leading north out of Oxford, they discourage through-traffic thus contributing to the seclusion and tranquillity of the neighbourhood. Although the general impression of the architectural style is neo-gothic or the more relaxed 'old English', many of the houses display that individuality of style associated with the wealthy middle-class suburb where the exigencies of speculation have not denied all possibility of choice. It could be said that North Oxford is an example of the mature type of nineteenth-century suburb as it had evolved by the end of the century.

But what is a leafy and spacious suburb like North Oxford doing within walking distance of the centre of the town? Usually the 'walking suburbs' of the towns and cities of England were formed at the end of the eighteenth and the beginning of the nineteenth centuries when a ring of terrace houses was built around the centre.[1] Describing Oxford as he remembered it in the early 1850s, the painter Burne-Jones testified to the absence of extensive suburbs around the city: 'It was a different Oxford in those days from anything that a visitor would now dream of. On all sides except where it touched the railway, the city ended abruptly, as if a wall had been about it, and you came suddenly upon meadows.'[2] Because those meadows remained innocent of houses during the first half of the century, there was no suburb of terraced streets to separate the city from North Oxford, most of which is within easy reach of the town by foot (Plate 2). An omnibus began to run in January 1860 between Oxford and Summertown, and early in 1882 a horse tram went into service up Banbury Road as far as St Margaret's Road.[3] But only those streets built at the north end of the suburb near Summertown needed

1 North Oxford, aerial view from the Radcliffe Observatory, 1907 (Local Studies Library, Oxford Central Library).

the assistance of omnibus or tram to make them readily accessible to the centre.

Another surprising characteristic of North Oxford is its extent and coherence. Some similar suburbs, because of a lack of sufficient land, give the impression that they are only a fragment of a larger, more complete development. Other suburbs though extensive, are formless, and lack a sense of place.[4] North Oxford, perhaps because it has the advantage of the physical boundaries to west and east of the canal and the River Cherwell, and is divided neatly up the middle by the Woodstock and Banbury Roads, has a definite sense of place as well as having enough room to be a complete suburb with a variety of house types and sizes.

Although changes have obviously taken place in the function of some of the houses and there has been a certain amount of new building, North Oxford retains its identity as much as does Bedford Park and Hampstead Garden Suburb in London. Despite covering such an extensive area and being so close to the centre of Oxford, two traits which make any suburb an easy prey to redevelopment, North Oxford has kept enough of its original streets, houses and gardens that no great stretch of the imagination is needed to recreate in the mind's eye what it must have looked like around 1914, by which time the greater part was built and beginning to mature. But besides

2 Map of Oxford (redrawn by Geoffrey Randell).

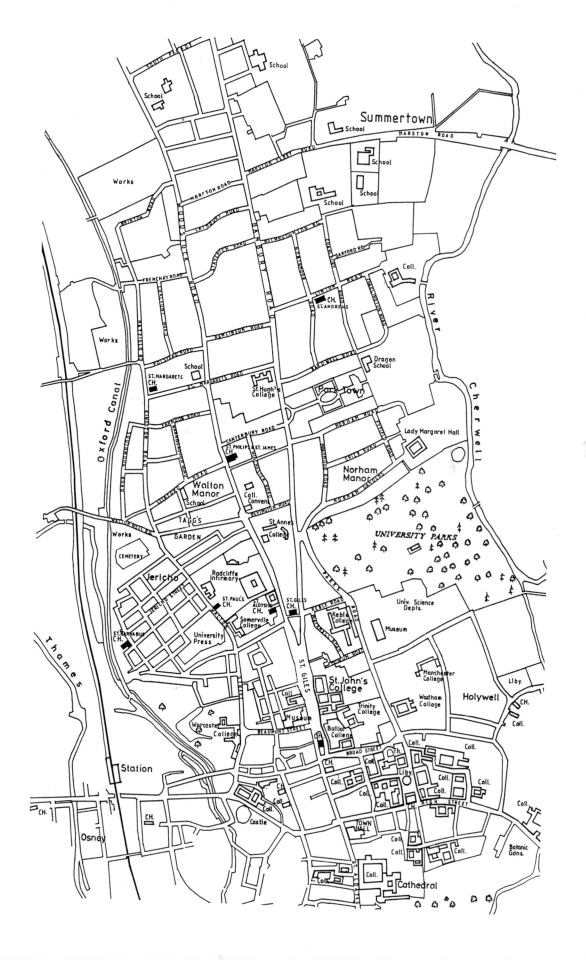

providing a welcome opportunity for observing the characteristics of the nineteenth-century suburb, North Oxford also raises questions about why Oxford did not follow the same pattern of development as did other towns during the nineteenth century.

One of the factors which decided when and where suburbs were built was the ownership of the land to be developed. As Donald J. Olsen has shown so well, the interests of the Duke of Bedford or Eton College determined when and how they developed their estates in Bloomsbury and Primrose Hill.[5] The original owner and developer of North Oxford was the College of St John the Baptist, and the College's decision to develop its land depended not just on the social and economic conditions of Oxford, but also very much on the sort of institution it was. Sometimes the decisions it made did not fit the existing market conditions and seemed to fly in the face of commercial common sense. As a corporate institution with well-established, long-term commitments it often found itself marching to a different tune from the entrepreneurs and joint stock companies. At the same time, the College gained a reputation, whether earned or not, for being a difficult landlord. Circumstances in the development of North Oxford which seem the result of chance become less puzzling when the needs and organisation of St John's are understood.

The College was founded during the sixteenth century for the purpose of preparing poor scholars for the Church and it depended for survival on the continued revenue it derived from its land. By its statutes the College was to support fifty fellows who were expected to take Holy Orders and accept a clerical living.[6] A royal edict of 1561 required that the fellows of all the Oxford and Cambridge colleges remain unmarried whether in Orders or not. Those fellows not yet graduated were called scholars and the graduate fellows, while awaiting their livings, tutored the junior members. The administration of the College rested in the hands of the more senior members under the guidance of the president. The communal life, an absense of luxury, and the emphasis on Holy Orders led to something approaching a monastic existence for the fellows. 'Commoners', or students not among those admitted under the founder's stipulations, could be accommodated on the payment of fees, but these fees made up only a small part of the College's income which came mostly from the revenue derived from its endowment.

The founder of St John's was Sir Thomas White, the son of a clothier and himself a prominent member of the Merchant Taylors' Company.[7] From 1523 when he was able to begin his own business with a £100 legacy, he advanced in the Merchant Taylors, becoming master in 1535. This success was followed by public office in 1544 when he was elected alderman of Cornhill in the City of London. White was an adherent of the old religion, and when Mary came to the throne in 1553, he served her well as Lord Mayor of London, especially when the city was threatened with Wyatt's rebellious attack early in 1554.

Perhaps conscious of the help given to him at the start of his own career, White established a loan fund to provide small amounts of capital for tradesmen in towns like Coventry and Bristol.[8] Such commercially based philanthropy was vital to ensure the continuation and growth of the nascent capital system. Another area of contemporary life where the philanthropist could have influence at this time was in education. Whereas most previous Oxford and Cambridge colleges had been founded by churchmen, White was one of the first of the merchant class to put his money into the foundation of a college. White received a licence from Queen Mary in May 1555 to found St John's in Oxford for 'the learning of the sciences of holy divinity, philosophy, and good arts'.[9] In 1554 he had bought from Christ Church the buildings of St Bernard's College, a former Cistercian house of study, closed in 1539 after the Dissolution of the Monasteries. He renamed his college after John the Baptist, patron of tailors and the Merchant Taylors' Company. Both his college and his loan fund depended on the only long-term investment then available, landed property.

There were two serious problems experienced by the young College. One was that founded in the reign of Mary and with orthodox sympathies, it lost some of its brightest members to the Catholics after Queen Elizabeth came to the throne.[10] The other problem was financial. White had intended the members of his college to live modestly as was suitable to their calling, but by the time of his death he had not been able to establish the finances on a stable footing, and the fellows experienced a degree of poverty not anticipated by the founder. Whether a college survived over the years seems to have depended on its founder guaranteeing its endowment,[11] and when White came to found St John's he took great care to establish an adequate endowment. In order to feed and clothe the fifty fellows allowed for under the statutes of the College, White purchased small manors around Oxford such as those of Long Wittenham, Warborough, Shillingford, Frilford, and Garford. Further land was bought in Northmoor and Cumnor along with various tithes. The income from these properties amounted to approximately £230 a year, whereas it was estimated that in order to run the College for the numbers proposed by the founder, £460 was needed.[12]

While White lived he was able to top up the income of the College although even this became difficult after his business declined from about 1562. At his death in 1567 it became evident that while his widow survived, the College would be poorly funded. An agreement was finally made with the widow's trustees whereby the College could have the £3,000 due to it under White's will and his London houses, thought to be worth another £3,000, as long as it allowed his widow during her lifetime the annual income earned from the capital. On her death in 1572 the College was able to claim the income for itself, and the position of the fellows began to improve from that date so that by the 1590s St John's had become well established.

White had wished that when the London property came to St John's, the College would sell it to buy land around Oxford. From 1571 until 1590 when the last of the London property was sold, the College continued to acquire land in the environs of Oxford, including 500 acres in Walton Manor, just to the north of the Oxford city wall and called St Giles's

Fields.[13] At the time of the Dissolution of the Monasteries, George Owen, physician to Henry VIII, had bought up a substantial amount of church property in north and west Oxford. In 1541 he acquired the manors of Wolvercote and Walton as well as the site of Rewley Abbey and Black Hall Farm. George Owen and his son Richard disposed of much of their holdings from 1549, and it was from Richard Owen that the College purchased St Giles's Fields for £1,566.13s.4d.in 1573, and the eventual site of the suburb of North Oxford became part of its endowment lands.

Although St John's relied upon the rents from its property for its income, it was not totally free to do as it pleased with that property. During the sixteenth century some members of the Church's hierarchy had sought to overcome the double evils of a reduced income and of inflation by leasing their lands on inordinately long leases for which they received a substantial cash payment called a fine.[14] This they kept for their own personal use. Because of the large fine the tenant would usually pay a very low, fixed rent for the term of the lease, and all those churchmen who came after could expect a poor income until the lease fell in, even if agricultural prices should rise. In order to protect the endowment lands of cathedrals and quasi-religious bodies like colleges from unscrupulous individuals, legislation was passed in 1576 and 1588 which prevented ecclesiastical institutions from leasing their lands on long leases and encouraged the use of so-called beneficial leases.[15]

Beneficial leases were short term, twenty years for land and forty for houses.[16] The principle was similar to the long lease in that at the commencement of the lease the tenant paid a lump sum or fine and then each year a nominal rent, usually in both money and kind. For example, a new forty-year lease was drawn up for one of St John's Oxford properties, Blackhall Farm Homestead, in October 1828. The fine was £500, but the annual rent was only £2 plus two bushels of wheat and twenty bushels of malt.[17] There were various ways of calculating the fine, one of which was to take a year and a half of the notional market value. If the landlord had received the fine only at the end of twenty or forty years when the lease fell in and another was negotiated, the income would not have been very great. In practice, however, the lease could be renewed, on land every seven years and on houses every fourteen, simply by paying another fine. This meant that the leases could be extended indefinitely, because each renewal was for the full length of the lease. After seven years, for example, the twenty-year lease on a piece of land could be renewed for a further twenty years from that date.

There were obvious drawbacks to the beneficial leasing system. The rents the landlord received were not as great as they would be if a rent based on the market were to be collected every year. This became more apparent during periods like the years of the Napoleonic Wars when inflation pushed up the market price of grain, but the surplus was being taken off only periodically and there was no guarantee that the landlord would benefit while the high prices obtained. The fines were also irregular, depending as they did on when the leases were first taken up, and there could be a considerable fluctuation from year to year in the income derived from fines. The money received from corn rents remained relatively constant over the period, but its proportion of the total income was reduced from 46.7 per cent in 1800 to 19 per cent in 1865. The value of the fines was less predictable, in some years contributing much more to the income of the College than in others as can be seen in the following table, derived from the College's *Computus Annuus*.

St John's College total income after land tax and percentage of fines, corn rents, and other sources of revenue[18]

	Total £	Fines %	Corn Rents %	Other %
1800	3,193	24.0	46.7	29.1
1805	4,442	24.8	38.0	37.0
1810	4,593	32.2	42.9	24.7
1815	6,784	59.4	24.2	16.2
1820	5,440	43.0	31.6	25.2
1825	6,224	31.6	33.0	35.2
1830	7,098	55.2	27.6	17.0
1835	5,263	33.8	34.5	31.6
1840	9,302	24.0	23.5	52.4
1845	6,586	32.7	33.2	35.4
1850	6,405	45.2	29.3	25.4
1855	7,128	27.4	29.5	42.9
1860	7,023	16.6	28.0	55.2
1865	9,516	17.0	19.0	63.8

The advantages of collecting each year the full economic rent, or rack-rent, were obvious to everyone, especially those outside the ecclesiastical institutions who wanted to see them run more commercially, and the growing proportion of St John's income after 1850 ascribed to 'other' sources was largely due to the gradual change from beneficial leases to rack renting.

Change was not so easy to bring about. Under a beneficial lease it was up to the tenant to maintain and repair the property. As long as the lease remained in the hands of one family often the bare minimum was done to improve the land and buildings. While competition in agriculture was at a low level, this would not matter over much, but with the repeal of the Corn Laws and the increased importation of grain from abroad, success depended much more on the quality of the land. Anyone willing to take a farm at rack rent would expect the property to be well drained and cleared, and buildings efficient and in good repair. To provide this after what might have been decades of neglect would require substantial expenditure on the part of the landlord. The other hindrance to changing from beneficial leases to rack renting was that the leases had to be allowed to run their course. If a college decided to regain possession of a leased property, it had to wait until the lease fell in. This would mean, depending on the type of property, twenty or forty years from the last renewal, and for that time the college would not receive any fines, only the very low annual rent. In order to facilitate the change, the government passed legislation to allow colleges to mortgage their property so that they could carry out improvements and supplement their income over the time the leases were running out.[19] Nonetheless, there was a great temptation to do nothing, and even in 1872 when a survey was made of the property held by the Oxford and Cambridge colleges, much of it was still let under beneficial leases. The opportunity to develop its suburban estate was a spur to St John's to discard the old system, and it must be said that in this it was not as conservative as some of the other colleges.

A change in the way the colleges leased their land was only one of the university reforms sought during the nineteenth century.[20] The growing pace of the country's economic activity was leading to the rise of different interest groups which up till then had been excluded from the older universities. The dissenting financier as much as the Anglican landowner wanted a university education for his son, but as the situation stood during the early decades of the nineteenth century that was not possible. Demand for reform focused on the perceived discrepancy between the power of the individual colleges and the relative weakness of the universities as institutions in their own right. In general the fellows of St John's were against change of any sort, especially if it interfered with their autonomy. When in 1837 the Earl of Radnor moved in the House of Lords that a commission be set up to enquire into the revenues and statutes of the colleges, the fellows promptly petitioned the Lords against the motion.[21] When a commission was finally set up in 1850, St John's along with most of the other colleges refused to make any formal submission. Despite the lack of co-operation the Oxford University Act was passed in 1854 by which the government appointed commissioners to assist the colleges in revising their statutes.[22]

The main point of contention between St John's and the commissioners was the question of closed fellowships. The College still adhered to the founder's statutes whereby its fellows were drawn from Merchant Taylors' School and schools in Tonbridge, Reading, Bristol and Coventry.[23] Although in the sixteenth century these schools had been charitable institutions intended for poor scholars – the 100 places at the Merchant Taylors' School being free – by the nineteenth century the boys were as likely to come from professional families as to be the sons of poor tradesmen.[24] Since many of the senior fellows had themselves gone to Merchant Taylors' there was a natural reluctance to weaken the College's ties with the school. They could also argue that although most of its boys were drawn from London and its environs, they were representative of the middle class that the reformers were seeking to get into the universities in greater numbers. Closed fellowships were, however, against the principle of a free trade in opportunity fostered by the reformers. Although St John's held out longer than all the other colleges, in the end it had to accept an imposed change to its statutes whereby it lost all its closed fellowships, but kept twenty-eight scholarships tied to Merchant Taylors' and the other schools.[25] The College would come to regret these scholarships when the agricultural recession eroded their income, for while other colleges could cut the number of their scholars according to their reduced circumstances, St John's had to continue its commitment.[26]

The Oxford University Act 1854 was the beginning, not the end of reform. Criticism now came from within the University where members, usually with liberal convictions, openly attacked the limitations of the 1854 legislation. Once more the problem centred around the strength of the colleges in relation to the universities. The argument ran that if the value of the colleges' fellowships were reduced and the number of professorships, especially in the new subjects like the natural sciences and modern history, were increased, the education offered at the university would be more effective and therefore more economical. Many people also believed that the time had come at last to loosen the hold of the Church and it was proposed that fellows need not necessarily take Holy Orders nor be celibate, and undergraduates need not subscribe to the 39 Articles of the Anglican Church. The Universities Act of 1877 gave the colleges the powers to change their statutes accordingly, and it also required them to give more generously to the newly set up professorships within the universities.[27]

In order to assess the amount of money they could expect the colleges to transfer to the universities, the government set up a Royal Commission in 1872 under the chairmanship of the Duke of Cleveland to gather information on the current revenues of the universities and the colleges. The report of this commission, submitted 31 July 1874, revealed the extent of the wealth of the colleges, and gave an insight into the management of their properties.[28] The report is particularly significant for the history of St John's North Oxford estate because it covers those years when their suburban development was just starting, and is a reminder that however important North Oxford became in terms of revenue, the rural estates were to remain significant for a very long time.

According to the returns sent into the commissioners by St John's, the College owned about 10,430 acres of land. Since the accounting system of the College changed about this time, it is not possible to make a direct comparison between the figures gleaned from the College's *Computus Annuus* given above and those found in the commissioners' report. However, it is clear that although the College was still receiving fines from the beneficial leases, the proportion of income they were getting from rack rents was growing.

St John's College income from corn rents, fines, and rack rents[29]

	Corn Rents	Fines	Rack Rents
1867	1,458	2,784	8,971
1868	1,298	2,020	9,168
1869	1,259	2,605	9,538
1870	1,180	7,151	10,280
1871	1,158	3,008	10,396

The bursar calculated that if in 1871 the College had received the rack rent for their land let on beneficial leases they would have enjoyed an extra £2,242, and £9,304 more if all their houses had been rack rented.[30]

The College had to undertake considerable work in order to entice lessees to take on the market rents after the beneficial leases fell in, and local people must have found great changes going on in those areas where the College owned land. In explaining an item for timber from the estates in Appleton, Fyfield, and Southmoor, the bursar wrote:

> The College has for many years been engaged in clearing its lands, formerly held under beneficial leases now expired, of all trees, bushes, and hedges, and has brought many hundreds of acres of useless land into profitable occupation. The timber mentioned before in this sheet forms a very large proportion of that sold, and no similar receipts can be derived from this source in future. Some of the coppices have been reserved to grow timber for repairs, and perhaps for sale, but all hedgerow timber has been cut down on arable lands.[31]

All this work had to be paid for initially by the College, and the extent of what had to be done is illustrated in this entry in the report for C.W. Edmonds's farm at Longworth:

> Farm formed on the expiration of various beneficial leases and the dropping of lives. The land was generally in a very bad state, and the buildings unfit for present occupation. In order to obtain a substantial tenant, the College covenanted to erect a good dwelling-house and a large set of farm buildings, and to remodel and repair the old buildings as far as practicable, as well as to drain the land and cut down all the copses and grub up many of the hedgerows. The expense of these improvements was upwards of 4,500*l*., which the College borrowed from the General Land Drainage Co., and pays for 31 years, for interest and principle, 6 per cent per annum. The operations have been entirely successful, and when the charge is paid off will be very profitable to the College.[32]

While this expenditure was being made on the College's estates, there was no slacking in their responsibilities as an Oxford college. Under the statutes of 1861 they had to provide for thirty-three scholars, and although the number of fellows had been reduced they had to wait for natural attrition, either through death or marriage, to bring their numbers down to twenty. As an educational institution, an upholder of the Anglican Church, and a landowner, the College also had a responsibility in the rural parishes where they held property to make donations to primary schooling and later, when the State took over education, to district nursing.

Given the task of turning beneficial leases into market rents, it is understandable that expenditure was outstripping income at this time. The bursar believed that the deficit would gradually right itself when the income from the rack-rented property began to compensate for the investment in improvement. But it would not have done to be too optimistic. The whole purpose of the commission was to give the government an idea of how much money they could expect the colleges to contribute to the universities in the future. To paint too glowing a picture of the health of the College's finances would only lead to a heavier commitment which might well become a burden. The bursar was quick to point out the uncertainty of the property market, especially in urban areas:

> ... it may happen that Oxford may cease to be a favorite place of residence, and then the value of the houses would fall, rapidly, or it may happen that houses may be erected on more eligible spots and then population now residing on the college property would pass there and a poorer class would occupy the present houses.[33]

In the event it was the rural property which suffered a profound drop in value during the agricultural depression of the 1880s, and upset the course of university reform.

From St John's report to the commissioners it can be seen that the College was a substantial landowner and by the time it began to develop its North Oxford estate it had embarked on an ambitious programme of land reclamation and rebuilding for its rural properties. Nor were all its fellows unworldly academics. Dr Adams, the bursar at the time of the Royal Commission, was a barrister and since 1866 Recorder of Birmingham. Still the development of a large residential suburb was not within their experience, nor had many other of the Oxford colleges had experience of developing extensive urban properties. Since 1776 Magdalen had owned land in Southwark which later became an important industrial area, and Queen's College had substantial property in Southampton.[34] In Oxford, most of the property within the city walls seemed to be owned by one college or another, but few colleges possessed blocks of land close enough to the city to develop them as a residential suburb. Christ Church had land in the western parish of St Thomas's, but this area was low lying and had already attracted the poor working class. Merton College owned property northeast of the city wall which they could have chosen to develop as a residential suburb, but they decided to sell most of this land to the University for the new science area and the University Parks. By 1860 only St John's was in position to develop a residential suburb which would appeal to the middle classes (Plate 3).

What St John's decided to do with its North Oxford property depended as much on the social life of Oxford as it did on its own needs. The testy relationship between the colleges and the city is legend, and the division between the two is summed up by the phrase 'town and gown'. The domestic economy of the colleges wove itself into every corner of the life of the city, and their peculiar character as corporate institutions, almost totally male except for the wives and daughters of the heads, affected the social life of the town in many different ways. At the same time as playing host to the University, Oxford had developed as a market centre for the surrounding rural area, providing the usual cattle, grain, and produce markets as well as the sorts of services required by farmers. But because of the college trade, there were also more shops dealing in luxury goods like wine and spirits, confectionary, tailoring, and fancy groceries, than might be expected in a

3 No 5 Norham Gardens, William Wilkinson, 1865.

market town.[35] The domestic life of the colleges required the services of a small army of people from butlers to washerwomen to keep them running smoothly, and it was their employment especially which posed a problem in the town. Although the upper servants could make a good living and formed a stable element in the lower middle class, for those at the bottom end of the scale the lengthy University vacations meant that work was seasonal and protracted periods of unemployment unavoidable. Many shops actually shut up during the long summer vacation and it is rumoured that grass grew in the streets.

Depression in the countryside during the 1820s and 1830s brought into Oxford many working people who settled in hastily built houses in the parishes of St Thomas's and St Ebbe's. At this time too St John's let off its first building leases, not in North Oxford, but on land they owned between St Giles's and Worcester College, and these leases were still of the beneficial type. The terraces built here were for a middle-class clientele, but before North Oxford could develop, there still needed to evolve in the city a substantial middle class. The prohibition against fellows marrying kept them in their colleges until they found positions elsewhere. As a market town Oxford had the usual solicitors, doctors, and bankers catering for the local gentry and landowners, but their numbers were small before mid-century. What was lacking was the sort of new money that was going into suburban developments in London and the industrial towns, and this would only occur with an expansion in the retail trade and a greater sophistication in the retail business. In 1850 St John's held 300 acres of potential building land within comfortable walking distance of the town centre, but it was constrained by the restrictions on long leases, and more importantly the College had to wait on changes in the social and economic conditions of the town before they could develop their North Oxford property as a residential suburb.

CHAPTER II
Early Estate Development

In 1853 when Jesse Elliston fell over dead in Banbury Road on his way to Summertown, *Jackson's Oxford Journal* mourned him as 'one of the earliest in working that commercial change which, in the shape of increased trade and spirited competition, has taken place in this city in recent years'. He was only forty-seven.[1] This sentiment was a far cry from that of nearly twenty years before when it was claimed at the Select Committee on the Railway Bill of 1837 that Oxford was 'always a century behind other towns'.[2] However, when William Morris in 1883 railed against 'the fury of the thriving shop and the progressive college' to his audience in University College Hall,[3] change in Oxford had been in motion for at least thirty years. Even as an undergraduate in the 1850s, he would have seen change if only he had looked, and certainly by then the commercial mentality, resulting in the later alterations to the city which so grieved him, had taken root in the minds of many local tradesmen.

It is now obvious that increased commercial activity will have an impact on the physical fabric of a town. Controversy arises with attempts to explain how this happened in English towns during the nineteenth century. One theory has it that successive tides of development washed over many towns laying down a sediment of ever increasing building density.[4] The rate at which this happened varied according to the accidental fortunes of the town, but as every wave passed it left behind a tendency for land values to rise as competition for central sites grew. Residential property which had once jockeyed for space alongside workshops and retail businesses, found itself squeezed to the point that house rents became prohibitive. Only the very rich and the poor could stay in the centre of the town, the poor by doubling up and sharing the rent. Those in the middle ranks looked for lower rents in the cheaper land of the suburbs.

Oxford, as a university town, was not typical in its development. Firstly the University and colleges had a restraining influence on commercial growth. They were interested primarily in continuity over the long run, and rapid change, which became more and more integral to nineteenth century commercial development, was antithetical to the ethos of conservation inherent in the way the colleges saw their role before the reforms of the second half of the century. On a practical level, the colleges were responsible for a transient population, made up for the most part of young men, and in order to maintain control, they had an interest in reducing disruptive change within the town to a minimum. The University dropped their opposition to the railway only when they were assured they would be able to check trains for undergraduates travelling without authority.[5] In the city they supported the closed system by which only freemen could practise trades, and although this system was largely abandoned by 1835, the year of the Municipal Corporation Act, its effects lingered.[6]

The second influence the colleges and University had on development was through the property they held in the centre of the town. Large sections of the centre were occupied by college buildings and their gardens as well as by University buildings. This property was not in the commercial market, so when there was competition for space in the centre, substantial areas were simply not negotiable. Added to this, the colleges also owned a sizeable amount of house and shop property in the centre.[7] When the colleges wanted to expand at various times during the century, they did so by reducing the amount of residential and commercial property in the main streets of Oxford.

The third influence the University had on town development was social. R.J. Morris has noted that the first suburban development around Oxford was for the working classes.[8] The population of the city rose sharply between 1821 and 1841 in line with the national population increase. Numbers rose, however, most markedly in the suburbs of St Ebbe's and St Thomas's, working-class districts close to the centre. Morris argues that the social structure created by the colleges concentrated the social elites in the centre of the town, close to the intellectual and professional activity of the University. The rule that voting members of Convocation, the legislative assembly of the University, must live within one and a half miles of the centre of Oxford may have reinforced this pattern,[9] and the retardation of commercial growth meant that there were not enough well-off tradesmen outside the sphere of the University to provide inhabitants for middle-class suburbs.

The University and colleges thus had a retarding influence on the development of Oxford, while at the same time contributing to the internal pressures for expansion within the town. When the colleges prospered so did the tradesmen who relied on them for custom. Accidents of geography, however, also contributed to Oxford's slow growth, since the city was surrounded on three sides by water, not just rivers, but water meadows and a high water table which could cause severe flooding. The only peripheral area not separated from the centre by water was directly to the north in the parish of St Giles's.

During the first half of the nineteenth century St Giles's was a 'working' suburb which was more useful to the town without houses.[10] The term 'suburb' had a technical meaning for a city like Oxford which had been a walled town. In this case the suburb provided a buffer between town and country and allowed all those activities which were neither urban nor properly speaking rural. When greengrocers grew their own vegetables and butchers raised their own meat, nearby arable and pasture land was

4 The Mount, Banbury Road in 1914, residence of G.P. Hester, now the site of St Hugh's College (Local Studies Library, Oxford Central Library).

a necessity. Likewise gravel and sand pits, brickfields and woodlands, provided essential raw materials for the town, especially before the railway made the transport of these materials easier.

The early suburb had an informality which allowed a number of productive activities to exist side by side. Another important role for the suburb was as a recreation ground, for formal games such as cricket and archery, or informal pastimes such as fishing. When building began these leisure activities were curtailed and located in specific places or abolished. From being an ambiguous area where many different sorts of activities could coexist, the suburb itself became a specialised area devoted almost entirely to residential property. The apparent sweet informality of the residential suburb was achieved by a radical act of regulation.

Even at the start of the 1850s, St Giles's seemed a long way from the regularity of suburban streets. A few successful men of business had moved to isolated villas up the turnpike roads and in Summertown (Plate 4). There was no inevitability, however, in the way the suburbs developed and the houses could arrive only after other changes in function had already taken place. The traditional productive use of the suburb could be removed when the railway brought coal, gravel and foodstuffs cheaply to the town from further afield. The decline in the traditional functions of the suburb coincided with pressure from the centre which needed cheap land for a variety of purposes such as cemeteries to replace overcrowded churchyards. Changes outside local control could also affect the suburb. The railway, for example, on its way from one centre to another could pass through a suburb, effectively changing the future character of the place. This might be an advantage for some suburbs, particularly later in the century, but when the railways

16

were first being laid down, the undeveloped suburb was considered just so much available land for passing lines.

Competition for suburban land placed the owners in a position where they could either react or initiate development of their own. As has been suggested some changes were beyond their control and set the future character of their property and therefore its value. Likewise any development they started themselves would also have an effect on the subsequent value of their property. Perhaps the middle-class residential suburb was one of the most unpredictable forms of development the owners could undertake.

Throughout the nineteenth century the middle class was in the process of converting itself into a recognisable group within society.[11] A general rise in wealth for this group coincided with an evolving cultural definition of the middle class, so that they could afford to express their view of the world in the way they clothed and housed themselves. The continuing evolution of their identity, however, meant that what might be acceptable middle-class behaviour at the start of the century was unacceptable by the 1880s. This continuing change had important implications for suburban house building.

Two building types prevailed in late eighteenth- and nineteenth-century suburbs. There were first the small country houses or villas in extensive, ornamental gardens, like those which had been built up the Banbury Road and at Summertown. The other form was the urban terrace, which must have seemed incongruous when it appeared among suburban fields.[12] These types represented two conflicting attitudes to the suburb. One emphasised the rural retreat from the city; the other stressed belief in future development and connection with the city. Anyone missing the mood of the moment could find himself burdened with the wrong type of suburb and declining property values.

The suburb was not simply townspeople moving out of the town centre to find greater space and air, although those early terraces stranded in fields may have had that purpose. A simple reproduction of urban domestic life would have been the goal of the first suburbs relatively near the town centres, but as waves of development transformed the city, so the concept of the suburb matured. The suburb altered the landscape around the town, but it gained its own definition from the town and not from the country.[13] It was sub-urban, not sub-rural. As the city became defined almost exclusively as the workplace, the suburb took on the connotations of home, and as the definition of the workplace became more precise and specific, so did that of the home. The suburb was constructed not so much as the antithesis of the city, but as its complement, supplying in its comfort and informality what the city lacked, while rejecting at the same time the louche diversity and essential inefficiency of the old productive suburb.

If rising land values in the town centre did tend to initiate suburban building, it must be admitted that values did rise in and around Oxford during the first decades of the nineteenth century.[14] Over fifty years, Magdalen College in the city centre, put up the fines on its properties in the High Street and Cornmarket as the table on the next page shows. This increase in values may have had more to do with the crisis in agriculture during the 1820s than development in the town, since the rise in fines tended

Swinbrook's		£		43 Cornmarket		£
127-9 High Street	1801	45		43 Cornmarket	1800	24
	1815	95			1814	45
	1829	145			1828	75
	1845	268			1842	95
	1857	288			1856	95[15]

to level off by mid-century after the large influx of people from the country-side in the 1820s and 1830s. Still in the early years of the century there seems to have been a genuine desire for development as pointed out by Henry Dixon in 1818. He was asked to survey land belonging to St John's College, then required by the Radcliffe Observatory, and in his report he wrote that 'Land has been for many years past and is now, in great request for Building'.[16] This perception led him to advise the College to ask a sub-stantial price for their land.

The first housing development in which St John's College was directly involved was the Beaumont Street area in the 1820s.[17] Beaumont Street itself was part of a road improvement scheme and was intended to form a much needed link between Worcester College and the rest of the town. Although the assembly of land for a road was authorised in 1774–5,[18] it was not until the beginning of the nineteenth century, and apparently on the initiative of Worcester College, that plans moved ahead. Worcester College may have felt that they were isolated from the other colleges in their position on the extreme west of the city, and without a decent roadway to the centre of Oxford, but the northwestern area beyond the old city walls had been accumulating a number of other institutions which transformed it from a rustic suburb to a modern centre outside the traditional boundaries of Oxford. Worcester College itself was begun only in 1720, then there was the Radcliffe Infirmary 1759, the Radcliffe Observatory 1772, and the workhouse in the same year. The Oxford Canal which was built in 1790, provided employment in the area through the various wharves along its bank, while more employment came in 1825 when the Eagle Ironworks were established near Walton Well, and after 1826 with the move of the University Press to Walton Street.

St Giles's the broad street between St Mary Magdalen's and St Giles's Churches, leading to the Woodstock and Banbury Roads, had from the eighteenth century some of the grandest, stone-faced houses in the city (Plate 5). The Beaumont Street development should be seen in the context of this handsome thoroughfare, the home at this time of many professionals as well as members of the University. Today the two streets are separated by the neo-gothic Randolph Hotel and the classical Ashmolean Museum and Taylorian Institute, but the style and materials of Beaumont Street suggest it was designed with the larger houses of St Giles's Street in mind.

Early in the 1800s, Worcester College was anxious to acquire some odd pieces of land around their entrance gate and to press forward with the road

5   St Giles, West Side in 1961 (SJC Muniments).

project. In 1804 St John's College who owned the land, was willing to sell to Worcester for five shillings 'enough land to make "an handsome road"', but not any more.[19] At the same time the College decided to take in hand Beaumont and Walton Closes, the fields in the area, so that new leases were not granted when they came up for renewal in 1809 and 1811. It would of course take another thirteen years at least for the beneficial leases to expire. In 1822 Henry Dixon, the surveyor, was asked to survey a road 60 feet wide from Worcester College to St Giles's, and in October of that year, the land on either side of the road for building leases.[20] In this year too, the architect (Wm) Garbett was paid £34.13s.0d by the College for 'Plans of Beaumont Street'.[21]

Advertisements for building land appeared in *Jackson's Oxford Journal* in April 1823. The land was to be let on beneficial leases, but of the kind usual for houses (Plate 6). The leases would run for forty years, instead of twenty, which meant that whoever took a lease paid a fine and then annual ground rent for fourteen years until another fine was due, in order to renew the lease for a further forty-year period from that date. In this way the College got around the problem of restrictions on long leases. The lease fines for the first plots taken by Mr Pinfold and Mr Chaundy were fixed at £128 and £117 respectively, with an annual ground rent of £5 each.[22] This compares with

19

6   Elevation of scheme for Beaumont Street, attributed to William Garbett, 1822 (SJC Muniments).

26 guineas, the fine previously paid for the whole of the Beaumonts. The development was obviously going to increase the income of the College considerably. However, the fellows had to wait till further leases fell in before they could let more land. In April 1824 they asked Dixon to survey the area of Beaumont Closes not yet let, and in June the same year they authorised that land near Worcester College whose lease had just fallen in also be let on building leases.[23] This was property facing Walton Street, on the western side. Although building started on both these sites in the mid-1820s, it was only in the early 1840s that the streets could be said to be complete.

These first streets of College houses were constrained by previous developments on surrounding land owned by others. To the south in Gloucester Green was the gaol and to the north the workhouse and the Radcliffe Infirmary.[24] Some of the houses in Walton Street were kept to two storeys so that their height would not interfere with the work of the nearby Radcliffe Observatory. The University Press building was contemporary with the Walton Street houses and closed off that development to the north. Functional change thus had begun in this northwestern suburb of Oxford some time before St John's College began letting its land on building leases.

Beaumont Street and its subsidiary, St John Street, were uncompromisingly urban. Garbett, the architect, had designed in 1822 the Catte Street facade of Magdalen Hall, now Hertford College, in a style combining classical formality and domestic ease. A drawing of the Beaumont Street development presumably by Garbett suggests the drama of a stage set by showing the classical fronts of Beaumont Street flanking an arresting perspective of St John Street centred on the tower of the Radcliffe Observatory behind the workhouse.[25] The entrances to the houses are more stylish than those built, but the proportions and materials are similar. The style of the drawing indicates a certain amount of grandeur rather than cosy domesticity, and it was evident from the first that these terraces in their regularity and scale were intended to have social pretensions (Plate 7). Behind St John Street was Beaumont Buildings of more modest brick, for those employed

20

7   Building Beaumont Street, 1832 (Local Studies Library, Oxford Central Library).

in serving the larger houses. In Walton Street the houses had small gardens in front and their facades had the same chequered brickwork as Beaumont Buildings. Although still urban in form, their greater retirement from the street presents a more suburban aspect than Beaumont Street.

Those who took building leases in Beaumont and Walton Closes were interested in the profits from development, the income derived from letting, or the houses themselves. Benjamin Hill, a hatter, took a number of plots in Walton Close, developed some himself and passed some quickly on to others. Builders like George Bennett and John Chaundy were active in Beaumont Closes, but so were George Kimber, a tallow merchant, and Crews Dudley, a solicitor, both residents of Summertown.[26] Those who took leases on the houses were a real cross-section of the middle-class population of Oxford, dominated by tradespeople. Many of the names in the leases can also be found in lists of the stallholders at the city's covered market.[27] Gentlemen and a few professionals participated, but only one member of the University, the Rev Philip Bliss DCL, took a lease in the early stages. On the other hand college servants were well represented. Prior accumulation of wealth was important in any venture where investment was required for future profit. When the Oxford Canal Navigation Company sought subscriptions at the end of the eighteenth century, they received them from a stratum of society above those investing in these Oxford houses.[28] Among the subscribers were members of colleges and in some cases the colleges themselves. The net they cast was also wider and included people from around Oxford, the surrounding counties, and even from London. During the 1820s and 1830s houses seemed to have been of much more local concern and drew money from quite modest sources.

Who lived in these new houses once they were built? From their size and form, as well as their position near the town centre, it would seem that these houses were intended for middle-class households. The Census for 1841 does indeed indicate that they were successful in attracting a middle- and lower-middle-class population.[29] The definition of class is extremely difficult, and it is even more difficult to determine in a prior age, since the concept of class is constructed year by year. The Victorian middle class recognisable in the 1880s was a long time forming, and required the conjunction of many circumstances to result in its peculiar characteristics. By 1841 however, the effects of the economic revolution since the Napoleonic Wars had permeated society far enough to influence domestic arrangements, but not yet to the extent of producing the great gap between one section of the middle classes and another.[30] In Beaumont and St John Streets the range of occupations among the heads of household suggests a promiscuous mixing of people whose incomes were derived from trade, the professions, and investment. As the century progressed, Beaumont Street filled a need by becoming the professional district of Oxford where doctors, solicitors, and architects took up residence.

One indication of a middle-class population in an area was the high ratio of women to men. This phenomenon followed from a number of circumstances dependent on middle-class family life. First of all the number of servants living in, particularly from mid-century, was especially high in middle-class districts, and since only very wealthy people could afford male servants, partly because of the high tax associated with them, most servants were women.[31] Second, single or widowed middle-class women had access to more wealth through family trusts, which allowed them to live independently on their incomes, sometimes with grown-up daughters or a female companion. And finally, increasingly during the nineteenth century in households with children, the sons would be sent away to school and professional training while the unmarried daughters remained as always at home.[32] In Hampstead, a London borough whose middle-class status grew during the nineteenth century, the ratio of women to men rose steadily until 1861, after which it remained high. In Shoreditch meanwhile, an increasingly working-class borough, the ratio steadily dropped:

	1841	1851	1861	1871	1881	1891	1901
Hampstead	1.33	1.41	1.60	1.58	1.58	1.55	1.58
Shoreditch	1.11	1.09	1.08	1.06	1.05	1.03	1.04[33]

In Oxford the average ratio of women to men in the central parishes was 1.03 in 1841, while in Beaumont and St John Streets, including Beaumont Buildings, it was 1.55.[34] A further refinement of the figures shows that the main thoroughfare, Beaumont Street, had a ratio of 1.87, while St John Street had one of 1.41 (Plate 8).

8   Beaumont Street, north side.

Although these ratios point to a largely middle-class clientele coming to inhabit the houses, it must be admitted that these relatively small developments took nearly twenty years to complete. Beaumont Street was begun in 1823–4 and the land in Walton Closes was authorised to be let in 1824, yet it was not until the early 1840s that all the properties were taken on lease. Although the shortage of houses intended for those middle-class families enjoying an income of from £500 to £1,000 was commented upon in the 1850s, this may not have been such a problem in the 1820s and 1830s.[35] The system of beneficial leases may also have discouraged potential developers since though the leases were for forty years, it was necessary to pay a fine as well as ground rent before the houses were built and leased. The question of beneficial leases was a technical stumbling block that had to be removed before the College could develop its land on a comprehensive scale. Before this particular difficulty was addressed the College had to deal first with the enclosure of the potential building land and not just the removal of common lands, but also the regulation of the existing property boundaries.

In 1825 the College requested Dixon, the surveyor of Beaumont Street, to survey St Giles's Fields and to put in place more boundary stones.[36] This may have been the first move towards enclosure. A survey of the whole parish of St Giles's is dated 1827 and notice was placed in *Jackson's Oxford Journal* in October that an application would be made in the next session

23

of Parliament to bring in a Bill of Enclosure for the parish.[37] It seems that the initiative for enclosure came from the various freehold and leasehold proprietors in the area, and in a petition to the Commons in 1828 the College indicated that there was no serious opposition to the enclosure of St Giles's

> ... the Inclosure of the said Lands was considered so essential as to have induced many of the Proprietors in the month of October last to petition the said College. . . . Proprietors of nine tenths of the said Lands have signed the petition presented to this Honourable House or signified their assent to the application to parliament and . . . not one of the Proprietors is known to be hostile to the proposed Inclosure.[38]

In such a petition it is unlikely that any dissenting voices would be recorded, though the one-tenth who did not express consent to enclosure do not seem to have actively protested. Still the questions arise why enclosure of St Giles's took place so late and why it was proposed in 1827.

Common land close to a town was very useful to those townspeople who did not own any productive land of their own. The gathering of wood, the grazing of animals, and the pursuit of leisure were all activities which could be carried out on common land near towns. In fact the common and wasteland in St Giles's was not of large extent, so that it may have been considered more politic to allow local people to continue using what there was than absorbing it into the fields.[39] However, as potential building land, St Giles's would be more profitable enclosed since then development need not be concerned with the odd areas of common land. If St John's was beginning to plan a great expansion in their suburban development, enclosure would be one of the first steps towards accomplishing this end. Freehold and leasehold proprietors too would be keen on enclosure, since this would not just increase their land holding, it would also regulate their boundaries, putting them in a better position in relation to the College when negotiations for building land began.

Not all went smoothly when the petition for the introduction of the enclosure bill arrived at Parliament. It seems that all procedures had been followed except that no notice had been affixed to the door of County Hall at the Epiphany Sessions in January of 1828.[40] The College's steward, Baker Morrell, had entrusted this task to one of his clerks who had neglected to carry it out. Morrell did not discover the oversight until it was too late, so the petition was sent to Parliament without all the requirements fulfilled. Although the College asked that the bill proceed after notice be given at the Easter quarter sessions, the House of Commons rejected their request.[41] This meant that they had to wait until the next year before they could present another petition for an enclosure bill, which was enacted on 22 May 1829.[42]

Henry Dixon was made commissioner for the enclosure and in October 1829 he began taking requests for allotments from the various freeholders and leaseholders in St Giles's.[43] Another of his tasks was to value the College's land in the parish. Notes in his manuscript report suggest that some leaseholders particularly in Tagg's Garden, may not have been happy to have their affairs known by the College.[44]

The Tagg family had for years been in the nursery garden business and held various pieces of land on the outskirts of Oxford. The piece of land called Tagg's Garden was immediately north of the Radcliffe Observatory, occupying the area between the Woodstock Turnpike and the road to Walton Well, as far north as present day Leckford Road. This land was leased in 1823 to Thomas Tagg and others on twenty-year beneficial leases, and they in turn let small plots to their tenants. Dixon did not take the word of the leaseholders when calculating the income they received from rents, but sent a servant of the College, William Glover, around to question the tenants themselves about how much rent they paid. Tagg claimed he received £29.12s.0d. in rent for his land, but a pencil note in Dixon's manuscript report records: 'The quantity of ground in Tagg's hands according to a valuation made proportionate to the rents which he received for gardens that he admits he *does* let, brings in about £50 a year. Though Tagg declares he does not let a great deal of this, yet it is very well known that he does.'[45] In another instance it was noted on the tenants' information that property claimed to produce £14 in rent, actually brought in £33.

Tagg's Garden was represented on a map of its own in the enclosure documents of 1832.[46] The development in this area was at such a density that it required a large-scale map to include all the necessary detail, and this fact in itself points up the different character of this area to the rest of St Giles's parish. Although the acres of Tagg's Garden were leased by six leaseholders, during the 1820s it seems that many cottages and other structures were being built by their tenants so that this area was becoming more and more a working-class suburb, but without any control being exerted by the College. In 1832 this phenomenon was confined to the limited area of Tagg's Garden, for the rest of the College's property in North Oxford retained its rural character and thus its potential for development. With pressure on land values, how long could this situation be maintained?

Tagg's Garden represented one of the functions of suburban land, the informal housing of working people for whom the confines of the town were unsuitable. It was not coincidence that many builders and carpenters found accommodation there. In September 1842, St John's requested the architect Henry Jones Underwood to make a valuation of the area and it was decided to lease the houses there on twenty-year leases.[47] This took the disposal of the houses out of the informal letting market into the control of the College. Underwood produced a map and survey of the area in 1843 and shortly after twenty-year building leases were being made on vacant plots in what was described as Tagg's acre.[48] Even if they had wanted to, it was too late for the College to stop the appearance of this working-class suburb in their North Oxford property. By introducing building leases, they could ensure that what was built was at least sound, unlike many of the Tagg's Garden cottages, and they could also control the rate at which development took place.

Could the College at this time have been considering the large-scale development of St Giles's Fields? It 1840 it was decided not to renew the beneficial leases held by the Duke of Marlborough on his extensive leasehold property immediately north of Tagg's Garden.[49] This was the first indication that St John's was interested in converting the beneficial lease of a substantial piece of land in St Giles's to rack-renting. The duke's leases had last been renewed in 1833, so in 1840 they had another thirteen years to run. Nothing could be done immediately although the College always had the option of buying out the remaining years of the leases. They chose, however, to wait, and by the time the leases expired in 1853, the land was ripe for suburban development.

As the 1840s and 1850s progressed, more and more beneficial leases in St Giles's were not renewed but allowed to run their course. In 1842 Joseph Parker's lease of land south of Horse and Jockey Road, now Bevington Road, was not renewed, nor was Crews Dudley's lease of land north of North Parade.[50] In the next year Dudley's lease of land south of North Parade was also not renewed.[51] Taking these three leases together meant that by 1856 the land between the Woodstock and Banbury Roads from the present Bevington Road as far as Canterbury Road would be rack rented and available for building. Similarly other leases as they came up for renewal were allowed to run the rest of their thirteen years, so that by 1865, the College had in hand practically all the land in St Giles's.

While the College was obviously keen to regain control of the land, the leaseholders too, may have been more than willing to relinquish their leases. Although the annual rent for a beneficial lease was often minimal the seven-year renewal fine could be quite substantial and over the years was increasing. The leaseholders were not necessarily themselves involved in cultivating the land in their leasehold. Crews Dudley was a solicitor who had been involved in building speculation in St Ebbe's and Beaumont Street, while Joseph Parker was a prosperous bookseller. As *Jackson's Oxford Journal* said in 1853, a different commercial spirit was abroad in Oxford, and land held on beneficial leases in the northern suburbs of the city may not have suited a new generation of tradesmen who wanted to invest their profits back into their businesses.

As Oxford grew and external changes began to impinge on the city, pressure was put on the Fields of St Giles's to perform hitherto unknown functions. Oxford had many parish churches within the old walls. As in other nineteenth-century towns, an increase in the resident population also increased the population of the dead who must be buried in the already overflowing churchyards. Added to this congestion was the competition for space as colleges wished to expand their buildings and businesses their premises. Under the circumstances the dead lost out to the living and in 1844 the Church and Burial Ground Committee approached St John's about buying some of their land for a cemetery.[52] The College suggested the land held by the Duke of Marlborough called Lark Hill, but the final decision put the cemetery in a less prominent place between the road to Walton Well and the canal, next to the Eagle Ironworks.[53]

Perhaps it was the railway, as in so many other towns, which initiated the

9 The Old Oxford Workhouse, on the site of the present Wellington Square, from a watercolour by J.C. Buckler, 1821 (Local Studies Library, Oxford Central Library).

greatest change in Oxford life at mid-century. As will be seen the railway played a dramatic part in the development of North Oxford, yet while lines were still being built for the Birmingham and Oxford Railway in Port Meadow, St Giles's provided the gravel needed to grade the tracks. In 1847 the College sold the gravel in Lark Hill to Messrs Sherwood, contractors to the Railway, for £800.[54] With every such decision to give over part of the land in St Giles's to yet another function, the College was creating constraints for itself which would eventually affect its house building ventures. Two projects which did not in the end materialise, would have irreparably established the character of parts of North Oxford and over both these schemes the College had no control. One was the proposed workhouse in Banbury Road and the other was the proposed railway line across St Giles's.

The old workhouse had been built in 1772 in what had become a built up area just behind the west side of St Giles's. With the increase in the general population and changes in the Poor Law, it was felt that need had outgrown the available facilities (Plate 9). There were two strong arguments against the old workhouse. One was what was termed lack of classification which meant that children were placed with adults and the able bodied with the infirm. This mixing of inmates was thought to lead to idleness through lack of supervision.[55] The other main objection was that the site was only 5 or 6 acres, and as such could not provide outdoor productive work which would train the inmates, especially the young, for work outside the institution.[56] A larger site was obviously needed.

At a meeting of the Board of Guardians in February 1849 it was suggested that an exchange of land be arranged with St John's College. In March it was announced that the Guardians were to have a 9 acre piece of land on the east side of Banbury Road belonging to New College.[57] The Guardians had selected three possible sites on St John's land near the Woodstock Road, including Lark Hill, but the College had not wanted to part with any of their land in that district. New College were then approached and they accepted an offer of £2,680 plus the exchange of some city property near the College. The treasury sanctioned the exchange in January 1850, but St John's were having second thoughts.

In June 1849 the surveyor, James Saunders, reported to them that if a workhouse were built on the east side of Banbury Road on the New College site 'a great depreciation in the Marketable Value of the Lands' belonging to St John's would result.[58] The strategy Saunders suggested was that the College offer to exchange the site in Banbury Road for one in Woodstock Road, roughly corresponding to the land about which the Guardians first made their enquiries. When the offer was made to the Guardians they were acute enough to realise the embarrassment their workhouse could prove to St John's in any suburban development they wanted to make. They refused Saunder's offer '. . . because they thought that St John's College had not duly appreciated the advantage of removing what would in their estimation hereafter prove to be a great annoyance to the College Estate.'[59] Secure in the knowledge that they had the New College site, the Guardians in June 1850 proposed that the College include additional land or £1,000 in the deal which Saunders believed would amount to £1,100 more than the College's offer.[60] The terms were turned down and the Guardians went ahead with their original plans.

Reservations about the Banbury Road site were expressed by one of the Guardians who thought the site proposed by St John's more appropriate and their offer generous.[61] He forecast problems in the foundations of the new building, but his doubts were cast aside and architects were asked to enter a competition for the new workhouse. The winning scheme was by H. Crisp of Stoke's Cross, Bristol, which nonetheless required alterations in view of a 'long string of objections' from the Poor Law Commission.[62] Although in January 1851 the Guardians' House Building Committee recommended that work proceed on the new workhouse, there were obvious continuing reservations about the site, the expense, and perhaps more seriously the expected government plan to compel Boards of Guardians to provide Industrial Schools for the young inmates of their workhouses.[63] In March 1851 Saunders reported that the Guardians had approached the College again to ascertain whether they would be willing to make the exchange originally proposed in June 1849 with the addition of 4 acres 3 roods and 4 perches used as the gravel pit for the railway.[64] Although Saunders recommended the deal, it became plain that the indecision of the Guardians would lead to an abandonment of the scheme.

In August 1851 it was decided to postpone the construction of the workhouse and to appoint a committee to consider the possibility of obtaining premises for an Industrial School. In the meanwhile the Banbury Road site was cultivated with clover and potatoes. When a site was chosen for the Industrial School it was 10 acres in Cowley for £600.[65] A committee formed in November 1852 to consider what was the best means of disposing of the Banbury Road site reported the next March.[66] They had asked two architects, S.L. Seckham and E.G. Bruton, to submit drawings and plans for the best use of the land, and they had selected those of Seckham. His scheme for substantial houses it was thought would meet a need in the area by providing houses for people with an income of between £500 and £1,000. So what had begun as a threat to St John's supposed ambitions for middle-class houses in North Oxford, ended as Park Town, a forerunner of their own later estates.

If it was thought that a workhouse would have lowered the market value of St John's land in North Oxford, the proposed railway line across St Giles's would have really affected the character of the future suburb. Oxford was slow to accept the railway, although it could be said that much of what happened in England during the nineteenth century depended on its spread.[67] Manufacturers supported railway expansion in the early years because they foresaw the means of greatly increasing their access to markets. There were few manufacturers in Oxford. Retailers were keen on railways to improve the flow of goods which enabled them to be more competitive. As has been noted, Oxford retailers were slow to adapt to a more competitive consumerism. Financiers welcomed railways as a good form of investment, but investment depended on the extensive profits being generated by manufacturing and competitive retailing. All classes would eventually benefit from the greater mobility the railway brought. For a town like Oxford which depended on transport to shift a significant proportion of its population several times a year from the colleges to their homes throughout the kingdom, any invention which made the journey more rapid should have been welcomed. The large transport industry in the city, including coach proprietors, carters, and the Oxford Canal Navigation Company were all against the invention. The only advantage was seen to be the transport of coal to the city, and it was thought the canal performed this task adequately.

Mobility, particularly among the middle classes, was to have a profound effect on how business and bureaucracy were conducted and how social contacts were made and maintained. Without the railway North Oxford might not have been able to sustain the number of relatively wealthy middle-class people needed to fill the very largest houses, since there was only a limited supply of successful tradesmen in the city. Nevertheless, at first the University were against the railway reaching Oxford.[68] Some colleges like Magdalen and Christ Church objected on the grounds that their land close to the colleges would be required for termini. Perhaps some of the more conservative noted that a man of reform like the Rev Francis Jeune, Master of Pembroke, and member of the dreaded University Commission, was a frequent user of railways.[69] Sensing that the social implications of railway travel would be profound, and not being able to foresee exactly what they would be, led the railway's opponents to assume the worst.

A compromise was reached in 1840 when the station at Steventon, 10 miles from Oxford, was made accessible to the town by a coach service.[70] The inconvenience of this arrangement, and perhaps the growing awareness that the railway could be quite useful, reduced opposition to the extent that in 1843 a Railway Bill to bring a line from Didcot to Abingdon Road was enacted.[71] After this initial line, others like the Birmingham and Oxford Railway and the Buckingham Railway Company connected Oxford to towns further north.

During the early 1850s, Oxford became caught up in the gauge war between the broad gauge Great Western Railway and the narrow gauge London and North Western Railway.[72] It seems that the subsidiary of the Great Western Railway, the Oxford, Worcester and Wolverhampton Railway, in order to gain access to London, proposed that it would petition the Commons to allow it to build a line from Wolvercote to Brentford in West London. This proposal may have simply been a strategy to shake the Great Western into agreeing a link-up in North Oxford between the two lines, which was another proposal made by the Oxford, Worcester, and Wolverhampton Railway. None of this would now be relevant to St John's and their North Oxford estate except that the line to Brentford would have run from a station at Walton Well, across St Giles's parish following a line just north of the present Bevington Road and Norham Gardens.[73]

No sooner had the notice for this line appeared at the end of November 1851 than St John's sent a petition to the House of Commons protesting against it.[74] The University Convocation also sent a petition against the extension bill in March 1852. The University opposition was not matched by the townspeople who called a meeting to approve a petition in favour of the bill. The petition put forward the city tradesmen's point of view:

> That the trade and property of your petitioners, and of the other inhabitants of the City of Oxford, has, for several years past, been greatly depreciated. That one of the causes of such depreciation is, as your petitioners believe, that Oxford has ceased to be the thoroughfare of traffic from Worcester and Wolverhampton, and other important towns and districts in the northwest of England, to London.[75]

One of the speakers in support of the petition noted that the University were against raising the turnpike roads 7 feet where the proposed line would cross because, he said, 'it would be very inconvenient to Doctors of Divinity to toil up such an ascent'. This comment provoked laughter among the obviously overexcited crowd.[76] G.P. Hester, the town clerk and local solicitor, declared he was in favour of the petition even though he lived in North Oxford, not far from the proposed line. Despite this petition the bill was thrown out by the Commons.

Another attempt was made the next year and another petition sponsored by the Town Council was sent in March 1853 to the Houses of Parliament.[77] The only dissenting voice was that of William Glover, the servant of St John's College. He claimed that the line would be dangerous and detrimental to North Oxford as well as to the rest of the city. The whole exercise had perhaps more to do with the competition between the wide gauge Great Western Railway and the narrow gauge London and North Western Railway than it had with providing a shorter route from Oxford to London. When this bill was rejected, there was another accepted by the Commons for a branch line from the London and North Western Railway's main line at Tring to Oxford.[78] This line would have followed the same route across North Oxford, but the bill was rejected later in the summer of 1853 by the Lords.

If either of these bills had passed, St John's College would have had to sell compulsorily the necessary land to the railway company. In February 1853 they drew up a provisional agreement with the London and Mid-Western Railway Company – the company formed by the Oxford, Worcester and Wolverhampton Company to forward their project – to sell 43 acres in St Giles's and Wolvercote for £20,000.[79] However, in April they also made an agreement with the London and North Western Railway Company to sell the same land for the same sum.[80] This was well before a decision had been made in the House of Commons over which scheme should go forward. Since only one company could be successful it was best to ensure the same terms with both companies.

As well as provision for the route across St Giles's parish, the contract with the London and North Western Company allowed for further compensation to the College for 'the erection of furances ovens or other works for the making and manufacturing of coke'.[81] However much a resident like Hester might think he and his family would be not be inconvenienced by a railway line running past the foot of their garden, the peripheral activities would certainly have proved obtrusive. The railway line would have had an effect on the development of the College's land, for although the suburb would have still been built, its character would have been different as well as its form. Rather than being divided by class east to west, the north of the suburb would more likely have been separated from the south. In the event the House of Lords suppressed the bill, so once again the College was saved from incorporating an intrusive development into their north Oxford property.

The two projects of workhouse and railway line faded into oblivion during the summer of 1853. From now on the construction of North Oxford as a middle-class suburb took on more purpose. The moment when the open fields were seen not as agricultural land, but as potential building land was a long time coming, and depended on outside influences. The one influence which probably tipped the balance was the prospect of financial gain, but this required the idea of the suburb to emerge first. Competition for the land by various functions presented the possibility of radical change and the possibility that the land could be used for more purposes than those traditional suburban activities marginal to the town. Some of the most active businessmen of Oxford had already begun to regard North Oxford as a middle-class place of residence by building substantial houses on land they had scraped together from owners other than the College. Thomas Mallam, a local auctioneer, pieced together enough land to build the Shrubbery on Woodstock Road.[82] Over on Banbury Road, Hester leased land from University College to erect the Mount and its lodge, and John Parsons, the draper, built the Lawn on land leased from Lincoln College.[83] When these men and their families stepped out of their front doors, they could enjoy the appearance of their own gardens, but the land around them belonged to St John's.

At this earliest stage of development two events started the gradual physical and psychological changes which launched the North Oxford estate.

10 Park Crescent, Park Town, Samuel Lipscomb Seckham, 1853.

One was the building of Park Town and the other was the campaign for and eventual establishment of the parish of St Philip and St James with its handsome church by G.E. Street. The Board of Guardians set up a committee to decide what to do with their Banbury Road site in November 1852, and by the time it reported in March 1853, the decision had been made to select the scheme of Samuel Lipscomb Seckham for a small estate of middle-class houses and central communal garden.[84] Seckham not only produced a plan, he also made an offer to the Guardians of £2,000 for about a quarter of the land. Here he proposed to build two crescents of eleven houses each (Plate 10). It occurred to the Guardians that it would be an advantage to get twenty-two uniform houses on the site at one time. If the land went for auction not all the lots might be sold, and those not necessarily in close proximity. This could have caused serious delay in developing the whole of the site. The cost of the roads and drainage into the Cherwell would be £430 which the Guardians planned to pay for initially, with the freehold purchasers repaying them subsequently.[85] The houses to be built would cost nearly £8,000 (£363 each) and 'would be a great improvement to that locality'.

In April 1853 Seckham made an offer for another portion of the estate for £1,200 on which he planned to build a terrace.[86] This offer too was accepted by the Guardians. Seckham seems to have had the backing at first of his father, William Seckham and his uncle, James Wickens, a wine merchant.[87] But the question must be asked whether there was enough money in Oxford for the building of a suburban estate of substantial middle-class houses. It has been noted that although members of the University invested in the Oxford Canal Navigation Company, they did not put their money into the Beaumont Street estate. With development starting in other suburbs around the city, could Seckham gather together enough capital from local tradesmen for the sort of coherent development now demanded by a middle-class clientele?

In order to entice investors into putting money into Park Town, Seckham and his backers set up a tontine.[88] A limited company, the Park Town Estate Company, was formed in September 1857 to purchase unsold land in the Park Town estate and to erect 'Residences, Reading Rooms, and other Buildings'. The nominal capital of £23,400 was guaranteed by the General Life Insurance Company, and Seckham's company planned to sell 780 shares of £30 each. Although mention is made in the prospectus of dividends, the main advantage of the scheme lay in the element of chance which formed its basis. Within twenty-one days of paying the £5 deposit on a share, the shareholder had to nominate a person resident in England and not less than fifty years of age at 1 August 1857. Then he had to insure the life of his nominee for not less than 30 guineas and not more than 40. This was to be done preferably with the General Insurance Company. For however long the shareholder held his shares he must keep up the premium payments on the life. When his nominee died, he lost his share and was out of the tontine, although he could regain his money through the life insurance policy. When the number of shareholders was reduced by the progressive deaths of the nominees to seven, then they would divide the remaining property of the company between them.

Was it so difficult to find investors for new houses that such an obscure form of enticement was thought necessary? In the end the scheme did not prove successful. At the close of the first year the company had sold 84 shares, and by 1860 only 278 had been taken up, bringing in £8,340, far less than the £23,400 they had hoped to raise.[89] The company went into liquidation in 1861.

Of the thirty-one shareholders in 1857, nine described themselves as gentlemen, nine as members of the building industry, seven as solicitors, and six as other minor professionals like accountants.[90] Most shareholders came from Oxford and its environs, although nine of these thirty-one came from further afield. Joseph Castle seems to have been the individual who took the most shares. He was an Oxford builder, but his nominees resided mostly in London and belonged to the gentry or lower aristocracy. Nothing in the prospectus said that the shareholders had to inform their nominees that their lives were being used in this way, and the advantage of the gentry was that their birth dates were well established and their deaths announced publicly. This would avoid any disagreement or misunderstandings.

The position of Park Town in St Giles's Fields may not have felt so isolated as might be supposed. Across Banbury Road was North Parade and the group of individual villas mentioned before, the Shrubbery, the Lawn, and the Mount. The urban character of the crescent and the terrace, would have emphasised the difference between the estate and the surrounding fields, but as long as the social and spiritual centre of peoples' lives was half a mile down the road in St Giles's Church, no sense of identity could develop in the newly colonised area. This thought may have been in the mind of F.J. Morrell when in 1854 as churchwarden for St Giles's, he petitioned St John's for the establishment of a new parish to supplement the church accommodation in St Giles's.[91] Morrell had just succeeded his father, Baker Morrell, as steward of the College and it was he whom *Jackson's Oxford Journal* later credited with advising the College to develop their North Oxford estate.[92]

Morrell's argument was that the population in the Tagg's Garden area and Summertown had grown substantially over the previous twenty years and that Park Town would add another sixty houses to the parish. An increase in the population though was only part of the problem in Morrell's view. Because the pews in St Giles's were assigned to those who could pay, the existing places were restricted to the wealthy members of the parish, while the poor, who made up the majority of the newcomers in Tagg's Garden and Summertown, had no opportunity of finding a place at the church services.[93] What Morrell recommended was a new church in a good location which could accommodate 800 to 1,000 people, preferably without pew rent.

Six months before, St John's College had embarked on their first attempt at suburban development. The layout Seckham had made for their land on Woodstock Road recently surrendered by the Duke of Marlborough included a church, and the College were willing to contribute to the building of a church or chapel of ease in this location. The church would have been in the middle of the proposed Walton Manor estate, away from the main road and surrounded by its own houses. For Morrell, this was unsatisfactory.

> ... the Church shown on Mr Seckham's plan having been obviously designed in connection with the erection of a number of new houses around it and being neither central in reference to the general wants of the Parish nor possessing any convenient access for the existing houses in its immediate neighbourhood can scarcely be expected to command any active support from the Parishioners ...[94]

The site that emerged as the favourite for the St Giles's vestry was one across the Woodstock Road, on a line with North Parade. Such a site would provide access from both Woodstock and Banbury Roads and be within easy

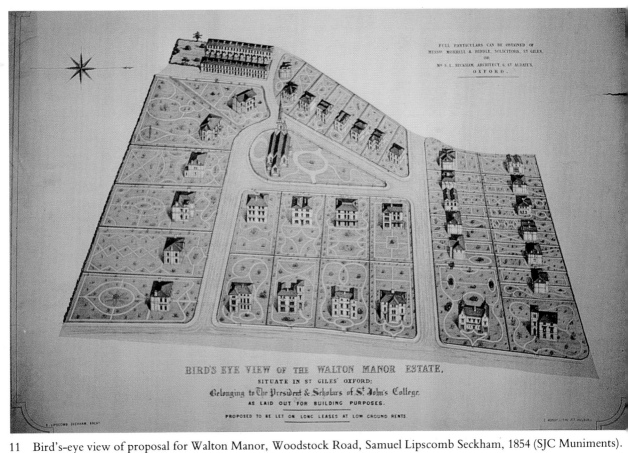

11 Bird's-eye view of proposal for Walton Manor, Woodstock Road, Samuel Lipscomb Seckham, 1854 (SJC Muniments).

reach of the poorer families in Observatory Street, St John's Road, and Plantation Road, those streets which had taken the place of Tagg's Garden.

By insisting on the Woodstock Road site, Morrell and the vestry were ensuring that the centre of gravity of North Oxford would be established in an advantageous position. If North Oxford was to develop comprehensively as a suburb it needed a focal point independent of the city, and yet prominent enough to establish a new sense of place. The leap of imagination necessary at this point was to see North Oxford covered by houses. The danger was to envisage the area developed in small pockets like Park Town with fields between. The scale of the undertaking had to be greatly enlarged in the minds of all those involved, and perhaps the insistence on the position of St Philip and St James was the first indication that this was taking place, at least among some.

The first venture of St John's College into the development of their North Oxford property did not have a propitious beginning. When the Duke of Marlborough's lease fell in, the College gave authorisation for the land to be let on rack rents.[95] This was in 1853, the same year that Seckham was negotiating with the Board of Guardians for the Park Town estate. As mentioned before F.J. Morrell became the College's steward in 1854, and it was probably his influence which led them to accept in that year a scheme by Seckham to develop the land previously held by the duke (Plate 11). The

35

estate was to face Woodstock Road with large detached villas of Italianate and gothic design disposed around a few short roads. There was also to be a more modest terrace at the rear of the estate on Kingston Road and a church in the middle.[96] The estate's position was on the western side of Woodstock Road, nearly parallel to where the Park Town estate was building, so again it would not have been as isolated as at first may appear.

Park Town was a freehold estate, and it became increasingly pressing that St John's be able to offer long leases on their houses in order to compete with freehold houses there and in other areas of Oxford. The forty-year beneficial leases were totally inadequate to cope with extensive development where it was necessary for the builder to recoup his losses through selling the lease with enough years to make it worth the buyer's while. At this time before the Universities and Colleges Estates Acts of 1858 and 1860, the College needed a private Act of Parliament in order to allow them to grant leases for ninety-nine years. In October 1854 authorisation to apply to Parliament for the necessary act was made and the bill was passed on 14 August 1855.[97]

The first building lease on the estate was made in October 1856 to John Dyne of Claremont Place, Wandsworth Road, Surrey.[98] The lease was for a plot facing Woodstock Road where Dyne proceeded to begin building a large semi-detached villa in the Italianate style not unlike many of the villas in Park Town (Plate 12). He took out three mortgages in September, October, and December 1856 for a total of £450 from the solicitors Morrell and Biddle, the former being the same F.J. Morrell who had so recently begun to encourage the College to exploit their North Oxford properties.[99] But by July 1857 Dyne had retreated and Thomas Winterbourne, a local builder, had taken over for £170 the lease of the houses which were 'now in course of erection'. Winterbourne sold the lease of the northernmost house of the two, 123 Woodstock Road, in August 1859 to the Rev Henry Renton. He demised 121 Woodstock Road to Louisa Pryor for ten years from September 1861 and sold the lease to her in January 1871. The price was £1,150, but £800 of this went to Rev Thomas Morrell, brother of F.J., who had held a mortgage on the property since 1862. And those were the only two houses built to Seckham's plan. An attempt was made in 1860 to auction off the part of the development facing Woodstock Road, but little building started in the area until the mid-1860s when Seckham had given up all interest in the scheme. By this time William Wilkinson had taken over as the supervising architect of the whole of the College's North Oxford estate.

Why was this first effort at development such a failure? Part of the answer might lie with Seckham himself who had returned to Oxford from London apparently intent on establishing himself as a developer, but perhaps with too little sensitivity to the local market. Although Park Town was not a financial success, it was a social success. If the ratio of men to women meant anything in the characterisation of a middle-class suburb, Park Town with 2.6 women to men in 1861 must certainly have been middle-class.[100] There were people both in Oxford and from outside who wanted to live in suburbs north of the city, but perhaps during the 1850s, when the population was

12   Nos 121–3 Woodstock Road, Samuel Lipscomb Seckham, 1856.

stagnant, there just were not enough. More importantly, the history of the Park Town tontine indicates that the organisation of investment capital in Oxford was not sophisticated enough yet to cope with a large development in that area.

We can only speculate on the moment when St John's College decided to develop St Giles's Fields into the residential suburb of North Oxford. The Beaumont and Walton Street developments could be seen as the continuation of earlier building in St Giles's Street rather than as a conscious move to develop the whole of their land to the north of the city. By 1840 the College had decided not to renew the lease of a large section of land held by the Duke of Marlborough, and certainly by 1849 when the Guardians were making plans for their new workhouse on Banbury Road the College's surveyor was warning the fellows about the adverse effect such a scheme would have on any future suburban development they might be contemplating. The pressure put on the old suburb of St Giles's Fields by such proposals as the workhouse and the Oxford, Worcester and Wolverhampton Railway line may have been the spur to the College to undertake the comprehensive development of their land in North Oxford. Nonetheless it seems to have taken F.J. Morrell, the new steward of St John's, to make the necessary conceptual leap from old style multi-functional suburb to single function, residential suburb, before the College could embark on the formation of their North Oxford estate.

CHAPTER III
The Beginnings of North Oxford

In the spring of 1883, the Oxford Building and Investment Company faced collapse after having provided investment for much of the suburban development around Oxford. The consequences were disastrous, not just for the directors and officers of the company, but also for the many small investors who had placed savings in their hands. It was the inability to find adequate investment capital that had led to the demise of the Park Town Estate Company in 1861. From its inception in 1866, the Oxford Building Company set out to provide that much needed investment for the house-building industry, but whereas Park Town had buyers and no capital, after seventeen years of the Oxford Building Company's operations, the Oxford housing market was suffering from an excess of capital and no buyers.

The failure of the Oxford Building Company marked the end of the first phase in the development of the North Oxford estate, so that the twenty-three years from 1860 to 1883 provide a convenient period within which to study the initial workings of the development (Plate 13). Speaking at the general meeting of the Oxford Building and Investment Company when its difficulties were first revealed, the chairman described how the suburb in North Oxford had 'sprung up like enchantment'.[1] For this 'enchantment' to take effect, however, circumstances had to have time to mature. It was not enough that St John's College owned 300 acres in North Oxford for the suburb to materialise, nor was it enough to make the decision to develop the land although that was an important step. Of more importance was the availability of investment capital, not just for building, but also for the occupation of the houses through the holding of leases and mortgages. The next requirement was the market, and for middle-class houses this meant families characterised by middle-class income and status. Finally the local network of builders, suppliers and labourers determined the success of any suburban enterprise.

In Oxford at this time there seems to have been no lack of those calling themselves builders as well as other building craftsmen such as masons, carpenters, bricklayers, plumbers, and plasterers. The colleges themselves attracted craftsmen to the city since from the middle of the nineteenth century work was almost continuous on the fabric of the college buildings. College work could cause a scarcity and put up rates of pay which would have made it difficult to build houses cheaply enough for the pockets of local

13   Map of North Oxford (redrawn by Geoffrey Randell); heavy black line delineates extent of property of St John's College.

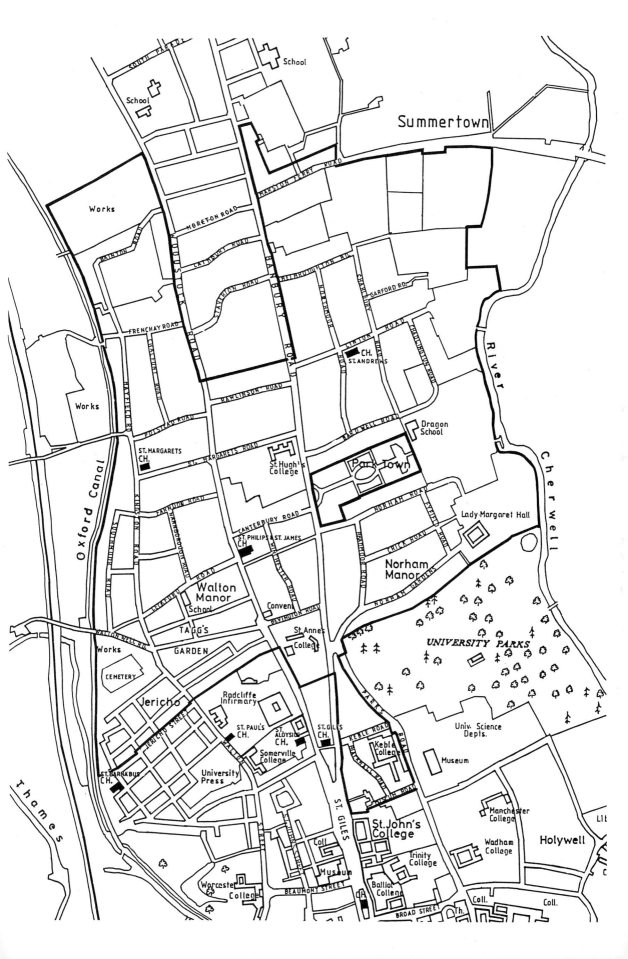

people, but there seems to have been no shortage of labour coming into the city. Between 1861 and 1871 males over twenty years involved in the building industry increased by 222, or 28 per cent.[2] Compared with another country town like Reading, there were far more stonemasons among the building workers in Oxford, a situation to be expected where both the restoration of old college buildings and the erection of new required much stonework. During the ten years from 1861, however, the number of bricklayers in Oxford increased from 57 to 141 or by 147 per cent.[3] Even the building of Keble College could not account for such a disproportionate growth without the added increase in brick-built suburban houses.

In order to erect houses the builders needed two things: first, access to capital and second, people who wanted to buy the houses once they were built. In the wealthy industrial or commercial cities like Birmingham or Liverpool the money for development was readily available from the profits of industry and commerce which gradually came into the hands of more and more people. In a town like Oxford, industry was not the main source of wealth, but even here up-to-date commercial practices and a rational approach to profits had begun to prevail. The general middle-class prosperity had also given those attending the University more spending power so that tailors, confectioners, wine merchants, bootmakers etc. experienced an increase in trade, and therefore enjoyed increased profits ripe for investment. All the builder had to do was to convince the tradesmen to invest in the new houses.

The small investor was essential for the amount of building necessary to ensure the success of the various suburbs around Oxford. The building society, although in its infancy, was one means by which small investors, particularly women, could invest in housing. The two organisations which were most active in the Oxford area at this time were the Oxford and Abingdon Permanent Benefit Building Society and the Oxford Building and Investment Company. The former was started in 1851 and was run on building society lines, while the latter increasingly provided risk money to local developers with dire results, but it could be argued that without these channels of funds, house building especially in North Oxford would never have reached the rate needed to produce a satisfactory suburb.

Just as in the Beaumont Street development there were people who took houses either for occupation or for investment, so there were in the later suburbs these two types of houseowners. Both the owner-occupier and the investor might need a mortgage in order to finance their purchase, which meant another group of investors was necessary to provide money for houses already constructed. The purpose of building societies and investment companies was to bring together borrowers and lenders, but local solicitors and banks such as F.J. Morrell and the London and County Bank were also useful in matching up interested parties, especially when it came to dealing with potential lenders from outside the locality. There were also professional money brokers like St Swithin Williams of the High Street, ready to advance money on deeds. Altogether these agents formed an intricate network providing the accumulated capital necessary to make the suburbs possible.

It might be expected that enticing people to occupy the houses would not pose a problem. It is after all a commonplace that the nineteenth-century middle classes moved out wholesale from the centre of their cities to the newly built suburbs. In 1860 a Mr Winstanley who had come to Oxford to speak on behalf of the Conservative Land Society presumed that the inclination of the population of Oxford was 'like those of other large towns and cities, to reside away from the places of business, in order to have the change of scene and air . . .'.[4] But Oxford was by general agreement a beautiful city and the absence of noxious industry meant that although it might be overcrowded through the expansion of the colleges and commerce it could still be a pleasant place to live. Even today central Oxford gives some idea of what it must have been like in the 1860s when business, social and religious life were concentrated in a very circumscribed area. There must have been a period when the drawbacks of the suburbs still outweighed their advantages. Before social connections could develop and when the services were still rudimentary, who would leave the conviviality of the centre of town for the inconvenience and isolation of the suburb? Thus the freehold land societies, sponsored by the Liberal and Conservative parties before the 1867 Reform Bill to increase the franchise through home-ownership, were agents in convincing Oxford people of their need for suburban houses as much as they were providers of the means for fulfilling that need.

Some men of affairs like Thomas Mallam, John Parsons, and G.P. Hester did retreat to North Oxford, while at the other end of the social scale, the working classes as shown in the last chapter moved into marginal areas to the west in St Thomas's parish, between Walton Street and the canal. But the concept of the middle-class suburb inhabited by young families had to evolve with the development of the middle class itself.

One area of Oxford where middle-class suburban life did begin to flourish in the 1860s was the new district on the eastern side of Magdalen Bridge. Here, in the parish of St Clement's and the new streets between Cowley and Iffley Roads, development gained momentum at the same time as a wave of redevelopment in the centre extended college buildings and expanded business premises into former living space. Between 1861 and 1871 the eleven parishes forming the central area of Oxford experienced a net loss in their population of 831, while the net increase in St Clements and Cowley was 2,167.[5] Commercial clerks and small tradesmen began to gravitate towards this new residential area and it is likely that newcomers to Oxford found it easier to find accommodation here than in the more congested centre. The land was largely freehold and taken in relatively small lots by local builders on a speculative basis. Development was a very stop-go affair, but over the ten years from 1855 to 1865 there grew up a network of speculators and investors who were well versed in the complex dealing necessary to produce a suburb.

As noted previously a lack of local connections and credit may have been one of the reasons why the first attempt of St John's College to develop their North Oxford property failed to succeed. It will be remembered that John Dyne, the London builder, who made the first agreement with St John's in

1856 for 7 acres on Woodstock Road, managed to start only two houses, and that with the financial assistance of the College's solicitors, Morrell and Biddle. By the summer of 1857, Dyne had assigned his interest in the houses to the local builder, Thomas Winterbourne, and no further houses were built on the site at that time. Without the close connections that existed between local builders and investors it would be difficult for an outsider to embark on the sort of development the College wanted for their Oxford suburb.

In the autumn of 1859, St John's appointed a committee to consider the best way to develop the North Oxford estate.[6] Such determination on the part of the College did not completely discourage new demands on North Oxford land for a diversity of functions. In 1859 the Board of Guardians once more appealed to the College for land on which to build a now badly needed workhouse, and in 1860 the proposal of a railway line across the suburb was again put forward. This time, however, the College was better prepared to defend its interests. The Guardians were given a flat no, but Dr Adams, a fellow of the College, subsequently became chairman of the Board of Guardians and successfully negotiated a site on the Cowley Road owned by Pembroke and Magdalen Colleges for the new workhouse.[7]

Dr Adams was also present in September 1860 at a public meeting to discuss the projected Wycombe and Thame Railway which it was proposed should continue on to Oxford.[8] Instead of condemning the line, he adopted a reasoned approach and sought to influence its route into Oxford. In contrast to the derisive laughter directed at 'doctors of divinity' in 1852, Dr Adams succeeded in eliciting applause from his audience by representing the members of the University as 'men of business'.

Railways and their stations were no longer seen as antithetical to residential suburbs and the two, it was thought by some, could exist side by side. A correspondent to *Jackson's Oxford Journal* suggested that a short branch line should be built with the express intention of providing a passenger station for the northern suburb on the east side of Banbury Road near the University Parks. The station would, he thought, enhance the value of the surrounding property, but must itself be controlled by the aesthetic requirements of the suburb:

> . . . I would suggest that it [the station] should be an elegant architectural building, in harmony with our University buildings. Indeed, I do not see why the Flemish-Gothic style should not be adopted, so that neither the building itself, or the purpose for which it should be used, should either be offensive to the neighbourhood, but the former an ornament, the latter a great public convenience.[9]

Nothing came of this proposal, but it showed that the residential suburb was now making the running and that North Oxford despite its few houses was no longer regarded as marginal ground waiting for a new function.

The committee of fellows set up by St John's in 1859 to consider the best way to proceed with the development of the College's property in North Oxford decided to try again to sell building leases on what was called the Walton Manor estate, alongside the two houses started by Dyne in 1856.

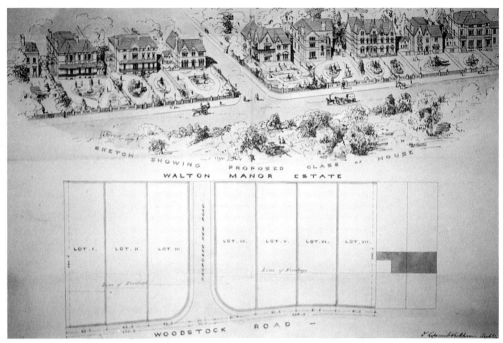

14 Bird's-eye view and plan of Walton Manor, Samuel Lipscomb Seckham, 1860 (SJC Muniments).

Once more Samuel Seckham, the architect, was to co-ordinate the scheme, but now only seven plots facing Woodstock Road were for sale, and on the drawing accompanying the prospectus a proposed turning at right angles to the thoroughfare was the sole suggestion that more streets were planned (Plate 14).[10] By this time it had been decided that the new church in the area would occupy a position on the east side of Woodstock Road, opposite the plots for sale. In 1853 the Board of Guardians had been pleased with Seckham's offer to buy freehold a large block of their land on Banbury Road because that meant they need not put it up for auction. Their fear was that only some lots would be sold and that development would be piecemeal, reducing the value of the remaining land. In 1860, St John's resorted to the auction sale of their building land with unsatisfactory results.

When the sale of the Woodstock Road properties came up in June 1860, five of the seven lots were sold, and some of these apparently went to speculators who could ill afford the ground rent, let alone the cost of building houses. Samuel Nicholls, after three years without any indication of building on his plot, pleaded extreme poverty, and gave up his building lease. Later John Galpin, a local surveyor, was to remember that what he called a 'very low class of people' took many of the College's plots and simply removed the gravel and anything else of value, before the College could regain control of the land.[11] In fact only two plots bought at the sale of 14 June 1860 were built upon by the successful bidders, while the rest passed through a succession of hands before the houses were started.

That summer the College also put up for auction a wholly new section of

43

15 Bird's-eye view of Norham Manor, watercolour attributed to William Wilkinson, *c* 1860 (Bodleian Library).

the North Oxford estate in the southeast corner, abutting the University Parks. This they called the Norham Manor estate. The layout for this area was made by William Wilkinson, an architect and member of a Witney family involved in building and property management (Plate 15). The College began by putting up for sale only the southernmost portion of the property which they owned in conjunction with the vicar of St Giles's since some of the land formed part of the St Giles's glebe land.[12] The auction took place at the beginning of July 1860, and the result seems to have been poorer even than that on the Woodstock Road site. Only two plots were taken by a Mr Thompson of St Giles's, but houses were not started and the plots eventually passed to another developer in 1868. The only houses to be built on the Norham Manor estate within the next two years were those of Professors Goldwin Smith and Montagu Burrows.

The College held at least three more auctions of building land.[13] The first took place on 30 March 1864 and was for four plots in Woodstock Road not successfully disposed of in 1860. Lots 1 and 2 may have been sold at this sale, but lot 3 passed from the builder John Dorn to William Lucy, iron founder, in 1865, and lot 4 was taken by Robert Hills in the same year. The second sale was held in August 1865 for the plots on the south side of the new Bevington Road. Of the ten houses subsequently built on these plots, only three or possibly four were put up by the original buyers. The third sale, in

44

July 1866, included land at the north end of Norham Manor estate on the south side of what became Norham Road and ten plots on the east side of the newly laid out Kingston Road. The Norham Manor property remained unsold and was even later considered for the site of a new church.[14] Nor was any of the Kingston Road property taken, and most of it had to wait another two years before development began there in earnest.

It must be remembered that what the College was auctioning at these sales were the building leases of the various plots and not the freehold of the land. The buyers bid on the ground rent, and whoever offered the highest rent for the plot gained the right to build, while paying the agreed annual rent. Depending on the length of the lease, whether ninety-nine or sixty-six years, the fixed ground rent had then to be paid yearly by the leaseholder until the reversion of the lease. The College had employed the auction sale in disposing of building leases during the 1820s and 1830s when they were letting the Beaumont and Walton Closes, but this type of sale may have been much less attractive in the 1860s when there was much more freehold land available, particularly in suburban Cowley. Why did they persist with the auction sale when it seemed to give only poor results? Galpin said that he had attended the sales on behalf of the College 'to assist in forcing the Land into the Market'.[15] If an auction did not succeed in disposing of building leases the run up to the sale with the series of newspaper advertisements and the excitement that any sale generated may have been a good way of presenting the College's plans to a wide public and of interesting people in the suburb.

It must be admitted that progress on the new suburb was slow despite newspaper reports that villas were 'springing up' in the area. During the seven years up to the end of 1866, fifty-nine houses were proposed and approved by the College, while thirty-seven leases were granted.[16] This last figure indicates the number of houses actually on the ground at the time, although they might not have been finished. For anyone accustomed to the rate of development going on in London during the same period, this seems extremely leisurely. At the end of seven years on Highbury New Park, a comparable estate in north London begun in 1853, two and a half times as many houses had been built.[17]

There were several reasons for the slow start in North Oxford, and one of these was the way the College managed its affairs at this time.[18] The member of the College responsible for its internal running as well as the administration of its estates was the bursar. His tasks ranged from buying and selling property to collecting the battels or college expenses from the fellows and scholars. Because the revenue from the College's estates was essential to its existence, the bursar's position was a demanding one and yet, like the other college offices except that of the president, it was held in rotation. Each autumn, when the fellows elected the officers for the coming year, a new senior bursar took up his post. Although some continuity was maintained by the custom of electing the current senior bursar as junior bursar for the next year, there was bound to be a certain amount of interruption in the work of the bursary.

16 No 18 Norham Gardens,
Frederick Codd, 1872.

The bursar had discretion in carrying out his duties, but the decisions of
the College were communal. A meeting of the president and fellows was
held quarterly throughout the year when they formally discussed matters of
policy and when decisions on a wide range of business were made. Until the
1860s the College managed to run its affairs through its regular meetings of
senior members and the ordinary exercise of the bursar's office. A growing
complexity, however, was creeping into its affairs. The change from beneficial leases to rack renting meant that extensive work was needed to be
done to improve the College's farm lands and buildings. This work had to
be carried out at a time when the college was no longer receiving the usual
fines from the now expiring beneficial leases. Twice during 1860 the bursar
was authorised to seek loans from the bank to pay for the ordinary expenses
of the College.[19] The development of North Oxford was yet another responsibility requiring an expertise not yet acquired by the College members,
so while the bursar took time to seek the advice and consent of his colleagues,
potential builders might be forgiven for believing that there was no real
necessity to press forward with the estate. In 1867 it was decided to change
the regulation so that the bursar could be elected for a period of five years
in order that he might maintain greater control over the ever increasing
complexity of the College's business and particularly of that connected with
the estates.

It was true that the College did not have the same need as the speculator to get on with building, and this was another reason for the slow pace of development. No matter what happened they would not forfeit their North Oxford property, so they could afford to wait for favourable circumstances. But the longer development hung suspended, the more contradictions emerged within the enterprise. Although not stated in so many words at this point, it is obvious from their actions that the College wanted to develop large areas of their suburb with first-class houses. One way of ensuring this was through high ground rents, to discourage the impecunious speculator and to encourage the wealthy who would want to get an adequate return on their investment whether they occupied the house themselves or let it to others (Plate 16). No one would build a house producing only £10 or £15 a year in rent on a plot with an annual ground rent of £10. On the other hand, house building needed to go on apace before the suburb became recognised as a desirable place to live. Lots left vacant while the College held out for high rents would become increasingly unattractive to the wealthy, and the temptation would be to fill up the empty spaces with lower quality houses. This happened constantly in suburbs where the market had a stronger influence on what was built. In order to avoid this situation, the College designated areas where cheaper houses could be put up and they then defended the segregation of house types with vigour, even if this meant waiting a period of years.

In October 1862 the College established an estates committee to handle the business connected with all their properties, whether rural or suburban.[20] Early on it was recognised that the North Oxford estate should be divided into two, the greater part dedicated to detached and semi-detached villas for the comfortable middle classes and the other built with terraces and smaller houses for the lower middle and working classes. When Samuel Nicholls could not afford to develop his Woodstock Road site in 1863, the bursar offered him an alternative: '. . . if your objection is merely to the size and style of the house which would have to be built on the site which you selected, the College has other sites upon which an inferior class of house might be erected and which would pay you better.'[21] It has been suggested that the College developed the lower-class side of their estate in reaction to the 1865 proposal by the Great Western Railway to establish their carriage works in west Oxford, just beyond the railway station.[22] But already in October 1864, the College fellows had asked the estates committee to consider the construction of cottages on their land, and cottage accommodation on the estate continued to be a concern at least until Hayfield Road was built in the 1880s, long after the idea of the carriage works had been abandoned.[23] The College still owned land near Worcester College and in Jericho, and admittedly they did ask Wilkinson to lay out this land for building in April 1865, the same month the railway directors decided to build their carriage works in Cripley Meadow. In May while enthusiasm for the works was still high, and before the backlash against turning Oxford into a manufacturing town, the College ordered a layout for what would become Kingston Road, from Walton Well to Heyfield Hutt (Plate 17). These two areas were on the far side of the North Oxford property, away from the

17   Nos 114–16 Kingston Road, C.C. Rolfe, 1872.

College itself. Already they had assumed a working-class character through their proximity to the railway and the canal, and through their association with the Tagg's Garden district. By accepting a lower class of development in the western portion of the estate, St John's were in a better position to reserve the streets nearer the College for handsome, high-class villas.

Although by embarking on the suburban development of their North Oxford property the College became committed to a commercial undertaking, their needs did not always coincide with the needs of development. The size and location of the houses had to be closely controlled as did the style and quality of building, so that pragmatic compromise based on commercial expediency could not erode the original intention of a first-class suburb. This was especially true in the early years when it was important to establish the character of the various areas, for what was appropriate in the sequestered roads behind the College was not always suitable for the more public thoroughfares. In 1868 the bursar, questioning the wisdom of Sleeman Lovis' building plans on a prominent site at the corner of Bevington and Woodstock Roads, wrote to the estate architect: 'I think the corner lot is an important one, and ought to be well filled up'.[24] Lovis subsequently gave up his plans and the houses were built later by someone else.

Eventually the estates committee adopted a procedure which involved control at every stage of the building process.[25] Whoever wanted to take a building lease had to present on a printed form the proposed site, ground rent, and rental value of the house. Ground rent varied considerably from one side of the estate to another. St Catherine's, Bishop Fry's house at 66 Banbury Road, was assigned a ground rent of £23 when the building proposal was made in 1869. That same year the cottages James Walter intended to build at the south end of Kingston Road were given a ground rent of £1.3s.0d. each. Similarly there was a great difference in the estimated annual rental values of these houses. The annual rental value of St Catherines was £120, while the rental of one of the cottages was only a tenth of that at £12. Once the proposal was signed by the supervising architect, then drawings had to be produced and approved before a building agreement could be prepared. This agreement was the first binding contract with the College. In order to instil a sense of urgency into the building agreement, the time within which the house was to be built was included. 'Time was of the essence', and if the house was not built within the usual two years, the agreement could be terminated. The College continued to hold the title to the house until it reached the first floor, so that if the builder went bankrupt or into liquidation at this stage, he could not use the house as an asset to pay off his creditors. This gave an added impetus for a quick completion. When the shell of the house was covered a lease of either ninety-nine or sixty-six years, depending on the type of house, would be granted to the builder or his nominee.

Four types of people took out building agreements and whether they also took the leases depended on their type.[26] First there were those who wanted to have a house built for their own occupation. During the first ten years of development, out of nearly 200 proposals, thirty-six were for purpose-built houses, usually designed by Oxford architects for local tradesmen and members of the clergy. These houses were concentrated in three specific areas: the west side of Woodstock Road, the east side of Banbury Road, and the west end of Norham Gardens. It is understandable why St John's encouraged such leaseholders because their personal interest in their own house ensured that the quality of building was superior and, while the design might be idiosyncratic, the houses were distinctive and set the character for the rest of the estate. James Hughes and Henry Hatch of Park Town both built in Banbury Road, as did two chemists, William Walsh and T.G. Cousins, and the corn merchant, John Weaving (Plate 18). Across the road from the new church in Woodstock Road appeared houses for Edwin Butler, the wine merchant, R.S. Hawkins, the lawyer, and Robert Hills, the photographer. Only five of these thirty-six houses were intended for members of the University and four of these were in Norham Manor. Professor Westwood chose to build in Woodstock Road, but

19   No 9 Norham Gardens, Charles Buckeridge, 1868, residence of Montagu Burrows, Regius Professor of Modern History.

Professors Goldwin Smith, Montagu Burrows, and Bonamy Price all built within close proximity of each other in what became Norham Gardens close to the Parks, and set a precedent which meant that in later years professors tended to live in this part of the suburb (Plate 19).

The second type of people taking building agreements were those who built a house in order to let it for the income it produced. At first this type consisted mainly of local tradesmen who took the smaller houses in Museum and Blackhall Roads. There were for example Frederick Irwin, hairdresser and perfume seller, John Sleeman Lovis, commercial traveller for a biscuit company, and Thomas Moses Allnutt, the head butler at St John's College. After the mid-1860s, builders replaced nearly all other tradesmen as those engaged in building houses expressly for their own investment. Some builders like John Dorn wanted a long term investment for the income it generated, while others were more interested in house property because they could raise collateral on loans to build other houses.

The type which produced the largest number of houses consisted of builders who took a building agreement, built the house, and then sold it within a short time to someone else. In taking the lease from the builder, the

18   No 64 Banbury Road, E.G. Bruton, 1873, built for the corn dealer John Weaving.

buyer became the College's lessee and assumed the reponsibility of paying the ground rent (Plate 20). The numbers of builders who got involved in this sort of development leapt up when the College released land in the west of the suburb on the newly laid out Kingston Road. Many small local builders took lots for terraces and semi-detached houses there, but only a handful of builders were involved in putting up the villas in the main part of the estate. One of these was Frederick Codd, an architect and builder, whose work dominated the Norham Manor and Canterbury Road areas until 1876. John Dorn was responsible for only slightly fewer houses, and other builders included John Dover, William Cross from London, and William Allsop Reynolds from Daventry.

The fourth type were the developers. These were the middlemen who were not builders themselves, but acted as brokers between the builders and the lessees, and who were important in arranging finances for loans and mortgages. During the early years, John Galpin, the local surveyor, was the only one seriously to pursue the role of developer. He and the builder, John Dover, were occupied especially with houses in the Norham Manor estate and the area around Warnborough Road. (Plate 21). In the mid-1870s a rival appeared in Walter Gray, the steward of Keble College, who had the sense to become engaged in both the smaller houses of Kingston Road and some larger ones in the adjacent streets. Galpin made the mistake of underestimating Gray, and as will emerge, suffered the consequences. Finally Frederick Pike, the auctioneer, should be mentioned here although his activity in North Oxford at this time was limited, albeit through no fault of his own.

The market for custom-built houses was practically exhausted by 1870 and speculation became the dominant pattern of production throughout the 1870s. Builders of both villas and cottages were able to get their capital from

20 (*far left*) Building Leckford Road in the 1870s (Local Studies Library, Oxford Central Library).

21 No 30 Norham Gardens, Galpin and Shirley, 1876.

the two local lending institutions, and building surged ahead. By 1883, 664 building proposals had been made for houses in North Oxford and 539 leases had been taken up. Of the proposals, 365 were for houses in the main part of the estate, from Norham Manor to Leckford and Warnborough Roads, while 299 were for houses on the west side, mainly in Kingston Road, but also in the newly laid out Southmoor Road which accounted for most of the 111 proposals made for this area in 1882 and 1883.

Building proposals and leases taken up to 1883

	Central Area	Kingston Road Area	Total
Proposals	365	299	664
Leases Taken	354	185	539

On the west side there was still vacant building land around the old gravel pit at Walton Well, but in the centre of the estate the houses had reached the old Hutt Road, later renamed St Margaret's Road, and the south side of Park Town. Both these roads seemed to have marked a notional barrier and until the College released more building land to the north, no further development could take place.

Builders and developers depended on the College to release building land, and when the best sites were taken, proposals dropped in number until new sites were again made available. After considerable activity up to 1874, new proposals slackened for the rest of the decade, while at the same time the number of leases levelled off. Although there was a steady market for houses in the area, it could not sustain the rapid rate of building enjoyed earlier. The College seemed reluctant to release more land until the development already begun was completed, possibly because the expensive burden of constructing the roads fell initially on them, whether the roads were built by a private contractor or the Oxford Local Board of Health, the body responsible for roads in the city. The College relied on their lessees to repay them through a road rate, but as the pace of building slowed, their chances of quickly recouping this heavy expense became more remote. The withholding of building land, however, put those builders locked into the North Oxford development in a difficult position. New sites generated new business, and competition for the few remaining sites in Warnborough and Farndon Roads became fierce. But while the builders fought over the remaining plots of land, it became apparent that the real problem was a lack of buyers.

The acceleration of building in North Oxford coincided with the establishment in 1866 of the Oxford Building and Investment Company which very soon began lending money to builders right across the suburb.[27] At first its prime purpose was to enable people without a great accumulation of savings to buy their own house for occupation or investment. It must be remembered too that they drew in money from small investors who might not have had enough savings to make a worthwhile loan to a builder, and who would not anyway want to take the kind of risk such a loan entailed. Of the company's 247 local bondholders given in a published list in 1883, 119 or 48 per cent were women.[28] As a group, women tended not to get involved in high-risk lending, so that the Oxford Building Company could bring them and other small capitalists into an area of economic activity they might not otherwise have entered. By providing loans for building they could also encourage small builders into a scale of development not otherwise open to them.

As far as money for building loans went, the Oxford Building Company and the Oxford and Abingdon Permanent Building Society split North Oxford between them. Up to 1883, 237 houses are known to have been built on borrowed money, and of these 182 were financed by one or other of the two companies.[29] Most of these houses were found in the Kingston Road area where small builders depended on corporate loans. Mortgage money, on the other hand, was concentrated in the main section of the suburb, and was provided chiefly by individuals. Only 58 houses of the 206 mortgaged by 1883 had a corporate mortgagee.[30] Again the two dominant companies divided nearly all this business between them.

Known number of houses up to 1883 financed through loans and mortgages

	Corporate		Individual		Total
Loans	190	80%	47	19.8%	237
Mortgages	58	28.1%	148	71.8%	206

Mortgages were made on already existing houses, when the bricks and mortar guaranteed security of investment, but in order to get those houses up, even in the wealthier parts of North Oxford, some mechanism was needed to ensure investment when the outcome was unsure. This was the role of the two loan companies.

From about 1870 to 1875, the man who dominated the estate in terms of houses constructed was Frederick Codd. He was an architect and builder from outside Oxford, having come originally from Norfolk via London where he had an office in the Adelphi in 1860.[31] Codd first appeared in North Oxford in 1865 when he applied on behalf of a Miss Frances Norris of Norwich to build a house in Banbury Road. Soon he was making more applications for plots on Banbury Road and Norham Manor, and in 1871 the *Oxford Chronicle* described these areas as 'the wealthiest site in Oxford where the taste of Mr F. Codd, as architect, reigns supreme . . .'.[32] Besides his speculative activities, Codd designed some custom-built houses like St Catherine's in Banbury Road for Bishop Fry, but he was also busy at this time on buildings in the town. Extensions to the premises of Mr Faulkner, a clothier in Cornmarket, and of Messrs Elliston and Cavell in Magdalen Street were included in the 1871 *Chronicle* report, as was a granary for Mr Weaving in Park End Street.[33]

Codd worked in conjunction with James Walter, a local builder who took plots himself in Kingston Road and was responsible for many of the terraced cottages there. Both Codd and Walter depended for their capital on the Oxford and Abingdon Building Society of which Codd was a member. The society enabled him to take building plots speculatively in Norham Gardens, Bradmore, Crick and Fyfield Roads, Bevington and Banbury Roads, the north end of Winchester Road and the whole of Canterbury Road. Most of the houses Codd completed successfully, but things began to go wrong in the mid-1870s. By March 1876 he owed the building society £16,047 in respect of advances on several unsold houses.[34] In order to pay back the advances and break even, Codd would have had to sell these houses at an average price of £1,337 each, about £200 to £300 more than was being paid for comparable houses at that time.[35] But worse than that, he does not seem to have been able to sell the houses at all.

In January 1876, the newspapers carried advertisements for houses in Canterbury and Winchester Roads, indicating that buyers were not already lined up.[36] Then in July, Codd himself took the leases of six houses and immediately mortgaged the property to the Oxford and Abingdon. This move did not stave off ruin, but only ensured his main creditor controlled most of his assets. By the end of September he was in liquidation and two sales of his building plant and equipment in Bradmore Road took place during the autumn.[36] In November, his own house at 39 Banbury Road was sold.

The year 1876 was a bad one also for the builder, James Walter, and for William Allsop Reynolds, who had been attracted to Oxford from Daventry in 1870 and had built houses in Norham Manor and Leckford and Kingston Roads. Both these men went into liquidation during the year thus adding their names to a growing list of tradesmen suffering the failure of their businesses.[37] Collapsing builders and a contracting housing market did not, however, discourage the acute entrepreneur. In December 1876, F.R. Pike, auctioneer and secretary of the Oxford and Abingdon Building Society, approached University College with a proposal for their property in North

Oxford, and started a correspondence which throws light on the state of development at this time.[38]

As noted in the last chapter, University College owned the land in Banbury Road on which G.P. Hester had built his house, the Mount, which is now the site of St Hugh's College. Hester died in 1876, leaving some years left to run on the lease, and Pike, in his capacity as auctioneer, had tried to sell the house for the family without success. Pike then came up with a scheme by which University College would buy back the lease and then grant a building lease for the land to be developed with villas to the value of £10,000. In writing to C.J. Faulkner,[39] the bursar of University College, Pike claimed that the growth of Oxford was stopped by the Mount, and the other residence in the vicinity, the Lawn. Faulkner rejected Pike's offer and added: 'There is obviously at present a glut of new houses in the neighbourhood of Oxford and so far as I can judge, it is not new houses that are wanted for tenants, but tenants that are wanted for the empty houses just built.'[40] Pike was not to be put off. He had been to America in the 1860s where he may have learnt persistence in commercial matters, and he seems not to have suffered from an excess of deference. After the third proposal, Faulkner's comment was that University College should take over the lease and develop the land in conjunction with St John's and let building sites 'directly to those proposing to live in the houses, and thus avoid the curse and cost of a middle man like Pike, who would simply put money in his pocket for doing nothing'.[41]

By this time St John's had a full-time estates bursar, T.S. Omond. Pike had also approached St John's about a scheme similar to the one he had proposed to University College, and after meeting Pike, Omond wrote to Faulkner:

> I do not wonder at your refusing to have any thing to do with it [Pike's scheme]. It is Pike in his most loathesome form. The ground is cut up into small villas, every available inch squeezed out. And the Colleges get no more for the land. They are paid so much an acre. It is simply to facilitate the Oxford builders' running up small cheap villas, and getting his profit out of them.[42]

Omond's opinion of the Oxford builders was less than generous when it is remembered that it was they who took the risk in building the houses while, in comparison, the risk undertaken by the College was much less. Codd's fate showed that when the College decided that the class of houses to be built must be more expensive than the market could sustain, the builder did not stay long in business. Omond also signalled dissatisfaction with the way the suburb had developed up until then. He thought more ground should have been included in the building plots, and that 'sometimes we have been hardly strict enough in the approval of architects and plans'.[43] Was this a hint that the dominant gothic style of the houses in North Oxford had become old fashioned by 1878 (Plate 22)?

Omond had replaced Dr Adams as bursar in 1877, and many of the understandings which had been made formerly between Adams and the

22   No 11 Norham Gardens, William Wilkinson, 1866, built for the solicitor, George Mallam.

North Oxford developers since he took office in 1872 were questioned by the new bursar. John Galpin, for instance, found that building land he thought had been 'booked' to him was transferred to others. In the past he had taken an option on land on which, although he was not actually paying ground rent, he could maintain the right of first refusal. This land he would dispense to friendly builders for a nominal fee. Now he was left with a lot in Farndon Road from which the gravel had been removed, and which required considerable expense to put right before building could commence. In his letter of protest to Omond, Galpin wrote: '... I do feel at a loss to account for this somewhat exceptional treatment and I cannot but think that from some quarter or other there is someone giving me a sly poke and that an inch or two below the belt.'[44] Competiton for sites had intensified since Galpin had made his gentleman's agreement with Dr Adams, and the rivalry was introducing a note of rancour among the developers of North Oxford.

   The insecurity of the times would have been brought home to St John's

College when their London bank, Messrs Willis, Percival and Company of Lombard Street, failed in February 1878.[45] This was one of the City banks which handled mainly country accounts, and it had suffered with the general decline in rural prosperity. What had begun as a few bad harvests at the beginning of the 1870s, had developed into agricultural depression when cheap American grain began to supply any deficiency in the market. There is a question, however, over the extent of the depression in Britain at this time, since a more complex economy meant that whereas fifty years before a decline in agriculture plunged nearly the whole country into depression, hardship was now selective.[46] Those in shipping and finance waxed wealthy and even those in farming able to turn their land to pasture were spared the worst. Oxfordshire farmers were in the grain belt and found it difficult to make the change from arable to pastoral production, and yet even in Oxford business did not grind to a halt. During an earlier interlude of poor harvests, in 1861, the chairman of the Oxford and Abingdon Building Society remarked that business had been better than expected, 'notwithstanding the general failure of the harvest, and the consequent great commercial depression'.[47] Poor returns from the land could mean a diversion of funds into suburban building, and indeed the problem the building societies had was finding enough business for their money to do. The slowdown in Oxford's housing market in the mid-1870s had badly affected individuals like Frederick Codd, but by the early 1880s the situation led to a more general collapse when the Oxford Building and Investment Company finally succumbed in their struggle to keep their business going.

The Oxford Building and Investment Company was registered in February 1866 not long before 'Black Friday', 11 May 1866 when the collapse of the large discount house, Overend and Gurney, with liabilities of £18 million, threw the City of London into panic. That they survived their first year against a background of financial crisis was a matter of pride for the directors of the Oxford Building Company when they came to make their first annual report.[48] The decline of the discount houses was symptomatic of a shift towards a different style of banking, whereby deposit banks took a greater share of the nation's savings while at the same time circulating this money more widely through loans.[49] The Oxford Building Company embraced this new style, and from the first conducted their business on bank overdrafts. Although they protested that none of the public's investments would be used for 'doubtful or speculative undertaking', the directors projected an image of daring and innovation. In 1871, one of the directors, Mr Luff, was reported as saying: 'He had heard it said that because they had such a small sum of money at their bankers the society must be going wrong, but that was quite a mistake, because instead of letting their money remain idle in the bank they let it out at interest.'[50] Luff compared the company's business practices favourably with tradesmen who, he implied, were rather cautious and narrow in their approach, while the company had the assets to be more expansive and bold. This attitude continued even as business began to contract, and while the Oxford and Abingdon Building Society prudently withdrew from North Oxford after Codd's difficulties in 1876, the Oxford

Building and Investment Company continued lending at a rate which led them into very doubtful practices.

At the first annual meeting in 1867, John Galpin, the secretary and surveyor of the company, was said to have been its 'main spring', and it was true that he drew to himself every aspect of the company's work. Galpin was born in 1825, the son of a carpenter who had come to Oxford from Somerset in search of work.[51] Galpin himself was apprenticed as a carpenter in Margaret Wyatt's building firm in St Giles's Street. He married young and moved to London where he worked with one of the large building firms there, returning to Oxford in 1854 at the age of twenty-nine to become the surveyor to the Paving Commissioners. His most substantial contribution as surveyor to the Commissioners was the design and construction of Hythe Bridge, but the inelegance of the structure bears witness to the fact that Galpin was not a talented engineer. From 1864 to 1868, he was surveyor to the Local Board and in this capacity had some responsibility for that most intractable of Oxford's engineering problems, the drainage of the town. Galpin then gave up these public positions to devote himself entirely to the Oxford Building Company and his own business interests.

Galpin claimed he had been in the housing business since 1858. In the 1860s he became involved in speculative developments in Cowley, which he undertook with the local solicitor, R.S. Hawkins.[52] His experience in Cowley may well have led to the establishment of the Oxford Building Company and to his selection as their secretary and surveyor. Galpin had other commercial ventures, however, all connected to the building trade. He was a partner with one of his sons in a timber business located at Abbey Wharf, and he was the manager of the Oxford and Berks Brick Company. Besides these enterprises he ran an auctioneering and estate firm in conjunction with another son. It was through the latter business that he took building land in North Oxford, and in his role as developer he worked closely with John Dover, who had previously done a substantial amount of contracting for the city, most notably the work on Hythe Bridge.

As the secretary and surveyor of the Oxford Building Company, Galpin held a key position. He accepted investments and handed out the loans, the amount of which was approved by the directors, but depended on Galpin's assessment of the value of the property to be built or purchased. The company found itself involved more and more in financing house building and Galpin did not make a strict distinction between the company's business and his own.[53] When a builder came to him for a loan to build a house, Galpin would arrange for the drawings to be made in his office, the bricks purchased from the Oxford and Berks Brick Company and the timber from J. & F.J. Galpin, timber and slate merchants. The expenses for these items would be deducted from the loan before it eventually reached the builder's hand. This practice was thrown up at Galpin by his critics as evidence of maladministration, but it may not have been so uncommon and it did nothing to stop the builders, who were advanced a total of £410,830 in the seventeen years the company was in business.[54]

The Oxford Building Company was a joint-stock company and did not register under the Building Society Act of 1874. The interests of the investors and the borrowers were not entirely mutual, since the borrowers did not have to hold any stake in the company. It operated more like a finance company which happened to lend most of its money for house building. At first, because of the scale of their business the company was able to offer annual dividends of from 8 to 10 per cent. Such advantageous rates drew in money from many small investors who tended to use the company as a savings bank.[55] 'The money flowed in like water', and as the rate of building eased off during the second half of the 1870s, new business had to be found to generate enough profit to keep the dividends up. Their profit, of course, was derived from the interest they collected on their loans, and as Galpin remarked in their defence, a company such as theirs loaned to high risk borrowers at 7½ per cent, whereas first-class borrowers got their money elsewhere for 4½ or 5 per cent.[56] By the very nature of their business, they risked a high rate of default. As the housing market collapsed, the company eventually found themselves in possession of 520 houses. Perhaps as a ploy to stimulate a flagging market, the company also began buying building land themselves and selling it off in lots. In 1877 they bought some land in Cowley, but they also came to own land in south Oxford at Grandpont and as far away as Swindon.[57] The Grandpont land belonged formerly to the Great Western Railway, and with the strong Great Western presence in Swindon the idea occurs that there might have been a railway connection in these purchases, especially since one of the directors and sometime chairman was Jason Saunders, Great Western's agent in Oxford. Yet the rate of building declined and, without a steady request for new loans, the company, no matter how much investment it drew in, could not generate the profits to pay the annual dividends. As in most companies in a similar situation, the directors hoped that the lack of business was temporary, and like others before them they paid dividends out of capital.

The holding operation required that the company borrow heavily, and yet retain the confidence of their investors until business picked up. Injudiciously, as it turned out, the Company sought a mortgage for £10,000 from a London bank in order to avoid panic in Oxford. Unfortunately the transaction was very expensive and took sixteen months to complete, during which time gossip began to circulate.[58] In December 1881, Walter Gray made a speech at a Conservative dinner at the Cape of Good Hope public house to the effect that through poor management the Oxford Building Company was in a very shaky state.[59] At this point party politics entered the picture. Although not exclusively Liberal, the company did have a preponderance of Liberals as directors and Galpin himself was a Liberal alderman on the town council. The Liberals had come to prominence during the 1850s, and their influence extended through patronage beyond the town council into many areas of public life.[60] Walter Gray belonged to a new breed of lower middle-class Conservatives who were emerging during the 1870s, but who found themselves excluded from advancement because they did not belong to what Gray described as the 'Building Society Clique'.

Gray was of another generation than Galpin, having been born in 1848,

23 Nos 11–12
Warnborough Road,
William Wilkinson, 1879,
two of the houses built by
Walter Gray.

but he too came from humble origins and was no stranger to financial insecurity.[61] His father was a failed farmer in Hertfordshire and after getting a job with a solicitor in Stevenage, the young Gray found himself without work when the solicitor went bankrupt. According to family lore, Gray became station master at Waddington, Lincolnshire where he met Colonel Shaw-Stewart, the future bursar of the newly established Keble College at Oxford. This contact enabled Gray to obtain the position of steward at the new college in about 1870. He obviously had a talent for handling money, and began in a small way to develop building plots in North Oxford. He first took land in Kingston Road in 1875, and in the same year he was also able to provide mortgage money for a builder. Gray was beginning his career as a developer just at the time others were retrenching, so he must have felt frustrated at the few sites available in North Oxford. It is likely that it was he who was in direct competition with Galpin for the land in Warnborough Road (Plate 23). Gray's speech in 1881 caused consternation, but was not widely reported because pressure was put on him to keep it out of the newspapers. As was pointed out at the time, not just Liberals put their money into the Company, but many loyal Conservatives, too.

The hoped-for improvement in business did not come and during 1882 the Oxford Building Company desperately tried to shore up their faltering enterprise. They had taken over the leases of a number of houses in North Oxford when purchasers could not be found for them. During 1882 and

1883 they mortgaged thirty houses in the area, mostly in the Leckford and Warnborough Roads, but also in Norham Manor. Eight of these mortgages were taken by Dr Bellamy, the president of St John's, while Morrell and Son, the company's solicitors, were very active in arranging others.[62] By borrowing money outside the company on the security of these valuable properties, the directors were in effect taking these assets out of the reach of the investors and, unbeknown to them, reducing the value of the Company.

Over one-third of the total amount lent by the company during their seventeen years in operation, in other words £105,795, went to John Dover.[63] His petition for liquidation in February 1883 should have been a warning that there was worse to come. Already the long-serving chairman of the company, J.C. Cavell, had resigned in August of the previous year, and there was a rumour that he had lent the company £10,000 on security of some of their property, but only on the proviso that he could take the deeds away with him. On 17 March 1883, the company held their annual meeting, the one at which the chairman spoke of 'enchantment'.[64] The directors declared that although there was ample capital in reserve they would not pay a dividend for the half year to March 1883. Alarm spread rapidly and the rush to withdraw their money by the bondholders which had begun on the publication of the company's balance sheet became overwhelming when in the course of two weeks requests for withdrawals amounted to £40,000. On the 5 April a petition for winding up the company was filed, although the directors hoped it could be reconstituted when its affairs were sorted out. Perhaps none of the directors really knew the actual state of the company's affairs, and besides what the chairman called 'rumours out-of-doors', the directors and officers seemed hardly aware of the hostile forces within the city now gathering against them.

On 17 and 18 April two meetings were held, one for the shareholders and one for the bondholders.[65] By this time a preliminary report had been drawn up by a London firm of accountants, Cooper Brothers and Company. But it was the report by the architects, Wilkinson and Moore, that caused the most consternation, because their estimation of the company's assets, based on the value of the various properties, was much lower than the company's own assessment and suggested that the company was £100,000 worse off than at first supposed.[66] Instead of facing a modest personal loss, the investors now faced possible ruin. Emotions ran high, and ugly animosities emerged. Walter Gray obviously held a grudge against Galpin who at a town council meeting had called him 'inexperienced' and had 'sat on' him. Gray now had the advantage over Galpin, because the latter was confined to his bed with gout. Gray led a section of bondholders who wanted liquidation of the company to be compulsory rather than voluntary, since they hoped this would lead to the control of the company's assets coming into their hands. Although voluntary liquidation was finally agreed upon, the bondholders were successful in replacing the court's first choice of liquidator with their own nominee, Walter Gray.

The heat of feeling spilled over into the streets when a public protest meeting of 6,000 was held at Gloucester Green to express lack of confidence in those councillors and aldermen who had been directors of the company.[67] An effigy in alderman's robes, clearly meant to represent Galpin, was paraded through the streets. The crowd intended to burn it after the meeting, but when they had displayed it before Galpin's house in Beaumont Street the police confiscated it opposite the Randolph Hotel. Galpin stood at the door of his house as the crowd surged past, but they did not touch him.

A subscription was started to help those who would be least able to withstand the loss of their savings, and St Swithin Williams was quick off the mark with newspaper advertisements offering loans to bondholders. After a dignified defence of his actions, Galpin bowed to the inevitable. The Oxford and Berks Brick Company went into liquidation in August and Messrs Galpin and Son followed in November. Gray moved into Galpin's offices in New Inn Hall Street, perhaps to be better placed to deal with the business of the now defunct company, but he also set himself up as auctioneer and surveyor. Through the sales of the company's property he was able to establish for himself a flourishing business, and over the next twenty years he became the dominant developer in North Oxford.

It took several years more before the affairs of the Oxford Building and Investment Company could be wound up, and the effects of the crash continued to be felt for some time. One February night in 1887 Cavell, the former chairman of the company and the proprietor of the largest draper shop in Oxford, was found lying badly injured in Magdalen Street outside his residence. It seems he had fallen from an upstairs window, and although the press were generous in reporting the accident, the doctor attending him believed that ill health, the recent death of his wife, and the failure of the Oxford Building Comany, with the accompanying blame assigned to the directors, had temporarily turned his mind.[68]

After the demise of the Oxford Building Company, the reason most frequently put forward for the collapse was Oxford's depressed housing market. Galpin put it like this:

> ... the time came when the requirements were satisfied, the gap was filled, houses ceased to let or sell, builders became bankrupt, traders suffered heavy losses therefrom, property was less satisfactory, dividends were reduced, a feeling of discontent arose, a want of confidence in the Company became apparent.[69]

There were those who regarded what had happened as something of a natural disaster, while others blamed the company for having distorted the market by encouraging builders to put up houses when there was no one to buy them. Although it was generally agreed that the decline in the market had precipitated the crisis, there seems to have been some confusion over who exactly constituted the market, especially in North Oxford. At the beginning of 1883, it was reported that there were in the suburb 'several hundred gentlemen's houses erected upon the ground, inhabited by senior members of the University, chiefly Professors and Tutors...'.[70] From the 1881 *Census Enumerators' Returns*, it can be shown that members of the University in fact accounted for only a small proportion of those living in

24 No 48 Banbury Road from the University Parks in 1913, the site of W.C. Marshall's Engineering Laboratory (Local Studies Library, Oxford Central Library).

the one suburb devoted to their class. Of the heads of households in the 286 occupied houses in the middle-class area of North Oxford, thirty-seven or 13 per cent were senior members of the University, while ten others were undergraduates.[71] The majority of houses were occupied by tradesmen, some clergy, and those living on income derived from investments, and it seems that by the late 1870s this market was largely satisfied. Family formation among members of the University had always been suppressed through the colleges' statutes forbidding their fellows to marry. In 1877 the Universities Act allowed the colleges to change their statutes but, despite the legislation, there was no great rush on the part of the fellows to buy houses and settle outside their colleges. Yet St John's continued to insist, even in the face of falling demand, that the builders on their estate produce houses suited to the needs and taste of the middle class (Plate 24). Who, asked one observer, is there in Oxford to occupy such houses?[72] The answer could only be those now living within the college walls, but it would take more than an Act of Parliament to change such a strongly engrained social convention, reinforced as it was by the financial organisation of college life. Until the large middle-class population within the colleges could be drawn out into the Oxford housing market, it would be difficult for St John's to find enough people to occupy their new North Oxford houses.

CHAPTER IV
The Formation of the Suburb

B Y 1860 WHEN St John's College began developing their North Oxford estate in earnest, the middle-class suburb as a form had reached a measure of maturity. The concept of the residential suburb did not spring up whole, but evolved along with the growing middle classes and the diverse modes of living they adopted from the middle of the eighteenth century. One of the most significant developments to affect middle-class life was the expansion of the towns at the end of the eighteenth and the beginning of the nineteenth centuries when a combination of increased population and the expansion of commercial activity forced the price of land up and the people who could afford it out of the centre. Ports, such as Liverpool and Bristol, were obvious candidates for fringe development with thriving docks and their ancillary buildings at the heart of the towns.[1] But country towns too could find themselves squeezed when new cattle and corn markets were required to cope with increased agricultural business. Even Oxford, with its tendency to be 'always a century behind other towns', could support the Beaumont Street development outside the centre.

The growing complexity of the general economy led to the pressures which pushed people out from the centres, but that complexity also provided the means to accomplish this move. Primitive as it was, the system by which capitalists could invest and builders could borrow produced the residential districts around the town. Now the terraced house came into its own outside London and Bath where it had first made its appearance.[2] The terrace suited so many of the interested parties from the landowner, who wished to let or sell a piece of land, to the developer, who wanted to get the maximum number of plots out of it. The builder too found that he could finance two or three terraced houses at a time and that the sale of these would pay for the next few. What the growing middle classes wanted were self-contained houses close to the town. Donald Olsen has borrowed that sobriquet of politics, the art of the possible, to describe the process of housebuilding during this period, and what was possible became desirable.[3]

There was another type of suburb as well as those built around the fringes of the towns, and that was the suburban village which for a long time provided the middle classes with a retreat and place of retirement. During the eighteenth century in the western environs of London along the Thames at Richmond and Twickenham, a community of small villas was built by the upper classes as a respite from fashionable society. Increasingly, successful members of the commercial and professional classes were able to take houses beyond the town in surrounding villages, where they could enjoy a semblance of country life without giving up their dependence on the town.[4] As wealth became more diffused throughout the middle classes, the suburban retreat became incorporated into the life cycle of the middle-class businessman. R.J. Morris has shown how it was usual for someone involved in manufacturing or commerce in Birmingham or Leeds to begin withdrawing from his business during his middle years so that he could finally retire in his fifties, usually to one of the surrounding suburbs.[5] To support his old age and his female dependents, he would transfer his capital from the volatility of business to houses which were considered a more steady investment.

The suburban villages became more closely tied to the towns, while retaining nostalgic links with the country. Even Mary Russell Mitford in her popular evocation of village life, *Our Village*, placed her village within sight of 'the elegant town of B-', despite her claimed preference for a 'little village far in the country'.[6] As the nineteenth century advanced, however, the town began to impinge more and more on the middle-class retreat. When a family sold up their house on the edge of a suburban village, the chances were good that a developer would buy it and build an estate of detached villas in the grounds, and either keep the old house to be let along with the others or demolish it.[7] A growth in population very often resulted in improved transport, even if only a more frequent coach service, and improved transport made it possible for those working regularly in the town to live in the outlying villages. This broke the assumption that life in the outer suburbs meant necessarily a retreat from the world of affairs, an assumption totally dispelled with the coming of the railway.

When the commercial methods of development which had resulted in town expansion were married to the amenities of the suburban village a new form of suburb appeared, the planned villa estate. There was the same task of carving from a finite piece of ground enough plots to give a sufficient return on investment, but the grid of terraces which made this relatively easy in the expanding towns was antithetical to a layout which mimicked curving country lanes and the generous gardens of the old suburban house. In order to find a compromise between these two forms the developer needed cheap land and a good architect or surveyor, since a clever layout was a means of reconciling the two. It took some while before the marriage was consummated. As Sir John Summerson has shown, a design for a planned suburban development of detached and semi-detached villas had been prepared for the Eyre estate in St John's Wood as early as 1794, but the houses were not built until the 1820s.[8] Even plans for the villas in Regent's Park were greatly truncated and Park Villages East and West, pretty as they are, seem only an experiment for a much larger picturesque suburb.[9] Some early examples of the villa estate are to be found in resort towns such as Decimus Burton's Calverley estate in Tunbridge Wells or the villas which climb the hill out of Torquay, but once the form caught on, it quickly made an appearance on the edges of large ports and industrial towns in such estates as Rock Park across the Mersey from Liverpool and Edgbaston outside Birmingham.

Since the villa estate needed relatively cheap land for its low density, it was usually found well outside the town centres beyond the influence of high land prices. There were some noted exceptions. In Nottingham a quirk of history meant that a site near the castle was not developed until the 1850s, by which time the villa estate had achieved such popularity that it was economically possible to build the Park estate close to the town centre. On the edge of central Birmingham, the Calthorpe family tightly controlled the development of their Edgbaston estate, ensuring that a large part of the suburb was built only after mid-century and that many of the houses were of the villa type.[10] Likewise St John's property, so close to central Oxford, could not be developed until 1855 when the villa estate had been adopted as the preferred middle-class suburban form. The picturesque villa, either detached or semi-detached, as well as a layout conducive to picturesque views, were necessary to evoke the rustic model of this new form of the suburb: but the exigencies of development meant that the lessons of that other model, the urban residential estate, with its carefully measured plots and its closely costed roads, could not be thrown away. Local conditions determined which model predominated in individual suburbs until the form matured enough that the models disappeared leaving the middle-class suburb as a recognisable type on its own.

As has been seen a few villas made an appearance in North Oxford during the 1830s, around the same time Richard Carr developed North Parade, a small freehold enclave of shops and houses between the Banbury and Woodstock Roads. These villas were the bridgehead which established a middle-class, residential presence in the suburb while its ultimate fate still hung in the balance. Park Town, begun in 1853 on the other side of Banbury Road from these earlier developments was the first planned, middle-class estate in the area, and Seckham's ingenious design was an attempt to reconcile the commercial and aesthetic demands of the scheme (Plate 25).[11] Seckham was faced with the problem of laying out a long narrow strip of 9 acres at right angles to the main road and enclosed by open fields owned by St John's. Such a small and confined site would have suggested the terrace as the only type of house possible to bring in the best return, but in order to attract the sort of people who could pay the £500 to £1,000 expected from the sale of the houses, a few streets of urban terraces would not suffice. Somehow Seckham had to produce the sort of picturesque design now considered the hallmark of the middle-class estate.

Park Town was a compromise between the terrace and the villa. The scheme depended on sacrificing large back gardens for communal gardens and planting in the central area (Plate 26). At the east end a terrace of relatively small houses closed off the estate and between this terrace and the central crescents were stables and semi-detached houses of a somewhat rustic design. The bulk of the estate was taken up by the two facing crescents which ran lengthwise down opposite sides of the site, while at the west

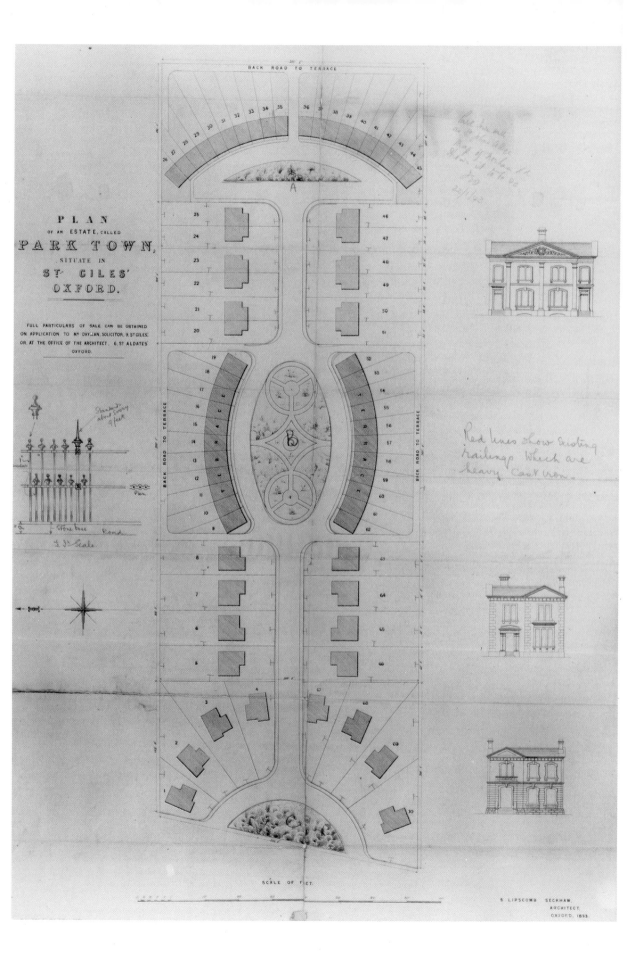

PLAN
OF AN ESTATE, CALLED
PARK TOWN,
SITUATE IN
ST GILES'
OXFORD.

FULL PARTICULARS OF SALE CAN BE OBTAINED
ON APPLICATION TO Mr DAY, JUN, SOLICITOR, 9, ST GILES,
OR, AT THE OFFICE OF THE ARCHITECT, 6, ST ALDATES,
OXFORD.

BACK ROAD TO TERRACE

SCALE OF FEET.

Red lines show existing railings which are heavy cast iron.

S. LIPSCOMB SECKHAM
ARCHITECT
OXFORD. 1853.

26 Park Crescent, Park Town, from across the central gardens.

end, fronting onto Banbury Road, were large villas standing in their own gardens. Planting on the Banbury Road side was generous so that the villas are now viewed through a screen of trees. The variety of house types and the change in road width, gave the illusion of a much larger estate, and the position of the houses and the planting contributed to the sense of seclusion and exclusiveness. It must be admitted that Seckham's design did not ensure the immediate financial success of Park Town, but this probably had more to do with the immaturity of the Oxford investment market than with the plan of the estate. By the 1860s all the houses were occupied and Park Town has retained its status and character ever since.

Park Town is a very satisfying example of making a virtue out of an unpromising site, but when Seckham came to lay out the first area of St John's North Oxford estate, he gave up any attempt at sophisticated planning. Seckham submitted his scheme for Walton Manor to the College at least by April 1854, not long after he had drawn up the plan for Park Town. The site, it will be remembered, was on the west side of Woodstock Road on land which had recently come into hand from the Duke of Marlborough. A lithograph of a bird's-eye view of the proposed scheme shows a variety of house types from the first-class villas facing the main road, to semi-detached houses behind, and finally small terraces on the west side along what would eventually be Kingston Road (see Plate 11).[12] There was no subtlety in the street layout, and the only hope for a picturesque effect would be when the gardens had grown up around the houses. A church

25 Plan for Park Town, Samuel Lipscomb Seckham, 1853 (Bodleian Library).   69

was included in the design, but as has been shown, this was considered completely the wrong place by the residents of North Oxford and those concerned with development there.

Much more attractive was the scheme for Norham Manor, that section of the College's North Oxford property directly north of the University Parks. The urban park, whether public or private, held an important place in the development of the middle-class suburb. This was the period when, in a last minute effort to preserve some open space, urban parks were being established in towns of any pretention.[13] Many of the parks were designed in conjunction with houses, usually arranged around their periphery. The houses might be only an adjunct to the park as they were in Victoria and Battersea Parks in London, or they might take up most of the site as in Nottingham with the park really an amenity for the adjacent houses in the Park Estate. About the same time as the College was starting to lay out their North Oxford estate, a competition was held in Liverpool for setting out the 400 acre Sefton Park, a large undertaking of which 113 acres would be given over to building sites around the park.[14] Building development often helped pay for the landscaping, but the proximity to the park also provided an ideal setting for the villa and gave scope for a picturesque layout.

In 1854 Merton College sold to the University 91 acres of their Holywell land between the Parks Road and the Cherwell. The new University Museum was built on a site facing the road, while the rest remained pasture land.[14] In the early 1860s it was decided to develop the park land by a programme of planting. James Bateman of Magdalen College drew up a scheme which was approved by Convocation in 1864 and planting soon began under the supervison of W.H. Baxter of the Botanic Gardens. Fussy flower gardens were avoided in the scheme, and specimen trees were arranged to provide quiet walks as *Jackson's Oxford Journal* reported in 1866:

> Numbers of ash, elm, and oak have been placed there, and numerous specimens of the interesting pine tribe are growing; in this way considerable progress has been made towards an arboretum, which, with the aid of further contributions, will no doubt be duly appreciated not only by the citizens of Oxford, but by visitors . . . A desideratum in the Parks is shade. This will be provided along the walks by the growth of the trees already planted; but the planting of others, in the central portions, is dependent upon the settlement of the College Cricket Ground question.[16]

The cricket ground did eventually occupy a substantial area which ensured an open prospect across the Parks.

Houses were not included in the development of the University Parks, so that St John's could take full advantage of this amenity in their layout of Norham Manor. A watercolour of a bird's-eye view of this estate shows how the houses along the southern border were intended to front onto the Parks in order to benefit from the view (see Plate 15).[17] As a whole the scheme displays those features which had come to be accepted as usual in the planned estate. Large detached villas faced the main road and formed an impressive screen to the rest of the estate which lay behind, accessible

70

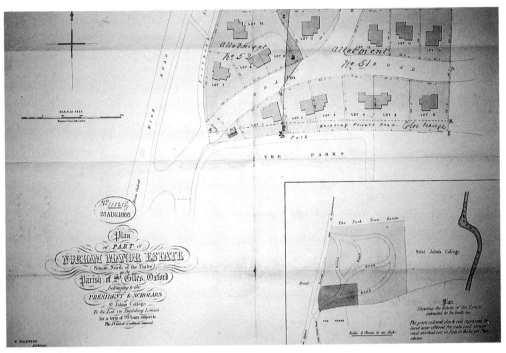

27   Plan for Norham Manor, William Wilkinson, 1860 (SJC Muniments).

only at two points at the south and north ends. The south end, obviously
the main entrance, was guarded by a gatehouse and a set of gates. The roads
formed informal curves around the site and the houses were placed so that
only a few could be glimpsed at a time. Every detached house had its own
front and back garden, although these seem rather small in contrast to the
size of the houses. At the north end of the estate, terraces ran along what
would be the border with Park Town, so that here too there was a variety
of housing types for different strata within the middle classes. Norham
Manor was given over totally to residential purposes, without even a church
to bring intruders in from outside the estate.

Like Seckham's lithograph of Walton Manor, the watercolour of the
proposed Norham Manor estate was probably meant to alert the public to
what St John's was contemplating for their property north of the Parks,
rather than to lay down strictly what they intended to build. Although the
watercolour has been ascribed to William Wilkinson, it is not certain who
was responsible for it.[18] When Wilkinson put forward the plan for the
auction of the first plots on Norham Manor, the scheme had been considerably simplified from the bird's-eye view.[19] Since at this time the College
was only interested in developing that land held by the vicar of St Giles's
this small area is the only one shown with any detail, but a sketch plan
of the rest of the estate shows a prefunctory layout which was basically a
peripheral road bisected by another at right angles (Plate 27). This was in
fact the layout adopted, so that now the only remnant of the original scheme
of the bird's-eye view is the south entrance to the estate where the roads

71

28 North Lodge, the University Parks, T.N. Deane, 1862, at southwest end of Norham Gardens.

meet each other in graceful curves and the northern gatehouse of the University Parks imparts a sense of place (Plate 28).

This is not to say that North Oxford does not share those picturesque qualities of the best nineteenth-century suburbs, but it must be admitted that the street pattern of North Oxford belies its picturesque appearance. The orientation of the site set down some natural limitations like the strong north-south axis formed by the Woodstock and Banbury Roads, and the resulting constraint on the road layouts in the long V formed by these two roads. On the west of the College's property was the canal, but on the east was the Cherwell and the meadows along the river which were liable to flood. The whole 300 acres were not laid out at one time, but the whole was divided into discrete areas which were developed loosely in relation to each other. Because of this and the fact that areas were developed sequentially, the different sections of the estate have their own character and integrity. Nonetheless the street pattern adopted was almost gridlike. What contributed most to the picturesque effect was the low density and the planting.

The density of houses in relation to the sites was laid down by the College in conjunction with the architect when the proposals to build were made. At this time the ground rent, dependent on the size of the site and the class of house to be built, would be decided upon, so that density was related to the expected return to the College. Low density meant high-class houses and high ground rent; high density meant a lower class of house and a correspondingly lower ground rent. There seems to have been general agreement early on that the west side of North Oxford would be developed at a higher density than the rest of the estate, and that the east side would be reserved for the highest class of houses. In between there was more flexibility, but even here, where the College had decided on detached houses of a certain value, they refused to allow cheaper houses to be built when the market began to falter.

Planting out a garden seems to have been one of the unspoken expectations that the College had of all its lessees. Most of the houses, even the cottages in Kingston Road had front gardens as well as back, and it is obvious that they were intended to be seen since the College insisted that to the front of the house the lessee build only a low wall surmounted by iron railings. Special permission was given for the building of a 6 foot high wall around the convent in Woodstock Road, but the College spent years of struggle before they could get the 'pallisade' around 52 Banbury Road replaced by a low brick wall. The residents of North Oxford gave business to a number of seed and plant retailers, such as Filsell at the corner of Banbury Road and the Parks, and Days Victoria Nursery further up Banbury Road near North Parade. Mature trees were kept where possible and the College required that a licence be applied for if a leaseholder wished even to lop a tree.[20] In 1871 when the residents of Bevington Road decided to improve the appearance of their rather bare street with a row of limes the College contributed £5 to the project. The damp English climate was the friend of the picturesque suburb, since after a few years the new estate would assume those desirable qualities of informal order and careless fecundity necessary for the picturesque.

Just as important as the views was the healthy aspect of the nineteenth-century suburban estate. An 1866 auction advertisement for plots in Norham Manor described them thus: 'The land in both situations has been laid out with great care so as to become the most pleasing environs of Oxford. The streets are spacious, the soil dry gravel, the air salubrious, the views extensive, and provision has been made for a perfect system of drainage.'[21] As the developers of North Oxford, the College was responsible for the infrastructure of the estate, and they had to involve themselves in the prosaic task of road building, sewerage, and drainage. The first houses to be built on the estate, in Norham Manor for example, had no sewerage and each house had to be provided with a septic tank. Since the cost of road building was substantial, the roads were not built until there were enough houses to make the expense worthwhile.[22] At first the College took out loans to pay for the roads built by contract, recouping a part of the expense from their lessees by a rate levied after the roads were built. Eventually these roads were taken over by the Oxford Local Board of Health, the body that had assumed responsibility for roads after the old Paving Commissioners. Before the board would take them over, the roads had to be of a certain standard which could be achieved either by the College having the work done themselves or by paying the board to do it. Later when the Corporation took over the duties of the board, they did the work of laying the roads and charged the College who by this time were incorporating the road rate in their ground rents.

Much of the roadwork on the first half of the North Oxford estate was undertaken during the 1870s, just at the time the colleges were beginning to feel the adverse effects of the agricultural depression. By the 1880s the financial affairs of St John's were in such a difficult state that the College could not afford to lay out any new roads. This situation brought to a temporary halt any comprehensive, planned development in North Oxford while the College turned inward in an attempt to overcome the very serious financial problems.

Anyone who derived their income from agriculture had to be reconciled to the ups and downs of good years and bad. St John's was no exception and the College's fortunes waxed during the boom of the Napoleonic Wars and waned during the troubled 1830s along with the fortunes of everyone else. It was usual to adjust the rents of their tenant farmers according to prevailing conditions. In 1882 the farmers of Wasperton were granted a reduction 'till agriculture shall become more profitable'. During the 1850s, when prices were good, the College considered raising the Wasperton rents on account of 'the rise in the price of produce'.[23]

Their endowment tied the fortunes of the College firmly to the land, but the system of beneficial leases, by which they received fines at irregular intervals, sometimes meant they were short of ready money. In 1834, 1851, and 1853 bank stock was sold to cover the immediate expenses of the College, and, as noted previously, in 1860 two substantial loans had to be organised in February and April in order to pay the fellowships.[24] At times there seems to have been contradictory perceptions about the state of the College's financial health. In February 1868 the bursar wrote to a fellow that 'the value of our Fellowship is certainly increasing year by year'.[25] In October of the same year the College's finance committee recommended 'Retrenchment'.[26] As a result of this recommendation more control was exerted over annual entertainments, such as the number of domus dinners and gaudies, but the apparent discrepancy of perception may have indicated a shift of resources from the communal life of the College to increased payments to its individual members.

The College's finances were divided into two accounts, the Internal which related to the College as an educational institution, and the External which covered their activities as landowner. Once the decision had been made to dismantle the old beneficial lease system, a growing proportion of the College's revenue was diverted towards the expenses necessary to make this change. In 1874, when the returns were made to the Commissioners appointed to inquire into the income of the universities, the bursar was cautious about committing the College to long-term expense, but generally there seems to have been optimism that after a few years of deficit, years of increased revenue would follow. From 1869 to 1877 the expenditure of the College averaged nearly £1,000 a year over revenue as they carried out the work needed to bring their farms up to standard.[27] Unfortunately these years coincided with the onset of the agricultural depression.

Controversy continues over how severe the effects of the depression were on the work of the colleges and the University, but there can be no doubt that as the scale of the depression grew, it became a serious concern for every bursary in Oxford.[28] From the letters sent to St John's by their tenants emerges a picture of growing distress. Dry years at the beginning of the 1870s gave way to wet years and flooding at the end of the decade. When yields were poor and prices should have been high, imported grain from America kept prices low, thus putting the farmers in the worst position of poor yields and low prices. In January 1877 Thomas Garner wrote on behalf of the farmers of Wasperton:

> I write to tell you of the losses we have again sustained by the bad seedtime of last year which made the Harvest late and unproductive the worst we have had for many years, this with the high price of Labour which has increased 25 per cent, has led us again to appeal to your liberality to help us in our present difficulties, and we will hope for better times.[29]

A longtime tenant of the College, J.W. Kimber of Fyfield Wick, contemplated in May 1879 giving up his tenancy if his rent could not be permanently lowered: 'Such a very great change has come over farming affairs during the last few years, and the outlook is so very gloomy, that it would be folly in me to promise to pay the same rent for a future term.'[30] It might be thought that the older tenants were unable to adjust to the new methods they were expected to adopt when the farms were rack-rented, but a more recent tenant at Frilford was also running into difficulty: 'I have now farmed for three years and if I had had my farm rent and tithe free I should have lost money therefore I think the day for farming in the old fashioned way is gone by in England.'[31] In some cases the College may have put too high a valuation on marginal land which had been forced into production when the farms were rack-rented. If this had been so, then profits should have improved once the rents were adjusted, but the depression continued and deepened. There was no escaping from the fact that American grain had changed the structure of the market and that even when the seasons improved prices would remain low.

At the same time as the state of agriculture was deteriorating there was a change in St John's bursary. Dr Adams who had been elected to a five-year term as bursar in 1872, and who had been actively engaged in College affairs for much longer, decided to retire in 1877 and subsequently died in December of that year. The practice begun in 1867 by which the bursar retained his office for five years, while ensuring continuity in the bursary, meant that the other fellows remained ignorant of the intricacies of College business. 'What will the College do?' asked a former bursar when he heard of Adams' retirement, and of course when Adams died he was no longer there even to advise.[32] The only one of the fellows willing to take on the post of bursar was Thomas S. Omond, elected fellow in 1872 and one of the first to be elected from outside the College under the statutes of 1861. Omond had previously been a fellow at Balliol and far from attending Merchant Taylors' School as had so many of the older fellows, he had been to school in Edinburgh and was thus something of an outsider from the first.

Dr Adams seems to have been a strong character who ran the bursary on 'understandings' like the one he had with Galpin about first refusal on building plots in North Oxford. Omond naturally wanted to establish his own authority, and tried to deal with everyone on a businesslike basis, but his authority was undermined when he married.[33] According to the statutes he had to resign his fellowship on marriage, but only fellows could be bursar, so a compromise had to be arranged by which Omond could be estates bursar without being a fellow. Even though he was elected principal bursar in 1882 when new statutes came into force, his position was ambiguous since he was still not a member of the College, but was in effect a paid employee.

The continuing development of North Oxford was an important responsibility for the new bursar, but the growing financial crisis, particularly by the mid-1880s, occupied much of his energy. After the College's balance sheet for 1881 was presented to the fellows in April 1882, a committee was established to advise ways of easing the College's financial position. The committee recommended that the fellows and scholars take a cut in their payments of up to 10 per cent.[34] For several more years the College continued to experience a shrinking income and, despite attempts to reduce expenditure, a rising deficit. In 1886, Omond reported to the president that the deficit in 1885 on revenue was £1,453.15s.0d., and it was estimated that savings of £1,500 were needed to break even over the next year, but when the bursar reported in the spring of 1887, the situation was even worse.[35]

One of the results of their economies was that part of the Canterbury Quadrangle collapsed through lack of maintenance, and the quadrangle could only be put right through the generosity of J.J. Moubray.[36] It came to be realised that cheeseparing was not the answer, and that a real reduction in the College's commitments was needed. Now they regretted the insistence in 1861 on appropriated scholarships by which favoured schools such as the Merchant Taylors' School, were guaranteed a fixed number of scholarships. Other colleges were free to curtail the number of scholars if their incomes could not bear the strain.[37] The fellows in December 1887 applied to the College visitor, the Bishop of Winchester, for help in lightening their commitments, and he granted them a 22 per cent reduction on all the payments they were required to make under the statutes to College members and the University.[38]

It is clear that the fellows at least partially blamed Omond for the state of the College's finances, since a committee set up in April 1888 to consider the expenses connected with managing the College's property recommended in October that Omond be requested to resign and leave the bursary the following March.[39] Omond readily accepted this arrangement, but in March 1889, just before his time had expired, the bailiff, Thomas Martin, absconded owing the College over £3,000. It had already got into the *Pall Mall Gazette* that St John's was experiencing financial difficulty, and it was not long before this new blow reached the pages of the local press.[40] Although Omond was in no way implicated in the fraud, he was held responsible for allowing practices in the bursary which had facilitated Martin's crime.

The difficulty in collecting the farm rents because of the depression must have played a large part in giving Martin the opportunity for his fraud. It was the bailiff's job to collect the agricultural rents, and since so many farmers found it difficult to pay on rent day, he had often collected rents long after they were due. These he deposited in his own bank account until he handed over the money before the books were made up. At some point Martin seems to have started paying off the previous year's rents with money collected in the current year.[41] The bursar had been warned about the large sums of money held by the bailiff, but he had been unable to change the practice. Martin had been bailiff since Adams' time, and he seems to have held an inordinate amount of power in the bursary. Omond's claim that the system was at fault did not receive much sympathy from the fellows, and by 1888 Omond was demoralised by his ambiguous relationship to the College. Since he was not a fellow, the authority of the College was not invested in his person, but at the same time the fellows did not fully support their employee. When Omond complained of this in 1885, the president did not seem to know what he was talking about.[42] The difficulty of Omond's position was tied up with the jealously defended principle of celibacy, so that no rational discussion could take place around the issue. A complete overhaul of the bursary which would have put it on a modern footing would have necessitated changes the College were not yet ready to contemplate.

In the event of another fraud occurring, the College took the precaution of requesting the new bursar, W.J.W. Glasson, to take out an insurance policy for £1,000.[43] Glasson had been a scholar at St John's but never a fellow. After taking his BA he had worked as a tax surveyor in Oxford and he was appointed bursar in his capacity as a 'professional man'. It is not clear what changes were made in the bursary after Martin's defalcation and the fellows may have hoped that once the bad apple was removed the bursary could function as before. Yet seven years later in 1896 it was discovered that Glasson had 'borrowed' nearly £3,000 of the College's funds and he was immediately requested to resign.[44] It must have been obvious by then that casual, old fashioned methods in the bursary were no longer adequate to cope with a more commercial approach to estates management, and that the room for slippage and loose accounting could easily lead from informal arrangements to dishonesty. After Glasson's embezzlement, the fellows returned to the safety of electing one of their number as bursar. H.J. Bidder, a fellow who had concerned himself with College business for some time, took control of St John's affairs until after World War I.

The agricultural depression was also blamed for the misfortunes of the Oxford Building and Investment Company. After the shareholders' meeting in March 1883 the chairman, Jason Saunders, was reported as saying: 'The failure of agriculture during the last eight or nine years had been very serious, so that millions of money had been lost to the landlord and tenant, and that naturally affected every trade and industry in the country, and of course it had affected the Company.'[45] Whether or not the depression caused

29 No 113 Banbury Road, H.W. Moore, 1888.

the company's collapse, it did emphasise the structural weakness of the company as it had the poor organisation of St John's bursary. But one effect which the collapse of the company did have was to bring Walter Gray to prominence in the local property business.

Gray, it will be remembered, eventually became the liquidator of the Oxford Building Company, and in this capacity he took over unfinished houses in Grandpont, Cowley, and North Oxford. Gray, the steward of Keble College, had already ventured into development himself when he took two plots for four houses in Kingston Road in 1875, and he had gone on the next year to take plots for ten more houses in the same area.[46] These small successes gave him confidence enough in his avocation to lease land near the canal for a builder's yard. Although Gray may well have prospered in the Oxford housing market regardless, his appointment as liquidator of the Oxford Building Company put him in a good position to establish his own business which was to become central to the development of North Oxford over the next twenty years.

Gray was obviously successful in managing money and attracted to himself a new cast of builders and investors. One of those who petitioned for Gray to be made liquidator was Harry Wilkinson Moore, the nephew of St John's estate architect and his partner from 1881. Gray looked to Moore to design the houses for his building plots on the estate, thus ensuring there was no delay in the acceptance of his house plans (Plate 29). Gray himself took out building agreements on 127 houses and a further 91 houses were undertaken by builders who were closely associated with him. John Money had already been working on his own in the early 1870s in the Kingston Road area and George Horne was the son of a local builder who had been engaged in the same area. Samuel Hutchins, however, had come to Oxford as a foreman carpenter with Parnells of Rugby who were the builders of Keble College.[47] These three builders erected houses especially in the northwest corner of North Oxford around Kingston Road and St Margaret's, Polstead, and Chalfont Roads. Already by 1885 Gray was lending money to these and other builders, and although fifty transactions were recorded there probably were many other informal arrangements.[48]

What was interesting about Gray's houses was that they were not long without leaseholders. Even in the case of his houses built in the late 1870s and early 1880s, when other builders were finding buyers scarce, only one or two years elapsed between the proposals being made and the lease being taken up. He had some help in the beginning, as for example in Warnborough Road where others were coming to grief, Gray sold the leases of his six houses to the Hon William Sackville West, the former bursar of Keble College.[49] Unlike the developers and builders before the collapse of 1883, Gray did not take many leases himself, so that his capital never remained tied up for long. He did seem to be particularly good at finding leaseholders for his properties, and he was one developer to benefit from the increasing practice of allowing at least some college members to live a married life outside the colleges and also from the 1882 reform of the Married Women's Property Act. This Act enabled married women from 1 January 1883 to hold property separately from their husbands, and fifty-two North Oxford leases were taken in the name of married women from this date. In September 1883 Walter Gray arranged for Elizabeth Hurst to take the lease for 23–4 Farndon Road, making the point that 'it is her desire that the lease may be granted in her name alone the purchase money being provided out of property under her own control and free from the control of her husband.'[50]

The decisions about the release of land for building and the size and standard of the houses to be built, still lay in the hands of the College. When he first became estates bursar, Omond seems to have wanted to influence the way the suburb was to progress. To Faulkner, the bursar of University College, he wrote in 1878 that he was keen to undertake a joint scheme on the land between Banbury and Woodstock Roads owned by the two colleges, and he expressed a critical opinion of development up to that time:

I am inclined to think that in Norham Manor we have hardly given enough ground – though some of the lessees prefer it so – & that sometimes we have been hardly strict enough in the approval of architect and plans. I am anxious to try what could be done in a new region, where the number of building plots is small, & where consequently the Colleges would not be in a hurry to let, by a larger & more liberal policy, combined with a stricter selection of lessees.[51]

The availability of building land was not the problem with nearly half the suburb yet to be developed, but, as has been seen, the real difficulty was finding the capital to cover the expense of laying out roads, especially as the College's revenues declined.

The Woodstock and Banbury Roads were already under the control of the Local Board so that building along these main roads could be started without commitment to great capital spending. It was decided in October 1880 that land abutting the Woodstock Road up to the corner with St Margaret's Road be laid out for building, and Gray took the plots in order to build four substantial, detached houses facing Woodstock Road.[52] In 1882 Gray had plans to extend his development in this same area of the College's estate and he waited on the success of the College to negotiate with the Local Board about the demolition of the 'Pest House' or smallpox hospital north of St Margaret's Road.[53] Suddenly everyone's plans came to a halt when the Metropolitan Railway proposed continuing their line from Aylesbury to Oxford, and North Oxford again became a potential site for railway development, including passenger and goods stations.[54] This time the College offered no objections to the proposal in principle, but they did want to have a say in what was built and they were determined to take full advantage of the increased value of the land in North Oxford. The revenue from the sale of their land would have been very welcome, and by 1882 the presence of a railway near a suburb was a less undesirable prospect than it had been even twenty years before. Development was to take place north of St Margaret's Road, and concern was expressed about the placing of the goods station on the Cherwell side of the property which they felt would be 'detrimental to some of our best land'. An amended plan was submitted in January 1883, and although generally approved, this plan was viewed with reservations as the bursar indicated in his letter to the surveyor acting for the College:

> It appears to me that the space proposed to be taken for a passenger Station is unduly large. It embraces nearly 11 acres, which must be far in excess of all possible requirements. It is true that, as you point out, the College would hardly care to retain the strip north of the Station. But I would not give them any more land south of the line than we can help. The farther north we can push them, the wider the space left to the college between Rackham Road [St Margaret's Road] and the station, the better for our building estate.[55]

Negotiations were entered into with the Railway Company, but in May 1883 the scheme was abandoned, possibly because the valuation of the land was much higher than the developers expected. Gray had been very disappointed at the check to his plans, and was quick to resume them in the autumn of 1883 when he started three houses in St Margaret's Road.

No land had been put onto the market since 1880 when the Woodstock Road site and a site next to the canal called Southmoor Road were released for building. In November 1883 Wilkinson and Moore put forth their plan for developing the east side of the College's estate, north of Park Town. There was general approval for it, but the state of the College's finances precluded any serious development which would require expenditure on roads and drainage. In response to the plan the bursar put forward the College's policy:

> Your plan for laying out the land north of the Crescent has been considered by the College, and has met with general acceptation. The College is not prepared to layout any new roads at present, so they have not considered your plan in detail, but they are prepared to receive proposals for a few sites fronting the Banbury Road, reserving a roadway to the east as per your plan. The wish of the College would be to reserve these sites for houses of the better class, & particularly for people wishing to build for themselves. They do not wish to force these sites into the market, but rather to reserve them for suitable tenants. They will also be prepared to receive proposals for the north side of St Margaret's Road, where single houses or pairs of semi detached of a somewhat less value would be allowed, say something like what Mr Gray is now building there.[56]

The policy expressed here was not fundamentally different from that followed by the College from the beginning of development in North Oxford when Norham Manor on the east side was reserved for the best houses, especially for those built by individuals for themselves. The decision of the College to follow this same policy with the land in the northeast while declining to build new roads, ensured that this area was slow to develop. Houses went up in Banbury Road, but the land behind, in what became the Bardwell Estate, was laid out only in the 1890s, while the rest of the area had to wait until after the turn of the century and the northernmost part until after World War I.

The idea that different areas of the estate would be reserved for different classes of houses and therefore of people was typical of urban development, but not of the village. Part of the charm of Miss Mitford's village was that the different classes, high and low, enjoyed a pleasant intercourse based on firmly drawn social distinction which allowed the picturesque proximity of cottage and villa residence.[57] In the purpose-built suburb, the distinction between the classes was geographically drawn. St John's had desired to provide cottages on their estate at least since 1864, and the early result of this desire was the cottage development along Kingston Road. In 1880 when they released land between Kingston Road and the canal for Southmoor Road, their intention was that cottages would be built on the site (Plate 30). The College was disappointed in the size of houses which ended up being let for a much higher rent than was intended. The bursar wrote to Wilkinson and Moore to express the College's displeasure:

30 Southmoor Road, Wilkinson and Moore, 1881.

I heard today on good authority that one of the houses in this new road was at first to have been let at £20, after the plans were passed it rose to £27, & the lessee is now threatening to ask £30. I think the college has grave reason to be dissatisfied that the stipulation so strongly insisted on has been disregarded so very much . . .[58]

In another letter to the architects Omond said that 'the College would not have gone to the expense of laying out the road except to supply the felt want of cottage accommodation in Oxford'.[59] Even £20 a year was not an insubstantial working-class rent at the time, and a correspondent in the local press commented that if houses renting for £12 or £15 were built then there would not be any houses left empty in the city.[60] However, one consideration that the builders must have had in mind was that letting out house room had become part of the economy of Oxford, so that houses intended for workers might be larger than elsewhere since the extra rooms could easily be let to people connected to the University.

The College had some cottage property which pre-dated the development of North Oxford and was now in a poor state of repair. When the lease on four houses in Plantation Road, part of the old Tagg's Garden area, came back to the College, they were found to be beyond repair.[61] Even the Oxford Cottage Improvement Company, a philanthropic organisation devoted to buying and repairing cottage property for letting at low rents, were unable to undertake the repairs and it was decided that departing from their usual policy the Company would demolish the houses and build seven new cottages.[62] This they did to designs by Wilkinson and Moore, and their unusual action pointed to the lack of cottage property for repair in North Oxford where the need for cottages at low rents was very pressing.

31   Hayfield Road, H.W. Moore, 1888–96.

Similarly when the dilapidated houses in Heyfield's Hutt came to the College in the autumn of 1883, cottages were considered suitable. On its west side the site ran down to the canal, and it lay well to the north of all except the few northernmost houses in Kingston Road and the new church of St Margaret's. Their experience in Southmoor Road did not encourage the fellows to trust the local building industry to produce houses small enough on the site, and in February 1885 the bursar was asked to obtain information on the cost of the College themselves building cottages to be let at not more than 4s.6d. per week while paying a profit of 5 per cent.[63] On making enquiries, however, the bursar discovered that the Land Commissioners would not give the College permission to borrow to build the cottages since the project was a speculative venture, an activity in which colleges were not yet allowed to take part.[64] Nothing more was done for a year when the Local Board was asked for an estimate to lay out a new road on the site to be called Hayfield Road and the College's architect was approached for plans for artisans' cottages.[65]

In February 1886 it was agreed to lease four blocks for ten houses each on the west side of the new road to the Oxford Industrial and Provident Land and Building Society. This society had started off as the Oxford Working Men's Land and Building Society, and unlike the Oxford Building and Investment Company was content to operate on a modest scale. All subscribers had to be members of the society and no one could have more than a £200 interest.[66] The society took the building lease on the land in Hayfield Road and then allotted the houses among their members by ballot. Members were limited by the number of shares they held, and many of the names of

33 (*far right*) Polstead Road, H.W. Moore, 1888–96.

32 No 26 Norham Road, Wilkinson and Moore, 1881.

the leaseholders were familiar from other properties in the Kingston Road area of North Oxford.[67]

The cottages were, according to the College's wishes kept small, although the bursar had to insist on the society keeping to the approved plans. 'Please make your members understand that we want cottages for workingmen ...', he wrote to the society's secretary, but slightly greater dimensions were allowed in the later houses on the east side of the road.[68] The houses had six rooms and ranged in price from £170 to £176, and despite the modesty of these cottages and their position tucked away in the far corner of the estate, the bursar still took an interest in their appearance (Plate 31). Omond pressed the society to drop the idea of building alternate blocks of red and white brick and insisted that they accept red as the colour of the bricks for the whole street.[69] The houses were without front gardens and exceedingly plain on the exterior, but still they were graced by Harry Wilkinson Moore's distinctive decorative motif.

The 1880s were a period of consolidation in North Oxford. The College released almost all their land on the west side of the estate for the small, semi-detached houses in Walton Well Road, the terraces in Southmoor Road, and the workingmen's cottages in Hayfield Road, and together these houses accounted for half the 462 leases taken during the decade.

Building proposals and leases taken up 1880–1915

	1880–1889	1890–1899	1900–1915	Total
Proposals	411	136	140	687
Leases	462	181	198	841[70]

The effects of the collapse of the housing market and more especially the failure of the Oxford Building and Investment Company were felt for some

time. Of all the 1880s leases, 116 were taken on houses begun during the 1870s, sometimes up to ten years before. Some of the new houses started were in old localities like Norham and Crick Roads in Norham Manor and Farndon Road, where plots had remained empty since the demand for houses had slackened at the end of the 1870s (Plate 32). It was Walter Gray who took the building agreements on these sites, and the houses built here and on his other plots in Woodstock and Banbury Roads were the only ones to go up in the main, middle-class section of the College's estate until the latter part of the 1880s. Then many of the houses in St Margaret's Road and Rawlinson Road were built, and Polstead and Chalfont Roads were started, largely under the auspices of Walter Gray and those builders associated with him (Plate 33).

During the 1890s work continued in Chalfont Road and the newly laid out Frenchay Road, both of which occupied sites that would have been considered too distant from the centre of Oxford before 1882 when the tram service was established as far as St Margaret's Road.[71] Each road added to the North Oxford estate took its place according to the formula which had evolved for the layout of the College's property. As has been pointed out, most of the roads had an east–west orientation between the strong north–south lines of the Woodstock and Banbury Roads. Where there was enough space a road parallel to the two main thoroughfares would be fitted in. The advantage of this simple plan was that the College could release building land according to their ability to provide the necessary services. The 1890s saw the start of the Bardwell Estate, the last substantial section of the College's North Oxford property, and an area reserved for the best class of houses. Here it might be thought that the plan would have shown more complexity, but the same loose grid prevails. Because this area was near the Cherwell, its subsoil was clay rather than gravel. As the only local source of

34   Chalfont Road in 1907 (Local Studies Library, Oxford Central Library).

gravel most of North Oxford had been well excavated before the houses appeared, and this meant that roads, such as Bevington and Polstead Roads, which would have been straight in plan were curved and hollowed, as the result of the removal of the underlying gravel. The streets of the Bardwell Estate, never having been excavated, were level and very nearly straight, but their width and the generous front gardens of the houses produced a character better suited to twentieth-century suburban taste.

In the midst of laying out the Bardwell estate in 1903, Moore, the College's architect was asked to resign his position. Moore had had some difficulty previously over issuing the certificate for R.H. Green's house in Bardwell Road.[72] The builder, D.J. Jarvis, was running into difficulty as he finished the house in 1893, and as R.H. Green wrote later, 'It is well known in Oxford that Jarvis was building against time to say the least'. Subsequently the chimneys smoked and plaster fell from the ceilings, and the fact that their architect had approved the work was an embarrassment to the College. The fellows expressed their discontent with Moore's work in 1897, but deferred any decision about his position. In June 1903 it was decided to terminate the association between Moore and the College, and in July N.W. Harrison was offered the post of 'surveyor to the North Oxford building estate'.[73] This was a less responsible position than the one Moore and his uncle had held, and since nearly the whole estate was now laid out, Harrison's duties were largely administrative. He did lay out Bainton Road around the west side of the College's cricket ground in Woodstock Road, but only Blackhall Farm remained to be developed on the Bardwell estate and that would not be done until the 1920s.

By 1915 when the North Oxford estate was nearly complete, the suburb had been building for fifty years and the area had absorbed the middle-class suburban ethos (Plate 34). The sequestered character of the suburban village had combined with the necessary conformity of the inner suburb, to produce that peculiar character which displayed itself in retreat behind walls and hedges and a jealous concern for accepted norms, whether laid down by the landlord's covenants or by local custom. This character now accepted as part of suburban life, was not achieved without conflict, as individuals adjusted their own social expectations to conform with the new ethos. In the mid-1880s two incidents occurred in North Oxford around the issue of stables, which signalled the transition to the new type of middle-class suburb.

The question of stables was one which concerned developers from the first. The horse ensured the mobility which was part of being middle class even in the age of the railway. In the urban suburbs around the city centres, stables had been included for example, in the mews behind the west end terraces in London. Since there was no expectation in these houses of a garden, the stables situated across a back yard from the house were not regarded as an inconvenience. Those who were the first to build in the suburban villages could afford land enough for a garden, stables, and possibly a paddock as well. However, when the planned suburb appeared with plots no more than an acre, and often much smaller, and where the garden assumed an importance in family life, the stable became less desirable.

St John's specified in their building agreements whether stables were allowed, and they usually gave permission only where the grounds were considered large enough to accommodate them. In 1875 Frederick Codd undertook to build stables at the east end of Norham Manor in Benson Place so that those in the immediate area could keep their own horse and carriage without disturbing their neighbours.[74] Ten years later in 1885, one of the first lessees in Bradmore Road, Thomas Allam, wanted to sell his lease, but the sale depended on permission to build stables on the premises.[75] Although the bursar pointed out that the stables in Benson Place were intended for the use of local residents, the fellows, with some reluctance, gave permission on condition the neighbours were consulted. This Allam neglected to do, and soon the bursar was receiving letters from anxious neighbours. The Rev Alfred Edersheim of 8 Bradmore Road wrote in May 1885, shortly after the sale of No 9, about the rumour:

I hope the rumour may prove to be unfounded, but I lose no time in explaining my strongest protest if such a proposal should be contemplated and the earnest hope that St John's college to whom the ground belongs could not give its consent to what would not only seriously injure the adjoining property, but render my own occupation of my present house *impossible*. Both my drawing room, the sitting room of my daughter, and my own study – not to speak of two bedrooms, look into the garden, and we have had a balcony built in front of the drawing room, especially to look into the garden, to have tea there, and to occupy it while tennis is being played.[76]

Mrs Clara Carden, on the other side at No 10, predicted that the enjoyment of her garden would also be ruined if the stables were permitted on her neighbour's property:

> ...I yet write at once to John's College to represent that a stable etc. in that garden would entirely ruin my house, and make it impossible for me to continue in it. I have taken great pains with my garden and [as] it is a source of great pleasure to me I find it difficult to believe that St John's College would deprive me of this pleasure and interest.[77]

In a subsequent letter, Mrs Carden pointed out that she had taken her house because she was 'attracted by the pretty gardens and the great quiet...' The dirt, smell, and general untidiness associated with stables had become inappropriate to the suburban setting.

In another incident about the same time, there was disagreement between Mrs Jeune and the bursar about accommodation allowed in her stables. One of the objections to stables in suburban developments was that they brought working-class people into proximity with the middle classes, especially when the stables were not used as such. They could soon be occupied as dwellings and workshops bringing down the social status of the nearby houses and lowering their value. Mrs Jeune, the widow of the Bishop of Peterborough and late master of Pembroke College, took the lease on a new house at 76 Banbury Road in 1885. The house had stables, but she wanted to extend the accommodation for her coachman and his wife. The bursar explained that it was the practice of the College where stables were allowed, to approve only one room for a bachelor groom. This was to prevent the stable becoming the home of a working-class family in a middle-class area:

> The very object of our regulation is to prevent the establishment of a married man, with clothes drying and all the objectionableness of a small cottage in a quarter where other people have built houses in faith that nothing but first class houses shall be allowed there. For this reason I was unable to approve the plans.[78]

Mrs Jeune could not understand the objection and in her opinion 'to secure the building of "first class houses" the provision for stabling is almost indispensible'.[79] She was of a generation when this would have been so, but she also came from a stratum of society whose members a generation before would not have lived in a suburban villa. To make the issue more puzzling to her the College had allowed her to build larger stables at her house on Woodstock Road which she had leased in 1871. What was different now? The answer was that a further fourteen years of suburban development had taken place, and the segregation of the classes had become entrenched in North Oxford as it had in other suburban estates. If the smells and muck of the stable, tolerated in the inner suburbs, were not acceptable in the villa suburb, so too the casual intercourse between the classes experienced in the village was discouraged. The middle classes of both town and country had to learn the ways of the new suburb where individuality and retreat were nevertheless dependent on mutually accepted conformity made necessary by the proximity of neighbours.

The first twenty years of building on the College's estate laid down the direction the physical development of the suburb would take, but the thirty years from 1885 to 1915 was the period when the social character of North Oxford became established. Although by World War I the suburb was not quite complete, those areas built up were acquiring an established air. A combination of the two models of suburban building, the town and village suburbs, had proved successful in laying out North Oxford. The town model met the needs of the College because it meant that St John's could keep some control over development, especially when their own finances prevented them from investing in the infrastructure. The village model met the desires of those who went to live there, and those desires were satisfied perhaps as much by the style of the houses and the prolific gardens as by the layout of the estate. The individual houses, because they were so vital to the character of the suburb, must be considered on their own.

CHAPTER V

The Architecture of the North Oxford House

NONE OF THE other Oxford suburbs abuts the town as does North Oxford. To reach Cowley and St Clement's it is necessary to go over Magdalen Bridge, while to reach south Oxford, Folly Bridge must be crossed. Only the broad, urbane space of St Giles's separates North Oxford from the colleges and the town, but the contrast between the well-mannered eighteenth-century facades and what has been described as the 'jungle of Victorian Gothic',[1] is as startling as any physical boundary could be. Tall gables of red and yellow brick, vast roofs of tile and slate emerge from a sea of vegetation, especially abundant in spring and summer, but green even in winter thanks to conifers and quantities of laurel. But what appears on first acquaintance as a homogeneous suburb spreading north towards Summertown, becomes on closer inspection a varied collection of houses demonstrating the major trends in domestic architecture from the 1850s up to the early years of this century.

Sir John Summerson has written about what he has called the 'lower school of Victorian designers' who were responsible for the design in most suburban developments during the nineteenth century.[2] Because architects of the first rank paid such little attention to the suburban house until the last decades of the century, the lower school carried on their work with little reference to the wider world of architecture. Although few first-rate architects were involved in North Oxford, those architects who were engaged there participated through their metropolitan contacts and through the architectural press in the dominant architectural culture of their time. Thus the houses of North Oxford have a special claim on our interest as exemplars of the emerging type of suburban house as well as including among them some distinguished individual examples.

Since, as has been shown, North Oxford was conceived and developed as a picturesque villa estate, the form and appearance of the houses counted for a good deal in the overall effect. But while the middle classes were evolving and consolidating as a social group, it was not always obvious what type of house was appropriate to their needs and aspirations, and the question of what constituted the middle-class house remained open until the end of the century. As long as the suburban villa was regarded as a retreat for a relatively small group of individuals, not too much energy went into considering how it should be designed. Most discussions in the journals and in books such as J.C. Loudon's *Encyclopedia of Cottage, Farm, and Villa Architecture*, centred on the question of style.[3] Style was thought important because it was the external manifestation of the individual taste of the proprietor. After long years of suppressing personal inclination to the necessities of town life, the retired businessman was in a position to indulge his architectural fantasies. But if he had not been brought up to develop his taste and exercise choice, how was he to choose from among the many styles available in the nineteenth century? Although Loudon himself did not favour one style over another, he did specify that '. . . a villa residence ought to be characterised by extent and irregularity'.[4] The constraints of the terraced house could be cast aside and if a picturesque style was chosen, there was no end to the variety that might be had in the size, number, and arrangements of the rooms. Increasingly the Italian style became a favourite for suburban building since it lent itself so readily to the picturesque without descending into eccentricity.

The first indication that the house was being taken seriously by architects came from those young men who were assuming the challenge of Pugin to build contemporary buildings in a suitable gothic style. Initially their ecclesiastical interests brought the parsonage to their notice, and the bad influence suburban building had had on its design:

> It would indeed be difficult to find, among those [parsonages] erected for many years past, any that do not resemble the Albert cottages and Victoria villas to be met with a mile or two out of London, and sacred to the retirement of its worthy citizens, rather than the 'Pastor's mansion' of a country village.[5]

Ecclesiologists like William Butterfield and William White, trained to study function in churches, turned their attention to houses when they were asked to design parsonages. White drew general conclusions from his experience in an article he published in *The Ecclesiologist* in 1853. The greatest fault he found with contemporary houses, even those purporting to be 'gothic', was that there was no connection between the external elevations and the plan:

> The smaller rooms and subordinate offices are so often made to hold the same place in dignity, with the larger and more important. Thus pantries and closets are, as it were, cut out of what would otherwise be a large square room like one of the others, and so they are formed four or five feet wide, and perhaps ten or eleven feet high, to the perceptible waste of good and valuable space; the upper part being comparatively useless.[6]

Since the varied functions of the house required a multiplicity of different spaces, its 'character' required that its exterior should be irregular: 'Not that every building *must* have irregularity to give it character, but a house must, because a house is a building that of undeviating necessity consists of so many different kinds of apartments, and it ought to be almost distinguishable from the exterior that each has its proper office and position.'[7] In this article White did not even begin to address the problem of the design of the house, but in pressing for the use of the gothic to the exclusion of other styles, White moved the discussion of the house beyond style.

Like White, George Gilbert Scott also thought that the gothic style was the one which was best suited to contemporary requirements. In his *Remarks on Secular and Domestic Architecture* of 1857, he was particularly scathing about current suburban house building:

> Look, again, at the rows of miserable houses in the suburbs of our country towns, and at the wretched creations of speculating builders in the neighbourhood of London: are they not vile beyond description? Look at the houses which grow up like mushrooms round the Crystal Palace, and which appear wherever a needy landowner begins to let out his ground on building leases: are they not perfect plague-spots on the landscape, instead of heightening its beauty, as they ought to do? And yet these display the vernacular style of house-building more truthfully than the forced productions of persons of more ambitious notions, and are, for the most part, much the same things denuded of a few ornaments, by which their natural ugliness is in a measure disguised.[8]

This opinion of suburban building was one expressed as well in the architectural journals of the day, which tended to publish illustrations of 'gentlemen's' houses, but neglected the suburban house or only found reasons to criticise its poor design and shoddy construction. It was very difficult in a modest suburban house to exercise all the subtleties of style which were the basis of architectural criticism in the 1850s, so that even though enormous resources of the building industry were going into suburban building, it was discussed very little. Scott's insistence on the suitability of the gothic for all contemporary needs meant that more attention could be paid to the function of even quite lowly building types, like the suburban house.

Robert Kerr was one of the first distinguished writers to take up the subject of the house, and despite a full discussion of style, it was his contribution to the plan which is remembered. In his book *The Gentleman's House*, published in 1864, Kerr took his readers meticulously through the plan, discussing every aspect of the domestic arrangements of the house. And yet this book would have been of only limited value to the suburban house builder, for although it was subtitled *How to Plan English Residences from the Parsonage to the Palace*, the 'palaces' predominated. The most important function of the plan was to separate the servants from the family: 'The idea which underlies all is simply this. The family constitute one community; the servants another. Whatever may be their mutual regard and confidence as dwellers under the same roof, each class is entitled to shut its door upon the other, and be alone.'[9] Within the family, however, the point of view is very much that of the 'gentleman', as Kerr made plain in a lecture to the Architectural Association in 1866.[10] The gentleman is the one to choose the style of his house because it reflects his *amour propre*; his special room should be placed so that 'people' – presumably women, children and servants – are not constantly popping in; and since children often give a

92

'good deal of trouble and annoyance', they ought to be shut away in the nursery which should have a lobby 'so that the nurse, in shutting the door, could not only shut the outer world out, but, what was still more important, shut the inner world in'. Kerr's ideal house was one of discontinuities in which privacy, especially of the master of the house, was held as the ultimate virtue.

Despite the obvious pride taken in the standard of housing enjoyed by many in the middle classes, during the 1870s some dissenting voices began to be heard about the effect the middle-class house was having on family relations. In an article on co-operative housekeeping, E.M. King, an active feminist, implied that the male proprietorship of the individual house led to abuses of power in the relations between men and women:

> Social reforms have a much stronger influence upon national character than political ones. No reform would have a more powerful influence than such a home reform [co-operative housekeeping], by bringing the masculine intellect more closely to bear upon the feminine, and the moral character of the women to bear more directly on the man; taking out of the man's hand, in a great measure, the power of domestic tyranny, so injurious to his own character, and so degrading to the woman's.[11]

W.H. White, that champion of the Parisian flat and not to be confused with the ecclesiologist White, also felt that there was a connection between the type of dwelling and the social arrangements of life, and his comparison between London and Paris was obviously meant to be to the detriment of London and the English middle class:

> French middle-class wives help their husbands in business; English wives of the same class often ignore office or shop. The Parisians cheat posterity [by producing few children], the Londoners overburden it. The Parisians live in Paris, the majority of Londoners live out of London. To generalise, Paris lives in a flat, London in a house of its own.[12]

Ironically this was written about the same time Viollet-le-Duc was extolling the virtues of the English custom of every family occupying its own house, and recommending that the French adopt this type of housing for the reason that it would encourage individuality and liberalism.[13] By the 1870s the middle-class house was becoming the subject of serious discussion in England, but a satisfactory form had yet to be found for it.

One model of the middle-class house suitable for the picturesque villa estate because of its rural associations, its size, and its relatively low cost, was the parsonage. Not as large as the squire's house, but more substantial than the farmer's, the country parsonage fulfilled the needs of the professional man and his family. The Pluralities Act of 1838 had encouraged the design of many new parsonages since it made less acceptable the practice among the clergy of non-residence in their livings.[14] Where the old vicarage or rectory had fallen into disrepair or had disappeared, new houses were built, sometimes with the help of the Ecclesiastical Commissioners. The Commissioners were prepared to make grants up to £1,500, comparable to the cost of a modest suburban villa.[15] It was recommended that the houses consist of drawing and dining rooms and a study on the ground floor together with kitchen and offices, while upstairs there should be at least four bedrooms. Where clergy could call on their own resources or those of the owner of their living, the house could be more elaborate. During the 1850s and 1860s the architects of 'muscular gothic' produced some startling and original parsonages, and gothic, with its ecclesiastical associations, remained the accepted style for rectories and vicarages well into the 1870s. Steep roofs, gables, and stout chimneys were combined with economical plans to produce houses both inexpensive and picturesque, just those qualities sought by the builders of suburban estates.

Although Seckham began the suburban development of North Oxford in an Italianate style it was gothic which triumphed during the first twenty years of building. All the villas he designed himself for Park Town were Italian, that is simple, rectangular blocks with wide eaves over small attic windows, the rest of their facades being regular to the point of plainness. Stone facing was used for some of the villas and the two central terraced crescents, but probably the financial difficulties of the Park Town Company led to the use of exposed yellow bricks and render in the end terraces, and render on some of the villas. The first of the College's houses in Woodstock Road, begun in 1856 by Dyne and designed by Seckham, were also Italian and a grander version of the Park Town villas, with cement rendering and similar details (see Plate 12). The plan Seckham had produced in 1854 for the Walton Manor estate included both the Italian and gothic styles, and the bird's-eye view of the proposed Norham Manor estate, attributed to Wilkinson, showed gothic gables and Italian belvederes in houses next door to each other (see Plate 15).[16] This mixing of the styles did not take place in North Oxford, and for the first twenty years of development the gothic dominated.

When development began on St John's North Oxford estate the Italianate villa had associations with retired tradesmen and the detached houses of Park Town had more affinity with those villas built across Banbury Road by the successful citizens of Oxford than they had with houses around the Italian lakes. The gothic house, on the other hand, had associations with the country. Scott noted with some chagrin that even the critics of gothic allowed that it was an appropriate style for the country.[17] Whereas Seckham had been formed by his sojourn in London, William Wilkinson, who eventually took overall control of the North Oxford development, was grounded in the country.[18] Born in Witney in 1819, he joined the family auctioneering business in 1838, just before his father's death. As country auctioneer, Wilkinson dealt with the full range of rural property, from furniture to livestock, but he also acted as land surveyor, estate agent, architect and builder. In a small town like Witney there was no demarcation between one type of business and another. Wilkinson began his career as architect in 1841 with his design for Lew Church, not far from Witney. During the next twenty years he continued to work mostly on church restorations and the design of farm buildings for the local gentry.

That Wilkinson worked for the rural gentry, rather than indulging in speculative ventures, made him more sympathetic to the ways of the fellows of St John's than was the entrepreneurial Seckham. The farm buildings Wilkinson designed in the late 1850s were not like the cottage orné of earlier decades, but were intended to be functional for farms run on capitalist principles. They included a model farm at Shirburn for the Earl of Macclesfield, farm buildings and a house for Henry Hippisley at Aston, and buildings for Sir Henry Dashwood at Northbrook Farm. These latter gained some notice when they were illustrated along with his work at Longleat Home Farm for the Marquis of Bath in J. Baily Denton's *The Farm Homesteads of England*.[19] He also entered competitions for cottages and farm buildings such as that held at the Leeds Agricultural Show in 1861.[20] Even after he became supervising architect to the North Oxford estate he kept up his work for rural clients.

Towards the end of the 1850s Wilkinson's career as architect began to overtake his other business interests. In 1856 he left Witney for Oxford and opened offices at 2 St Giles's, moving later to 5 Beaumont Street. By 1857 he had taken over from J.C. Buckler as architect to the Oxfordshire Police Committee and in the next year he had jobs in Oxford for Grimbly Hughes and Dewe's new grocery premises in Cornmarket, now disappeared, and for the University Gymnasium in Alfred Street. In 1860 he designed his one building in London, a set of offices for Messrs Soane and Page called Crosby House in Bishopsgate.[21] Probably Wilkinson's best-known work is the Randolph Hotel which competes for attention with Cockerell's Ashmolean at the top end of Beaumont Street. This was begun in 1864 and completed two years later. But his largest, single commission was for St Edward's School, Summertown, which he started in 1872 and continued working on until he retired in 1886.

At the beginning of the development, Wilkinson was one of several involved in laying out the North Oxford estate. Seckham, of course, had been connected with Walton Manor since 1854, and a Mr Fisher of Messrs J. and W. Fisher, the College's surveyors, laid out the land in Walton Street and on the south side of Bevington Road.[22] Gradually all the work of the estate passed into the hands of Wilkinson. In April 1865 he was asked to prepare a plan for the area around what was to become Kingston Road and it was he who negotiated with the Local Board over the new road to replace the old Hutt Road.[23] At least by the end of 1866 or the beginning of 1867, Wilkinson had assumed responsibility for approving all the suburb's building proposals. The College inserted into their building agreement a clause which ensured that every house be built in brick and stone, without the use of commercial cement or render.[24] This suggests that the fellows too favoured the 'true' materials of the gothic over Italian, and in Wilkinson they found the man who was in sympathy with the sort of suburb they hoped to build.

During the 1860s Wilkinson had numerous commissions for small country houses, parsonages, and farm cottages, as well as for houses in North Oxford. In 1870 he published a volume illustrating his domestic work under the title, *English Country Houses*.[25] Significantly he included four of his

North Oxford houses in this collection without making any distinction between them and the country houses (Plates 35–7). This suggests that in Wilkinson's work there was a common origin for the small country houses, often parsonages, and the suburban villas he designed for his clients in North Oxford. The illustrations were drawn by a local architect J.W. Hallam who provided perspectives for *The Builder* of the work of such well-known architects as William White. Wilkinson's own work appeared from time to time in the architectural press, and it could be said that although he was a

37   No 31 Banbury Road, plan (*English Country Houses*, 1870).

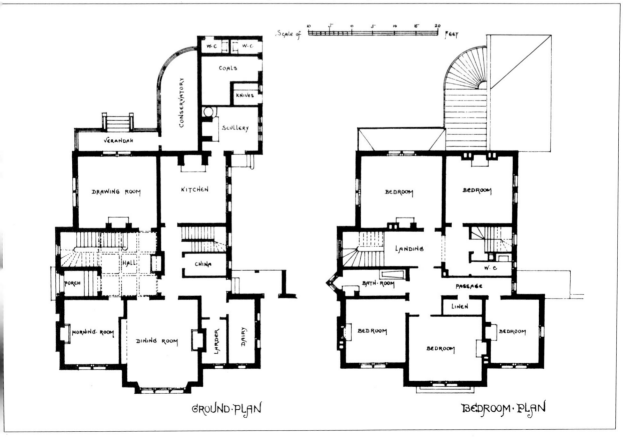

facing page
35 (*left*) No 31 Banbury Road, William Wilkinson, 1866
built for George Ward (*English Country Houses,* 1870).

36 (*right*) No 31 Banbury Road in 1966 before being
demolished (Local Studies Library, Oxford Central
Library).

38 No 113 Woodstock Road, William Wilkinson, 1863
built for the wine merchant, Edwin Butler (*English
Country Houses,* 1870).

provincial architect, he was not working in isolation but had connections
with contemporary architectural ideas.

    The historian and critic Goodhart-Rendel in his Slade lectures of 1936,
particularly praised Wilkinson for the planning of his houses, and Wilkinson's
internal planning does indeed deserve attention (Plates 38–40).[26] Generally
he adopted the country custom of placing the kitchen on the ground floor
while the basement, if there was one, was reserved for storage. Wilkinson
followed Kerr's recommendation that the service area of the house be

39 No 113 Woodstock Road, plan (*English Country Houses,* 1870).

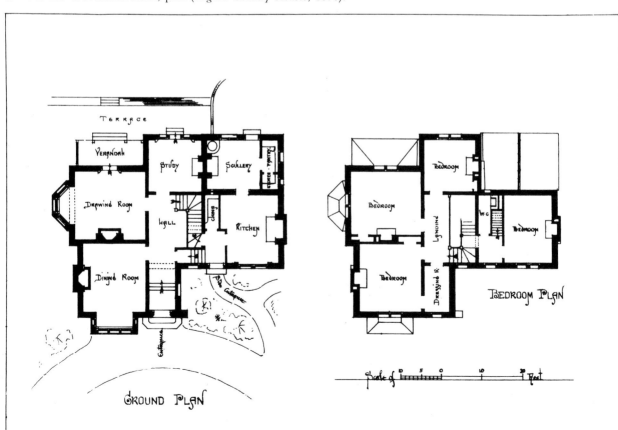

40 No 113 Woodstock Road in 1967 before being demolished (Local Studies Library, Oxford Central Library).

separated from the family rooms, something of an achievement when the kitchen shared the ground floor with the main reception rooms. There were usually three family rooms on this floor, the drawing and dining rooms, and a study or morning room. Between these rooms and the service area was the staircase and hall, sometimes graced by a fireplace, but always substantial in proportion to the rest of the house.

Beyond the door leading to the kitchen and its ancillary offices was a separate realm, often with its own corridor and stair. Where possible each domestic task was given a generous space so that what in later houses would be allotted a cupboard, here had a room of its own. The china store, the larder, the coals, lined up alongside the scullery and the much larger kitchen. Even in a moderately sized house like Chadlington House in west Oxfordshire, orginally built as a parsonage but never used as such, the proliferation of offices included a dairy and laundry, turning the house into a place of domestic production.[27] When the house was large enough to have a back stair, the division between the family and the services was carried through to the first floor. One good sized bedroom and a WC beyond the main landing on this floor would be reserved for servants or the nursery.

The parsonage like the country house, was intended for a family whose male head pursued much of his work within the house. In addition to the separation of family and servants, it was also important to ensure the detachment from family life of the working study where the parson could write his sermons and attend to parish business. The study usually took up one of the three corners on the ground floor occupied by the family, close to either the

41   No 60 Banbury
Road, William
Wilkinson, 1869, built
for the chemist,
Thomas Cousins.

main entrance or a side one, so that visitors on business need not pass into
the private areas of the house. This plan was followed in the North Oxford
villas where the first purpose-built houses were intended for professors or
local businessmen with political interests, both of whom needed space within
the family home for their own work.

From the moderately sized house in the country, Wilkinson evolved his
basic plan, but for his clients in North Oxford he succeeded in designing
houses of considerable originality. Of the four he illustrated in *English
Country Houses*, two have been demolished, Edwin Butler's house in
Woodstock Road and George Ward's in Banbury Road. The house
Wilkinson designed for T.G. Cousins still stands at 60 Banbury Road and is
a fine example of his work, built in yellow brick with a well proportioned
turret over the front door and neat hipped roofs (Plates 41–2). The house for
T.F. Dallin at 13 Norham Gardens, though much altered in 1906, remains
and both it and its neighbour No 11 are good examples of the adaptation of
his small country houses to the confines of the suburban plot.[28]

The first houses in Norham Gardens were built on the south side next to
the newly laid out University Parks. Nos 1, 5, 7, 11, and 13 are probably by
Wilkinson, and all turn their backs on the road so that their domestic offices
face north while the family rooms are arranged on the south side,
overlooking their own gardens and the Parks. Dallin's house was purpose
built for an academic at the start of his career. The front door was on the
west side of the house so that the street facade is rather flat and business-like,
broken by some tall gables. The plan allowed for a study to the left of the

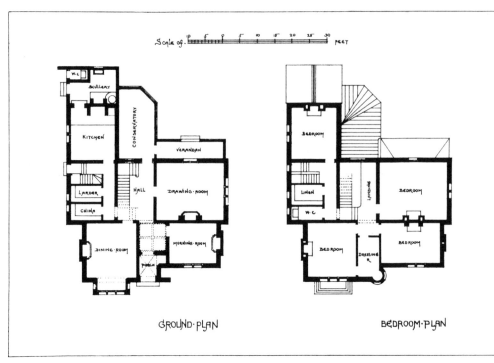

entrance hall, on the same side as the offices and kitchen (Plate 43). This meant that the drawing and dining rooms could take advantage of the southern aspect. The dining room, not usually placed facing south, was sheltered by a verandah. There was also access to the garden from the dining room which often in the middle-class house doubled as a family room. At

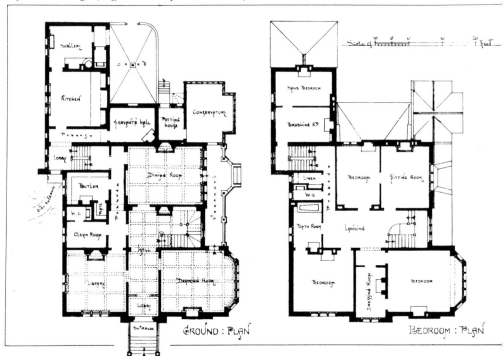

the end of the verandah a conservatory provided an opportunity for enjoying the garden, even during a drizzly Oxford summer.

The northeast corner of the Dallin house beyond the backstair formed the servants' area approached by a service passage separate from the main hall of the house and with its own entrance on the street front. Kitchen, scullery, and servants' hall were grouped around a courtyard, separated not just from the rest of the house, but also from the garden, so there was no danger of the servants overlooking the family while they enjoyed the garden. On the first floor the separation between the family and the servants was maintained with bedrooms for servants behind the backstairs. On this floor too, besides the main bedrooms, was an additional drawing room which may have been intended for Dallin's mother who was living with him and his young wife in 1871.

The fabric of the house was red brick with crisp stone dressings bonded into the brickwork around doors and windows. The larger windows were mullioned while the smaller were simple sashes, and the arch made its appearance mostly as segmental relieving arches in brick over the larger openings. The ground plan of the house, which was composed of two interlocking rectangles, might be expected to generate a rather bland elevation. The gables at roof level avoid this by defining the separate sections of the interior. It was expensive to include so many hips and valleys in the roof design, but not as expensive as straying very far from a rectangular plan. The size and complexity of this house aligned it closely with Wilkinson's country houses, and together with its neighbours it set the character for the type of house preferred by the College. 11 Norham Gardens next door was a similar house in yellow brick for George Mallam, and at 111 Woodstock Road, Wilkinson designed a handsome redbrick house for Robert Hills, the photographer, which also turns away from the street with entrance and offices on Leckford Road but living rooms facing the garden.

Viollet-le-Duc illustrated five of Wilkinson's designs in his *Habitations Modernes* of 1875, including Dallin's house.[29] This compares with one each for the better-known architects, Waterhouse, Norman Shaw, and Burges. What seemed to please Viollet-le-Duc about Wilkinson's designs was the rationality of the plan and the arrangement of the spaces for their appropriate functions. He was particularly impressed with the way the English dispensed with symmetry in their search for comfort and convenience.

Viollet-le-Duc had the illustrations from Wilkinson's book redrawn for his own, and the changes he made are telling. The people who inhabit the illustrations by Hallam appear to be typical of the late 1860s. As might be expected the inhabitants of the middle-class houses have ample leisure to wander about their gardens or enjoy a family game of croquet. The illustration for Dallin's house shows a group gathered around the croquet lawn, everyone dressed as if for a bracing walk in inclement weather. The women still wear hooped crinolines and hats as well as being buttoned up to the chin. Wilkinson did not change these illustrations for an expanded 1875 version of *English Country Houses*, although by this time the costumes had become decidedly out of date. Besides making adjustments to the design of

44   No 13 Norham Gardens, perspective (*English Country Houses*, 1870).

the house by increasing the symmetry of the verandah and by replacing the rectangular conservatory with an octagonal one, Viollet-le-Duc's illustrator changed the actors in the scene (Plates 44–5). Gone is the croquet party with their stuffy clothes and in their place is a gentleman greeting a lady who is wearing a bustled, low-necked dress and carrying a parasol on whose ferrule have been tied ribbons which flutter pleasantly in a light breeze. The amount

45   No 13 Norham Gardens, perspective (E. Viollet-le-Duc, *Habitations Modernes*, 1875).

of garden growth has been noticeably reduced and a sunny summer day is suggested rather than the doubtful weather of the croquet game. The house is also set among other similar suburban dwellings whereas Hallam's house gives the appearance of being set in its own country grounds. Both the lighter atmosphere and the frankly admitted suburban setting are more in tune with developments in house design of the 1870s.

During the early years of the suburb there were a number of other local architects designing for specific clients. Charles Buckeridge who will appear again as the architect of the Convent of the Most Holy Trinity was responsible for 3 and 9 Norham Gardens. Buckeridge was a pupil of Scott and during the 1860s before his untimely death in 1873 he was engaged in mostly ecclesiastical building and restoration work, employing a thoroughly gothic style. *The Ecclesiologist* of 1863 was especially complimentary of 9 Norham Gardens, designed for the recently appointed Professor of Modern History, Montagu Burrows:

Mr Buckeridge has designed a house in *The Parks, Oxford*, for Professor Burrows, which deserves great praise. The style is pointed, and the material brick, with arched and monialled windows of stone, and hipped tiled roof. We admire the arrangement of porch and hall, the bold window for the staircase, – a feature too often minimized in modern Gothic houses, – and the placing of the 'garderobes' in an external circular turret...[30]

Like Wilkinson's houses in Norham Gardens, Buckeridge's houses turn their backs on the street and present strong facades to their gardens and the University Parks. A very large later addition on the west side of No 3, although it reflected the original design, overbalances the garden facade. Buckeridge's three dimensional composition of No 9, despite an unsympathetic addition on the east side, can still be appreciated from the garden where the turret and the hipped roof of the street side are glimpsed in conjunction with the garden front and its prominent rear window arches with their plate tracery. Buckeridge's designs were more obviously ecclesiastical than Wilkinson's.

E.G. Bruton, another local architect, built his own semi-detached house in Woodstock Road, now gone, and also Nos 62, 64 and 33 Banbury Road.[31] These are substantial villas in the strong gothic style favoured by Wilkinson and the College. No 62, the most original of Bruton's houses, was the residence of the Rev R. St John Tyrwhitt, vicar of St Mary Magdalen and local patron of the arts. The entrance bay is given prominence by a gable that rides up over the roof line, and the entrance itself was disinguished by a sculpted relief attributed to J. Hungerford Pollen. All the houses on the east side of this part of Banbury Road were built for individual clients and they form something of a showpiece of distinctive villas at the entrance to the suburb.

Another architect who designed three houses prominently positioned in this section of Banbury Road was John Gibbs. Initially he had been in Oxford before moving in the early 1850s to Wigan and then Manchester. From here he published two books of gothic designs, intended as models for details in churches and houses.[32] The short text accompanying them suggests how gothic was finding its way into the popular consciousness. The text of Wilkinson's book was a practical treatise on house building, relying to a great extent on the 1865 Oxford Building Regulations for its content. No mention was made of style and the merits of the gothic. Gibbs, however, in his books dated 1853 and 1855, was writing at the time when the fight for gothic was still to be won. He equated British with Christian, and Christian with comfort. His argument was that without Christianity one could not expect to be comfortable, and that the gothic style united at the same time what was British, Christian, and comfortable. For this reason gothic was the style of the future which he saw in apocalyptic terms:

> Schemes of enterprise are visible in every city, and the apathy that once clothed our ancient towns with so much sluggishness, is giving way to the demands of modern culture; even the obscure village is become the recipient of a gratifying ambition proportionate to the chances of speculation. Impatient minds are flashing on amidst the thickening foam of an overwhelming tide, one that bears upon its waves the still to be dreaded darkness of an unknown future.[33]

Gibbs himself designed a number of memorials in the gothic style, including Banbury Cross in 1859. He was also the author of a novel, *The Old Parish Church: with the Ghost of Merton Hall*, published in 1861, in which he attributed the narrator's taste in gothic architecture to his college days in Oxford.

Gibbs returned to Oxford from the north in the 1860s when he designed houses for Thomas Arnold, the son of the famous headmaster of Rugby School, for Henry Hatch, bootmaker, draper and theatre proprietor, and for William Walsh, a chemist. The house for Arnold, 54 Banbury Road, is now greatly altered by the additions built after it became Wycliffe Hall, but it would have been similar to No 58. This latter is distinguished by its narrow, roundheaded windows and the dark red brick of the walls with very little stone in the understated detail (Plate 46). Despite Gibbs' obvious interest in the gothic this house displays a style more distinctly of its time than any pastiche of the medieval. Goodhart-Rendel found the house 'more interesting than all the others put together', and was particularly struck by the originality of the composition:

> Its character is marked, and lies entirely outside that general course of English Victorian architecture, suggesting rather that some traveller in the South of France or in Spain had wished to graft upon our current habits in house-building the peculiar simplicities of those regions . . . The silhouette arises naturally from the plan, but is extraordinarily well balanced. The tall narrow windows are of nineteenth century England and give to this design its peculiar novelty and – indirectly – its greatest merit. Whether such windows are convenient or not we need not now consider; at the time when this house was built they were preferred, and are here contrasted with the marked horizontality of the rest of the architecture in a way as skilful as it is successful.[34]

46 No 58 Banbury Road, John Gibbs, 1867, built for the chemist, William Walsh.

47 No 56 Banbury Road, John Gibbs, 1867, built for Henry Hatch and the longtime residence of E.B. Poulton, Professor of Zoology.

The almost geometric composition of this house distinguishes its sober design from more facile attempts at producing a picturesque effect with an array of gothic details.

No 56 for Hatch was extended twice by its subsequent owner Professor Poulton, but even so its yellow brick facade with its plate tracery and elaborate stone porch is much less restrained than that of No 58 (Plate 47). Like its neighbour, its main chimney is placed on the front facade, with the added feature of a niche containing the statue of William of Wykeham by the sculptor, W. Forsyth of Worcester. The house made a strong impression on *Jackson's Oxford Journal*:

> In this conspicuous illustration, Mr Gibbs has forcibly endeavoured to show that when Gothic architecture is fully carried out, it is the style best adapted for buildings of a similar description. The gothic here exemplified is early, and somewhat Continental; and we are informed that the elaborate style adopted can be treated as economically as its rival, the classic . . . Indeed 'Wykeham House' may be regarded as a very satisfactory piece of architectural design, in which is embodied a new and useful development of the Gothic, not unworthy of repetition.[35]

This comment signals the acceptance of the gothic character of North Oxford which was not to be questioned for another fifteen years.

All the houses mentioned so far were designed for specific clients and when an architect designed a purpose-built house in North Oxford, he knew the requirements of his client. An architect designing for the speculative market could not always be sure he was getting it right, especially when there was outside pressure being put on him to produce houses of a specific value. When the households inhabiting the purpose-built houses in North Oxford are examined in a group, it is evident that even the architect designing for a specific family had no small task in accommodating a range of people with differing, but overlapping interests. A quick glance at the *Census Enumerators' Returns* for the twenty-three purpose-built houses occupied in 1871 show that although these were houses designed for middle-class families the characteristics of individuals living in the households cut across age, class and sex.[36] For example, two-thirds of the inhabitants were female, but three-quarters of these were children and servants. A third of the residents was under the age of eighteen, but this included children of the families and teenage servants. Because of the high number of resident servants, two-fifths of all household members were working class, both male and female, adult and adolescent. Through social codes and custom, reinforced by the disposition of space, the different members of the household, as Kerr had pointed out, could be accommodated in the middle-class house. By dealing with one family at a time, the architect of the purpose-built house could concentrate on the needs and projected needs of one household. The speculative builder, however, had to form out of his experience a notional, middle-class family, and the emergence of the suburban house type depended on successive attempts by architects of speculative ventures to design in a way which would suit the generality rather than the individual.

Probably the most interesting architect of speculative development in North Oxford was Frederick Codd. As noted in chapter 3, he was born in East Dereham, Norfolk in 1832, but some time before 1857 he went to London where he was established by 1860.[37] He was still in London in 1863 when his fourth child was born there. Then in 1865 he was in Oxford applying to St John's on behalf of Miss Frances Norris of Norwich to build a detached house in Banbury Road. At first he lived in Cowley Road, St Clement's, across Magdalen Bridge, but he soon built his own semi-detached house at the corner of Banbury and Bevington Roads, next to Miss Norris' villa. Codd established a busy practice in Oxford and was responsible for many of the shop refurbishments and commercial developments in the city during the 1870s, such as the speculative shops and offices in the new King Edward Street built in 1871–5 for Oriel College. It is his suburban houses in North Oxford, however, which remain his best work.

Over the ten years that Codd was occupied with house building, he evolved a repertoire of motifs that he could put together to produce a statisfying composition for a medium sized, gothic house. The villa he designed in Banbury Road for Miss Norris showed him to be already a competent designer. The house, No 37, is without basement and sits wide and comfortably on its site (Plate 48). Gables break into the roof and different roof levels reflect the variety of spaces within. The fabric is yellow brick with red and blue bricks delineating the voussoirs over the pointed arched windows, a rather old fashioned detail by this time and soon dropped

48   No 37 Banbury Road, Frederick Codd, 1866, built for Miss Frances Norris.

by Codd. There is very little stone detail in this house with only some short columns and carved capitals between the double arched windows and plain lintels over the straight-headed openings. In his own house next door, the parapet detail of the two storey bays was formed in brickwork. The reluctance to use stone may have been an economy, or Codd, coming from London, may not have been accustomed to the availability in Oxford of skilled masons to do the crisp stone detailing found in his later houses.

During the late 1860s and early 1870s Codd was fully engaged with houses in Banbury Road and Norham Gardens. None of these houses, even the largest, contained all the features characteristic of the Codd house, but all have some. In Norham Gardens, for instance, the window openings in Nos 15 and 16 are pointed arches, while those in Nos 14 and 18 are straight-headed with mullions. Nos 15 and 18 have the distinctive stone course which forms a hood-mould over the upper windows in the gable. In Nos 14 and 16 this has become a simple contrasting double course of red brick across the

50 (*far right*) No 17 Norham Gardens, plan, Frederick Codd, 1874 (SJC Muniments, redrawn by Geoffrey Randell).

49 No 66 Banbury Road, detail of entrance, Frederick Codd, 1874, since removed. A new balustrade has recently been added to the porch and tower (SJC Muniments).

gables. The two-storey bay window with stone detailing at the parapet appears in nearly all the houses, and in No 18 it even continues an extra storey. The little barge-board dormer, which makes its appearance so often that it could almost be considered essential, is missing in No 16. The porch too takes different forms, from the elaborate stone aedicule placed symmetrically at No 18 to the simple wooden shed constructed over the entrance to No 14 (Plate 49).

In these houses Codd put the kitchen and offices in the basement, a decision which enabled him to enclose the whole villa within a simple rectangle, as can be seen in the plans for 17 Norham Gardens (Plate 50). The large square hall and staircase held a prominent place at the centre of the house, with a fireplace positioned opposite the front entrance. The hall was flanked by a study and lavatory on the left and a morning room on the right. These rooms faced north and were smaller than the two south-facing rooms, the dining and drawing rooms, with the latter graced by a broad bay window overlooking the garden. On the first floor the staircase and landing took up a large amount of space, but still there were four good-sized bedrooms and a dressing room.

There is, however, an unease about these Norham Gardens houses. They are big in order to accommodate the requirements of the middle-class family and some of them were enlarged still further after they were built,[38] but they are also sited well forward on their plots to allow for large back gardens. Under these circumstances the houses have an uncomfortable relation with the street, especially now that the front gardens are bereft of their iron railings and have lost much of their planting to facilitate the parking of cars.

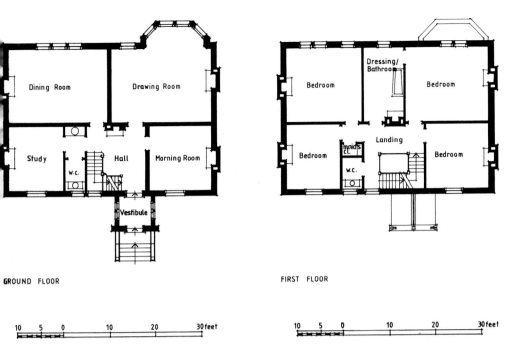

GROUND FLOOR

FIRST FLOOR

| 10 | 5 | 0 | | 10 | 20 | 30 feet |

| 10 | 5 | 0 | | 10 | 20 | 30 feet |

52 Banbury Road, set in a generous triangle of garden, shows that given enough space, even Codd's larger houses could produce a very satisfactory effect and the position of this particular house is especially important because it forms the introduction of the North Oxford estate at the south end of Banbury Road. The houses Codd designed in Canterbury Road, Bradmore Road and further north in Banbury Road did not have to be so large as those in Norham Gardens and generally they are more successful. All the same details are there: the gables, the hood-moulds, the bay windows, the dormer, the porch, but the reduced scale of the houses seems to have inspired Codd to compose his facades with greater assurance and the details are handled with some subtlety. The range of houses formed by 14 to 17 Bradmore Road is particularly effective in giving that sense of variety in homogeneity which has become one of the hallmarks of the middle-class suburb (Plate 51).

The search for variety and distinction characterised the houses of the 1860s and 70s, even those undertaken by speculators like Galpin and his builder John Dover. One of their more distinctive houses was 20 Bradmore Road which was subsequently extended extensively in 1889 (Plates 52–3). The kitchen and services of this house were also put in the basement, but perhaps the most surprising feature of the plan was the extent of the circulation area which filled nearly the whole of the southeast corner of the ground floor. Part of this space was taken up on the first floor by the bathroom, but on the ground floor, instead of the four rooms that might be expected in a double fronted house with the kitchen in the basement, there were only three. Galpin's architect was George Shirley who designed most of Galpin's houses at the east end of Norham Gardens on the north side, Bradmore on the west side and Crick Roads on the south side as well as the later houses in Warnborough and Farndon Roads. However, there is not the consistency in

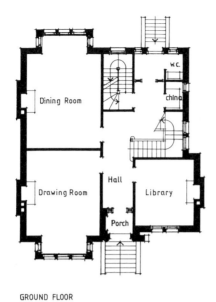

GROUND FLOOR   FIRST FLOOR

52 No 20 Bradmore Road, plan, Galpin and Shirley, 1873 (SJC Muniments, redrawn by Geoffrey Randell).

51 (*facing page*) No 16 Bradmore Road, Frederick Codd, 1872.

53 No 20 Bradmore Road, Galpin and Shirley, 1873, subsequently enlarged.

54 Nos 18–19 Bradmore Road, Galpin and Shirley, 1873.

the Galpin houses that there is in those by Codd, so he may have depended on more than one architect. Similar designs do turn up in different streets like 26 and 28 Norham Gardens, 11 and 12 Norham Road, and 17 and 18 St Margaret's Road where the double course of red header-bricks sketched out on the yellow brick facade arches and string courses. A feature of some of Galpin's semi-detached houses, for example 18 and 19 Bradmore Road, was that they were designed asymmetrically (Plate 54).

One builder whose houses were almost inevitably semi-detached was John Dorn. It appears that the designs for his houses came out of Wilkinson's office and they can be found in the smaller streets of the southern part of the estate, in Museum, Norham and Winchester Roads. These houses were cheaper than Codd's or Galpin's, but their facades were nevertheless decorated with red brick voussoirs and with herring bone patterns within relieving arches, while like the larger houses window and door details were executed in stone. It is easy to pick out those houses Dorn built in Norham Road after an examination of 5 to 10 Winchester Road (Plate 55). Earlier houses by Dorn in Museum Road, though different in detail, are basically the same. Once it is known that Codd ran into trouble over his lots in Fyfield Road, the presence of Dorn's characteristic three lights over the front doors in 2–4 Fyfield Road signals that it was Dorn who eventually took over the building of these houses. Stylistic anomalies in North Oxford often point to the difficulties of individual builders or a change in the players involved in the development of the suburb.

Just at the time that Codd was running into difficulties, a new architectural style was gaining favour, even in gothic Oxford. In 1876 T.G. Jackson won the competition for the Examination Schools in the High Street and

112

55 Nos 5–6 Winchester Road, William Wilkinson, 1875, a typical house built by John Dorn.

introduced his version of the English Renaissance.[39] Jackson had given his opinion of the gothic revival in 1873 in his book *Modern Gothic Architecture*, where he urged architects to move on from the project to forge a contemporary style from medieval models. He wrote: 'We, too, have been like alchymists, grasping at a shadow, dreaming of an actual restoration of Medieval art dreams from which we are beginning to awake, to find them as delusive and idle as those of the philosopher's stone.'[40] Although Jackson was in favour of returning to the past in order to develop a new style, he thought the severe gothic of the previous generation too limiting and found excitement in those early experiments in classicism that English architects and builders had undertaken at the end of Elizabeth's reign and during the Stuart period.

In the realm of domestic architecture a similar change in perception was taking place. In the early 1860s Richard Norman Shaw and William Eden Nesfield had together evolved a style which has been called 'old English' since it was forged from details found in those old houses remaining in the

113

villages and towns of the southern counties of England.[41] In the architectural press by the mid-1870s the 'old English' style began to become the dominant style in the illustrations of small and medium-size houses. Architectural attention was at last turning to the small family house, with the result that interest began to gather around its style and planning. The so-called 'Queen Anne' style attracted to itself some controversy, and the architect, J.J. Stevenson, found himself its rather bemused defender.

The Queen Anne style was a version of the vernacular revival, but its models were those seventeenth- and eighteenth-century town houses whose artisan builders had decorated them with simple classical motifs in moulded brick.[42] The challenge for the nineteenth-century architect was to design his house with so much sophistication that it captured the charm of the naive attempts of the unlettered builder to reproduce classical detail in a material antithetical to that purpose. Those who took up Queen Anne did not want to lose the freedom the gothic style had given in the planning of the house, but they believed their eclectic style would be even more suited to contemporary living. Stevenson published in 1880 his two volumed *House Architecture* where he pointed out that Scott's plea for the use of gothic in domestic architecture on utilitarian grounds had not proved sound. 'Difficulties not anticipated have shown themselves in adapting the style to modern use, and there is a feeling that the question whether gothic is the most suitable style of architecture for modern domestic use needs reconsideration.'[43] It must be said too that middle-class life had changed since Scott was writing in 1857. If the tradesmen of the towns had learnt the culture of the suburbs, so had the gentry, whose work in the professions drew them into the towns from the country. Their expectations needed to be lowered as much as those of the shopkeepers had to be raised. Although the concept of the separate spheres for men and women in some ways was becoming more entrenched through the sentimentalism surrounding mothers and children, the relations between the sexes were easier and contact between children and adults was greater. It was also becoming more difficult to keep women within the home. The reduction in the birth rate among the middle classes gave women more freedom and released space in the house previously given over for long periods to the nursery. Servants continued to make up part of the middle-class household for many years yet, but though they were more prevalent, there tended to be fewer of them per household.

Omond, the bursar of St John's, had expressed reservations in 1878 about the quality of the architecture of the houses on the College's estate.[44] When a building site at the south end of Banbury Road became available in 1880, he called on his brother-in-law, who happened to be J.J. Stevenson, to design for him a house in the new Queen Anne style. He also persuaded T.H. Green, Whyte's Professor of Moral Philosophy, to have a similar house built next door.[45] The fabric of the houses is a bright, orange-red brick, not much seen in Oxford up to this time. The houses are broad rather than tall, and the passerby is struck by the dormers set in wide roofs rather than by high gothic gables (Plate 56). Decorative details are in fact few with most of the interest in the facade coming from the moulded and rubbed-brick details,

56 No 29 Banbury Road, J.J. Stevenson, 1882, residence of Thomas Omond, bursar of St John's College.

especially around the segmental arched openings on the ground floor. The architect has included some deliberate archaisms like placing the frames of the straightheaded sash windows flush with the brickwork, and he has used wooden details rather than stone. On the front of No 27, which was to have been Green's house, there is a brick plaque on which are depicted the initials of Green and his wife, Charlotte Byron Green (Plate 57). Dallin had had a stone plaque affixed to the street side of his house, but he only included his own initials. This small detail suggests the change in sensibility from the expected proprietorship of the male head to the shared responsibility of the companionate marriage. This responsibility fell abruptly onto Green's wife when he died suddenly before they could move into the house and she had the task of arranging a mortgage.[46]

The plan of No 27, which was the larger of the two houses, is a variation on that of the standard Oxford villa (Plate 58). On the ground floor, within the main block of the house are the dining room, drawing room, and kitchen. There is no space on this floor for a study since the vestibule, hall and staircase, and cloakroom take up the rest of the main block. In this house

58 (*below*) No 27 Banbury Road, plan (SJC Muniments, redrawn Geoffrey Randell).

the hall has become a real room of meeting, rather than a neutral area where
strangers are separated from intimate callers. The study is found in a south-
facing room on the first floor whose dimensions are extended by a large
projecting window bay supported on iron columns. Despite his tight plan,
the architect managed to include all the usual domestic offices and a servants'
hall by building a one-storey range on the north side of the ground floor,
divided from the main block by a passage from the kitchen. This is by no
means a small house, but its proportions and composition recall the
overgrown cottage rather than the reduced country house which had been
Wilkinson's model (Plate 59).

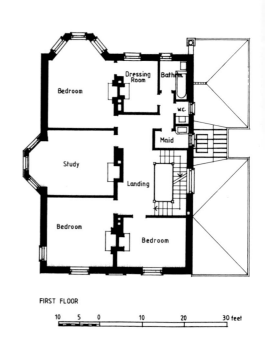

GROUND FLOOR

FIRST FLOOR

116

59 No 27 Banbury Road.

Stevenson's designs signalled a change in the style of the North Oxford houses, a change which had nonetheless been brewing even in Wilkinson's office. At the end of the 1860s his nephew, Clapton Crabb Rolfe, designed the rows of cottages on the east side of Kingston Road in a style which, though gothic in spirit, included some striking vernacular elements like the first floor windows which break up through the eaves, the patterned and

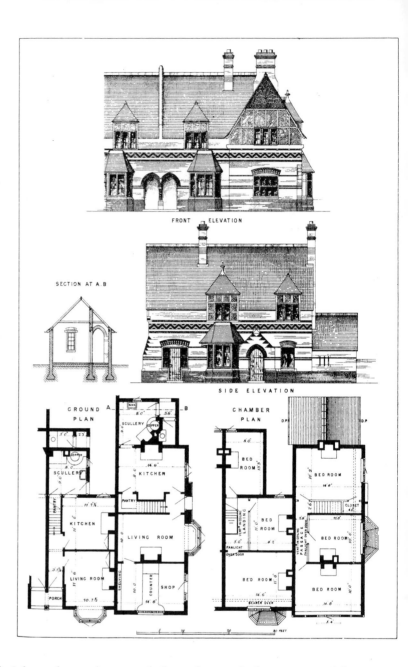

FRONT ELEVATION

SECTION AT A.B

SIDE ELEVATION

GROUND PLAN

CHAMBER PLAN

60 Nos 159–64
Kingston Road,
C.C. Rolfe, 1870
(*Building News*).

herring bone brickwork, and ground floor bay windows capped by steep tiled roofs (Plate 60).[47] In 1875 Wilkinson reissued his book *English Country Houses*, with sixteen additional illustrations drawn by Maurice B. Adams, who was by this time working for *Building News*.[48] Adams had acted as draughtsman for Norman Shaw and other 'aesthetic' architects like J.J. Stevenson, R.W. Edis and E.W. Godwin and he was also involved in Jonathan Carr's Bedford Park. Thus it could be said that by association Wilkinson was on the margins of what was being called the aesthetic movement. The designs for 23–4 and 25–6 Leckford Road by Wilkinson's chief clerk, F.J. Connell, give some evidence of this since they show him discarding gothic gables to experiment with Dutch.

61 No 36 Norham Road, F.J. Connell, 1880. The ball and cap have been removed from the front gable.

In 1881 Wilkinson made his nephew, Harry Wilkinson Moore, a partner and they continued to work together in partnership until Wilkinson's retirement in 1886. Once on his own, Moore illustrated a number of his Oxford schemes in *Building News*, and they show him a convert to Jackson's English Renaissance style.[49] They included the parish buildings for St Clement's Church, a residential building for Somerville College, a tutor's house for University College, and an extension to the Pusey Memorial House, 61 St Giles's. Even before the nephew took over the supervision of the North Oxford estate, however, houses designed with a new repertoire of details began to appear in the suburb.

Walter Gray, the college steward turned developer, complained in 1883 that the houses built under the auspices of the Oxford Building and Investment Company were ugly.[50] He took especial exception to the yellow brick supplied by the Oxford and Berks Brick Company. Galpin dismissed this complaint as trivial, but he simply did not understand that Gray was using style to establish his ascendancy on the estate. After 1883, in the second wave of building, Gray and Moore joined together as developer and architect to produce a substantial new section of the North Oxford suburb.

Gray began his activities in Kingston Road, but he was soon busy elsewhere on the estate, especially where other builders had abandoned their options. For example, at the east end of Norham Road, a semi-detached pair 24 and 25, and 26 stand out from their neighbours as different in style (see Plate 32). These houses are built of red brick and have very strong, stone details which include palladian windows and that feature so redolent of the seventeenth century for the late Victorians, the ball and cap. Nos 36 and 37,

62   No 78 Woodstock Road, Wilkinson and Moore, 1882.

also built for Gray and designed by F.J. Connell, have even more features which suggest the seventeenth century (Plate 61). The ball and cap and the palladian windows are there, but also decorative brick pediments and the proportion of wall to window contribute to the picturesque evocation of the seventeenth-century house.

Banbury and Woodstock Roads continued to be the areas where the most expensive houses were built. There is no more yellow brick, and stone continued for some years yet to dominate the decorative system of the facades. The model for 74 to 80 Woodstock Road seems to be the seventeenth-century houses built in what Sir John Summerson has called 'artisan mannerism', with a much more regular disposition of the windows than in the gothic houses and with the employment of Dutch gables (Plate 62).[51] Further evidence of a seventeenth-century influence can be found in the porch at 74 Banbury Road which is vigorously decorated with stone strap work (Plate 63). These houses are reminiscent of those evocative paintings of suburban houses by Atkinson Grimshaw, for example *Sixty Years Ago*, 1879 and *November Morning*, 1883[52] and they indicate an acute awareness of the picturesque qualities necessary for the success of an estate like North Oxford in the 1880s.

120

63   No 74 Banbury Road, detail of front porch, Wilkinson and Moore, 1882.

As Wilkinson and Moore took on sole responsibility for the design of Gray's houses, they evolved plans which are well exemplified by the houses they designed during the 1880s for St Margaret's Road. The houses were oriented firmly with the street and for the most part lacked basements so that the plan of the ground floor included the careful separation of the kitchen and offices from the living rooms as Wilkinson had done in his earlier houses. The big bay windows which are a feature of these houses ensured that the main rooms were well lit, and the plain stone frames around these

64 No 2 St Margaret's Road, ground floor plan, Wilkinson and Moore, 1884 (SJC Muniments).

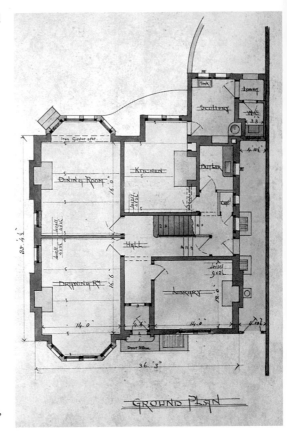

65 No 2 St Margaret's Road, elevation, Wilkinson and Moore, 1884, now site of St Hugh's College (SJC Muniments).

windows dominate the facades, often both front and back (Plates 64–5). A decorative motif which occurs frequently in Moore's houses is that of two abutting scrolls linked by a swag. This motif appears in every class of house from the largest villa to the cottages built in Hayfield Road for the Oxford Industrial and Provident Land and Building Society.

Gray's success as developer depended on his ability to produce houses for the wealthy on the prominent sites while building lower middle-class and artisanal houses in the back streets behind Woodstock Road. But whereas the College's lower-class terraces in Kingston Road had been completely different in style from the villas on the rest of the estate, Gray maintained a continuum from the high-class houses to the lower, and he did this through his architect who used the same red bricks and stone details in the houses in Polstead, Chalfont and Frenchay Roads as are found in the larger detached houses in the Woodstock and Banbury Roads.

Before the end of the century the North Oxford house went through another stylistic change. The brick and stone of Moore's houses of the 1880s gave way to a style which included many more different sorts of materials like hung tiles and render; those same elements with which Richard Norman Shaw had experimented as early as the 1860s and had used to great effect in some of his country houses and in the houses he designed for Bedford Park. One house in North Oxford which exemplified this style to the extent that it was formerly attributed to Shaw was 80 Banbury Road, designed by R.W. Edis in 1884 for A.V. Dicey, Professor of Law.[53] Edis was a London

67 No 80 Banbury Road, plan (SJC Muniments, redrawn Geoffrey Randell).

66 No 80 Banbury Road, R.W. Edis, 1886, residence of A.V. Dicey, Professor of English Law, now demolished (Local Studies Library, Oxford Central Library).

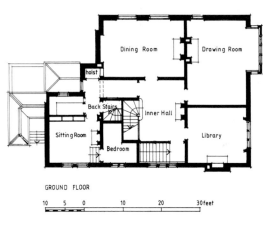

GROUND FLOOR

68 No 2 Northmoor Road, E.W. Allfrey, 1903–8, residence of Charles Firth, Professor of Modern History.

architect who had gravitated towards the 'aesthetic' styles of the 1880s. In 1880 he gave the Cantor lectures before the Society of Arts which he published the next year as *Decoration and Furniture of Town Houses*, and here he agreed with Jackson and Stevenson about the failings of the gothic for contemporary design and advocated a more eclectic approach.[54] He designed a distinctive house in Tite Street for Dicey's artist brother, Frank in 1879, and 80 Banbury Road, although very different, was also striking (Plates 66–7). Its unusual form was due to the ground floor being completely given over to the domestic offices of the house while the main rooms began on the first floor. The entrance led into little more than a vestibule, but a large inner hall with fireplace was situated at the top of the stairs which ran up just to the right of the front door. Such an arrangement completed the

Library

Drawing Room

Landing

Lin.

w.c.

Sitting Room

FIRST FLOOR

Scullery

Kitchen

store

larder

Dining Room

Servant's
Sitting Room

Lobby

Boots

Back
Stair

Hall

Lav.

Coals

Wine

Pantry

W.C.

Vestibule

GROUND FLOOR

| 10 | 5 | 0 | | 10 | 20 | 30feet |

69   No 2 Northmoor Road, plan (SJC Muniments, redrawn Geoffrey Randell).

transformation of the hall from utilitarian circulation to an additional social space. On the outside, these two floors were expressed in brickwork, surmounted by another storey of half-timbering which gave the house a high, broad form unusual for North Oxford houses of this period.

Most of the North Oxford houses up to this time had been designed by a very few architects, and especially during the 1880s and 1890s Harry Wilkinson Moore dominated the estate with his designs. Although Omond had hoped that individuals would build in the Bardwell estate, many speculative houses were built. There were, however, some examples of individuals building their own houses. Charles Firth, Regius Professor of Modern History, commissioned E.W. Allfrey, a local architect, in 1902 to design 2 Northmoor Road. This is a very attractive and important house in the suburb, displaying an innovative composition with eclectic details (Plate 68). The wooden sash windows set flush in their segmental-headed brick frames, which themselves have prominent keystones and aprons, refer to the Queen Anne style as does the rich orange-coloured brick. The front gable on the other hand is reminiscent of the seventeenth-century manor house style, but the semi-circular bay afixed to the facade with flat roof, bands of smallpaned windows and rendering suggests something more along the lines of designs by Baillie Scott or Voysey. The arts and crafts motif is carried through in the front door, surrounded by ashlar with a canopy supported on brackets. The rear facade is also impressive, and since the south-facing bay lights the rooms on the left side, the architect could use the main chimney stack as a prominent feature. On the right the double-height bay through the

70   No 2 Northmoor Road from the garden.

first and second storeys, almost entirely glazed with small panes, balances in its lightness the flat solidity of the chimney.

The eclectic approach to the exterior design of 2 Northmoor Road is matched by its internal arrangement which like Dicey's house has the kitchen and offices on the ground floor with the main rooms above, but with the difference that the dining room is also on the ground floor next to the kitchen (Plate 69). This solved the problem of how to arrange the kitchen and dining room in proximity, a problem which plagued house design whether the kitchen was in the basement or on the ground floor but separated from the family's rooms. Allfrey's solution would have led to a procession through the house when guests came to dinner, but this would no doubt have added to the occasion.

Another feature of Professor Firth's house was its great size when the tendency was towards smaller, more compact houses (Plate 70). The basement was now discarded completely in the houses of North Oxford, and the kitchen and domestic offices, though still extensive were strictly separated in what amounted to a small domestic wing. In order to include the domestic offices on the ground floor and a good sized hall with fireplace, the houses built in the 1880s and 1890s were broad as well as high. Rawlinson Road has some examples of houses with this profile together with a greater freedom in

71   No 6 Rawlinson Road, Herbert Quinton, 1889.

the use of materials, for example No 6 by Herbert Quinton (Plate 71). On the Bardwell estate Moore continued to build high and broad, but he too varied the details by including along with the stone lintels and mullions, tile hanging, half-timbering and turned wooden balusters as he did at 10 Northmoor Road (Plate 72). The broader composition appeared also in semi-detached houses like 2–12 and 26–8 Bardwell Road, designed during the 1890s by a Birmingham firm of architects, Radclyffe and Watson (Plate 73). But with the turn of the century the move was away from really large to moderate sized houses, even on the Bardwell estate.

8 Linton Road, called the White House, was designed in 1899 for Mrs Katherine Hopkins by E.T. Marriott, a London architect, and this modest house exemplifies an increasing simplicity of design, while still keeping the multiple functions of the house (Plate 74).[55] The hall and stairs continue to dominate the centre of the house, and the hall, though only 10 feet wide, has a fireplace. On the ground floor are the drawing and dining rooms besides the kitchen and offices, with the client's studio on the first floor, placed

72 No 10 Northmoor Road, H.W. Moore, 1904.

73 Nos 10–12 Bardwell Road, Radclyffe-Watson, 1894.

74 8 Linton Road, plan (SJC Muniments, redrawn by Geoffrey Randell).

FIRST FLOOR

75 No 8 Linton Road, E.J. Marriott, 1899–1901, built for Mrs Katherine Hopkins and called 'the White House'.

76   No 11 Chadlington Road, Frank Mountain, 1910.

above the kitchen and appropriately facing north. The exterior is rendered
and depends for effect on the free arrangement of the windows, rather than
on any richness of the materials (Plate 75). The house, as it was built,
incorporated the rooms on the west side into the large front gable which
gave a simplified profile.

Although Moore continued to design houses on the Bardwell estate after
he was dismissed by the College as the surveyor of North Oxford, other
architects replaced him as the dominating influence.[56] The architect who
took over from Moore as surveyor, N.W. Harrison, had been a pupil of
Moore's but does not seem to have adopted his vigorous approach to design.
His houses are to be found mostly in Charlbury and Chadlington Roads. An
architect with more flair was F. Mountain, who was responsible for 14–16
Northmoor Road and 11 Chadlington Road (Plate 76). His distinctive stone-
battered buttresses combined with rough-cast and half-timbering are un-
characteristically strong for this part of North Oxford. More typical is the
work of George Gardiner who designed an attractive group of houses in
Marston Ferry Road and 19–27 and 16–20 Linton Road, as well as Cherwell

77   No 23 Linton Road, George Gardiner, 1909.

78   No 7 Linton Road, A.H. Moberly, 1903.

House for H.B. Haldane, now replaced by Wolfson College. Gardiner's houses are recognised by their render, which has remained unpainted in most instances, and by the red roof tiles (Plate 77).

A.H. Moberly's design for 7 Linton Road, right across the street from Marriott's No 8, introduced the neo-Georgian style to North Oxford, a pre-war indication that the freer 'old English' was beginning to be played out (Plate 78). Red bricks and sash windows with small panes have already been seen on the estate, but what is distinctive about this house is its regular form. The windows of ground and first floors are aligned one above the other and the front facade is balanced by two bays symmetrically placed at either end. Only the front entrance has been placed asymmetrically.

After World War I when only the northern section of the Bardwell estate was left to be completed a new generation of architects became involved in the design of the houses. Among these were Fisher and Trubshaw, Mills and Shepherd, Arthur C. Martin, Frederick E. Openshaw, and Thomas Rayson.[57] The most active of these was Christopher Wright, a London-based architect, who had studied at the University of Liverpool School of Architecture and had trained with Niven and Wigglesworth in London.[58] In the early 1920s the College released the land on the north of the Bardwell

130

79 No 26 Northmoor Road, Christopher Wright, 1925.

estate which still remained undeveloped, and it was in the newly extended
Northmoor and Charlbury Roads that Christopher Wright began his work
in North Oxford. He adopted the now popular neo-Georgian style, which
suited the greatly reduced size of the suburban house, but in his designs he
avoided the blandness which resulted so often from the application of this
style to the small house.

Wright's houses are characterised by their simplicity, but this did not
mean that they were without embellishment. In 1924 Wright used an
L-shaped plan in Northmoor Road, for example in Nos 22 and 26, and
a carefully detailed chimney marks the juncture between the intersecting
sections of the house (Plate 79). One feature which recurs in Wright's houses
is the almost square first-floor windows which push up under the eaves of
the hipped roof. The red brick walls are articulated by raised bands between
the bays which can be seen as pilasters or the bays can be considered cut back
from the main wall surface. No 24 presents a straight seven-bay facade to the
street, but the roof profile is similar to the one used in Nos 22 and 26 (Plate
80). The first-floor windows also push up into the eaves, and the brick walls
are treated in a similar way.

The houses that Wright designed subsequently, for example in

80 No 24 Northmoor Road, Christopher Wright, 1925.

Belbroughton and Garford Roads, show a variety of forms and details but all within the neo-Georgian style, and Howard Colvin in *Unbuilt Oxford* has commented on these by writing that 'Only in Belbroughton Road will the connoisseur of neo-Georgian find a small group of houses worth his attention . . .'.[59] No 1 Belbroughton Road is basically a simple rectangle made distinctive by the three arches and by the contrast between the brick-work and the rendering within the arches (Plate 81). The plan of this house demonstrates how house design was changing during the inter-war years. The amount of space given over to circulation has been contracted into a relatively small area and the hall, though still at the centre of the house, acts only to connect the rooms and leads to the enclosed stairs at the back of the house (Plate 82). There is nothing unusual about the arrangement of the rooms on the ground floor except that an additional entrance to the dining room brings it within easy reach of the kitchen. On the first floor again the circulation is functional and the six bedrooms fitted into the rectangle of the house with the minimum amount of wasted space.

H.S. Goodhart-Rendel in his lectures on the architecture of North Oxford singled out 1 Belbroughton Road as an example of the neo-Georgian successors to Wilkinson's gothic and Moore's Queen Anne, and could not help feeling some regret at its 'more calculating charms':

The house of which I now shew you a picture will seem much more agreeable to most of us than those that have hitherto been upon the screen.

132

81   No 1 Belbroughton Road, Christopher Wright, 1926.

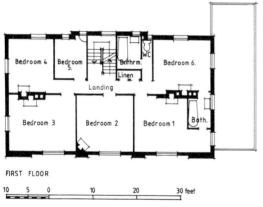

FIRST FLOOR

10   5   0   10   20   30 feet

GROUND FLOOR

82   No 1 Belbroughton Road, plan (Local Studies Library, Oxford Central Library, Oxford City Engineer's Deposited Plan, redrawn by Geoffrey Randell).

83 Nos 2–4 Charlbury Road, Stephen Salter, 1910.

Its details are carefully studied, its proportions satisfactory and its aspect is genial and inviting. It is in fact, one of the most charming little town halls I have seen, and I have no doubt that it has been adapted so as to make a delightful house. But I wonder what Mr. Wilkinson would say.[60]

Indeed, Wright's houses were a long way from Wilkinson's country vicarages and the versions of them he adapted for North Oxford. His task was also simpler since he was designing at a time when the middle classes had evolved a less complex social life, requiring less segregation of function and of household members. While there were still references to the country in these houses and the others built at the same time, it could be said that they were, regardless of style, adapted to the requirements of the suburb and the middle-class life as it had evolved.

Because the most prominent houses in North Oxford are still those ex-emplifying the nineteenth-century domestic gothic, the suburb is identified with this style, but a comprehensive range of domestic architecture from the 1850s to the 1930s can be found in its streets (Plate 83). More than this, the houses display the development of the suburban house from Italianate to the gothic, from gothic to the 'old English' and Queen Anne, from 'old English' to the neo-Georgian. Most of the houses were built speculatively, but nevertheless many of these were designed by architects, such as Codd and Shirley, and of course by Harry Wilkinson Moore. Among the North Oxford houses there are some distinguished examples of suburban houses of their time, and although the suburb rarely led the fashion, it does illustrate extremely well contemporary trends in domestic architecture over the period of its building.

CHAPTER VI
North Oxford Institutions

DESPITE THE DEMANDS of various railway companies, gravel contractors, and bodies such as the Board of Guardians, St John's succeeded in establishing a residential suburb in North Oxford. The open fields north of the town had already provided space for the Radcliffe Infirmary, the Observatory, and the University Press, but when North Oxford was designated a residential suburb, notice was tacitly given that any future institutions would have to conform to the residential character of the area. Still the suburb continued to draw those wishing to set up institutions in the environs of Oxford, not only because they found the land cheaper there than in the overcrowded centre, but also because they saw positive advantages in establishing themselves in the new suburb.

There were two types of institution which made their appearance on the estate. First, were the churches and schools which served the residents of the suburb. Second, were institutions whose trustees were attracted to the area as congenial to their purpose, although this might have only a coincidental relationship to the suburb. St John's need not have sanctioned anything other than the churches and schools which were essential for the success of any middle-class suburb, and it adopted a pragmatic approach by which it accepted whatever other institutions seemed in the long-term interests of the suburb and therefore of the College. Most of the institutions were either religious, educational, or both, and many of the second type had a strong residential element. All of them could be said to be in some measure experimental and reflected developments in the wider world of middle-class life outside the suburb. For this reason they are worth considering, but they were also significant in the development of North Oxford since whatever effect the suburb had on them, they most certainly affected the character of North Oxford.

The first institutional building to be erected and the one which did most to set the tone of the early developement was the Church of St Philip and St James, situated on its commanding site between Woodstock and Banbury Roads (Plate 84). For a suburb to succeed in the nineteenth century, it was necessary that there be at least one church in the immediate vicinity, as much for social reasons as for spiritual. Social status and forms of Anglicanism were subtly intertwined, and it was important to have the right sort of church service to attract the right sort of people. The old association of trade and

84   St Philip and St James, George Edmund Street, 1862.

commerce with the dissenting religions still held to a certain extent, but even within the Church of England various factions had arisen during the 1840s and 1850s which gave an opportunity for the different strata within the middle classes to form their own religious allegiances.

Religious controversy ran strongly through middle-class life and nothing that went on in the parishes of Oxford was probably any more disturbing than, for example, the long and bitter struggle waged by the Evangelical vicar of Islington in North London against ritualists in his parish.[1] And yet for several reasons the parishes of Oxford were particularly sensitive to the different shades of opinion within the Church of England. At mid-century most members of the Oxford colleges still took Holy Orders and the colleges continued to be among the foremost patrons of the Church. Besides supplying clergy for their own livings, however, the colleges of both Oxford and Cambridge at this time produced most of the priests and hierarchy of the established Church, so that any version of Anglicanism developed within the walls of the colleges found its way eventually out into the parishes of the country, often starting with those in the immediate neighbourhood. Religious controversy in the parishes of Oxford was to be expected, and in order to ensure the success of their suburb St John's had the task of steering a course through the differing religious preferences of the occupants of North Oxford.

Within the city walls, Oxford was well endowed with parish churches, but once beyond the confines of the town, church accommodation at mid-century was less abundant. St Giles's was the parish church for North Oxford and in the early 1830s it had been thought necessary to divide the parish into the districts of Summertown to the north and St Paul's to the west. Once sure that North Oxford would be developed as a residential suburb, the Bishop of Oxford asked St John's to set aside a site for a church, and on Seckham's Walton Manor plan of 1854, a church was given a place at the centre of the houses.[2] Almost as soon as Seckham's plan became public, St Giles's vestry put forward an alternative site as more desirable for the parish as a whole. It was noted in chapter 2 that the man behind the suggestion was F.J. Morrell, churchwarden, but also the new steward of St John's College, and someone interested in the way the College's estate in North Oxford would develop. It has already been suggested that Morrell's insistance that the church be built in a more central position on the estate helped to establish an overall concept of the suburb at a time when development could have gone ahead in small, discrete pockets such as had already begun with Park Town.

In September 1854 St Giles's vestry submitted a petition asking that St John's authorise a site in North Oxford for a new church to augment the capacity of the parish church and that the College make a donation towards the building.[3] Morrell seems to have been largely responsible for drawing up the petition which contained three specific points. The first was the patent need for a new church in the locality given the recent increase in the population and the proposed plans for developing the North Oxford estate. Morrell used the *Census Returns* for 1831 and 1851 to prove that building in the vicinity of the old parish church had greatly increased the number of people to be accommodated at St Giles's. Summertown in the north of the parish had also grown lately, and although a new church had been built in that district, full services were not yet being held there. The second point was related to the first, since most of the increase in population was among working-class people who could not afford to pay pew rent every Sunday. It was still traditional to collect pew rents at St Giles's, but during the 1850s a movement had grown up to abolish pew rents altogether, or at least to reduce the proportion of pews assigned a fee. Although some of the other churchwardens would not go so far, Morrell believed that pew rents should be abolished in order to remove an obstacle to regular working-class attendance at church. The third point was that the site indicated in Seckham's plan on the west side of Woodstock Road was not as central as the one between Woodstock and Banbury Roads suggested by the vestry. There was, it was claimed, an immediate need for a church which could accommodate from 800 to 1,000 people, and there was little sense in linking the new church to the eventual building of additional houses in Walton Manor.

Those signing the petition included Thomas Mallam, G.P. Hester, and John Parsons, the three men who had already built themselves houses in North Oxford, and among the others involved were Montagu Burrows, James Hughes, and Edwin Butler, all future residents of the College's estate. The College was cautious in their response. For some time they maintained that since provision had been made for a church in Seckham's plan no other site need be considered. They were, however, prepared to contribute to the erection of the church and its endowment. In the meantime the site of the church had become the main issue with the members of the vestry. In October 1855 the College offered to donate £500 towards the erection of the church along with the site in Seckham's plan or £1,000 without a site.[4] The vestry found this offer ungenerous and argued that the College should provide the site in Woodstock Road plus £1,000. Morrell tried some moral persuasion in his letter to the College's president in April 1856: 'Few can really tell the extent of the evils of our present deficiency of Church room. It may not occasion a very loud out cry, but it does create a great deal of dissatisfaction and alienation from Church and Constitutional Authority.'[5] The next offer that came from the College was for a donation of £1,000 towards the church building. They also agreed that two-thirds of the seating could be free, while the revenue from the rented one-third would go towards the endowment of the minister.[6] They still held out for Seckham's site.

It was not until 1858 that the College accepted the vestry's preferred site. By this time it was obvious that there was not going to be a great rush of people to build in the newly laid out Walton Manor estate, so that the site on Seckham's plan now really did seem isolated. The College added a condition to their agreement that the parish raise a 'sufficient' amount towards the completion of the church.[7] In 1856 Morrell had sought the help of the architect, G.E. Street, to draw up plans for a modest church of one aisle which later could be enlarged. The amount he had in mind at this time was between £1,800 and £2,000. By 1859 the plans had changed to provide a complete church with a capacity of 600 at an estimated building cost of £4,500.[8] The vicar of St Giles's, G.M. Bullock, immediately set to work raising a subscription with a circular to his parishioners.

The approach that the vicar took was a materialist one. In the circular the vicar sent out in April 1859 he exhorted the parishioners of St Giles's thus:

> I also appeal to you who have been laying out your money in the purchase or erection of houses, to assist heartily and liberally in this work, which, merely in a worldly point of view, will be of great benefit to yourselves, your property, and your tenants. I ask you to see that you cast not on others a burden which is properly your own, but that you take a just share

of the cost of building this House of God, which will be for your own convenience and benefit; and permit me to remind you that such share should bear some fair proportion to the amount of capital expended on your own houses, the existence of which has rendered the Church necessary.[9]

These words did not have as much effect as could be wished, especially with the houseowners of the newly built Park Town, which was the largest concentration of middle-class houses at this early stage in the development of North Oxford. Morrell wanted to try something stronger. In June 1860 he drew up a draft circular intended for the owners and tenants of the houses in Park Town. Over a short period of just six years sixty houses had been built at a capital expenditure estimated by Morrell to be approximately £50,000, but what, he asked, had the proprietors and occupiers of the property at Park Town subscribed towards the new church?

An examination of the present subscription list amounting to £2,900 it is found that Park Town has given and promised only £166 of which £74 has been given by six occupiers not being owners . . . Surely we have all freely received and have we so entirely to learn the precept 'freely give' that those who have laid out tens of thousands of pounds in a permanent investment for their own earthly benefit should offer to God for a Church in the immediate neighbourhood of this investment the scant measure of less than a tithe of a single year's interest of their capital? On the one side £50,000 on the other side £164![10]

The circular was subsequently amended before publication and Morrell's words were tempered.

It was Easter 1856, long before the College had approved the Woodstock Road site, that G.E. Street was asked for a preliminary plan. Street was the diocesan architect for Oxford, but his general approach also seemed to be in sympathy with that of Morrell. For example he was a member of the Council of the Free and Open Church Association, the group which sought to increase the number of free places in Anglican churches.[11] He was also a High Churchman and an ecclesiologist, interested in developing church design to accommodate an Anglo-Catholic ritual, and as will be seen those involved in the establishment of the new church in North Oxford were inclined towards an Anglo-Catholic position.

When St Giles's vestry asked in 1856 for a church with only one aisle, Street provided them with a design in what he described as an early pointed style.[12] Later in 1859 when they asked for a complete church he produced a design in which he adopted the later, early decorated style, and incorporated some features reminiscent of French gothic such as the very large, foliated capitals. Because Street was such an active member of the Oxford Architectural Society while he resided in Oxford, St Giles's vestry may have been surprised when on submitting Street's scheme to the society for comment, the society refused to give their approval.[13] There was, according to them, too much of a foreign element in the design. They found that on the exterior the spire was too short for the very large spire lights, and on the interior the pillars were disproportionately stubby. The arrangement of the clerestory they criticised because, as it was placed over exceptionally wide aisle arcades, it defied the rule of masses over masses and voids over voids. But what they really took exception to were the red sandstone bands set horizontally in the hammer-dressed walls of the exterior. A key to the strength of the society's criticism lay in the words 'This horizontalism partakes more of Lombardic than Gothic architecture'. Lombardic architecture was the *bête noir* of the president of the society, J.H. Parker, and he had been in contention with Street for almost a year over foreign elements in contemporary architecture. The conflict between Parker and Street came out into the open in January 1859 when Street challenged Parker's opinion that Scott's design for the new Foreign Office was too Italian.[14] There began a brief but heated exchange in *The Builder* and *The Building News* in which Parker argued that as English medieval architects had not been directly influenced by Italian gothic, so contemporary architects should avoid including in their buildings any Italian details.

Two weeks after the Architectural Society's criticism appeared in the local press, Street was given the opportunity to respond. He denied that his design was foreign, an accusation he felt was made because he refused to produce copies of known medieval examples which could then be commented upon by the archaeologists: 'As to the foreign character of my design, I must say I dispute the fact. I have always protested vigorously against the common practice of copying old buildings in the servile manner so much encouraged by many of those who have been active in the revival of medieval art.'[15] One by one he refuted the other criticisms of the society and concluded by taking exception to the claim that their remarks were offered in a 'most friendly manner'.

Although this incident was only an echo of a dispute in the wider architectural circles of the day, the preference for an 'English' gothic style may have had a local significance. Whereas the English style was acceptable to most protestants, the introduction of Continental elements, especially from Italy, could be construed as a dangerous inclination towards Roman Catholicism. This dimension to the controversy emerged through a letter of F.C. Hingeston to Morrell dated 11 November 1859. He wrote 'I regard the criticism in question as quite a party attack; and, it is calculated to injure the promoters of the church among whom (I understand) you hold a conspicuous place.'[16] Hingeston was a fellow of Exeter College which had just been accused in the press of straying from the Prayer Book into ritualism when they dedicated their new chapel in October 1859.[17] This was also the year when the anti-ritualist riots at St-George-in-the East in London were widely reported and causing upset throughout the Church.

Although Morrell must have favoured an Anglo-Catholic position, he acted as a moderating influence. When it came time to name the new church, Morrell thought that those names first suggested, St Martin-in-the-Fields and St Augustine, were too controversial since they were outside the protestant canon of accepted saints. In May 1860, only weeks before the dedication service, Morrell wrote to the vicar of St Giles's about his concern over the name:

> But the form of service requires the name of our new Building, and therefore especially I write. We all agree that to call it 'St Augustine' or any other than an Apostolic name is likely to add considerably to the suspicion with wh: we are already looked upon and that it will be most desirable to call the Church after some Apostle or Evangelist. The Stone will be laid Octave of St Philip and St James – There seems therefore to be more reason for calling the Ch: after them than any other . . .[18]

The dedication service took place in what was in effect open fields so that anyone could attend and indeed there were 1,500 guests at the ceremony. This may have been why the organisers thought that it was necessary to draft in ten special constables and to seek the assistance of six police constables, but they may also have wanted to avoid any disruption of the ceremony.[19]

The church was consecrated 8 May 1862, although it took another four years before the spire was completed. Not long before consecration Street offered to design a reredos for the the altar of the new church, and the motif he chose was a crucifixion. Once again Morrell stepped in to avert possible controversy, as he indicated in a letter to Street in February:

> I must confess my first impression confirmed by a nights interval is that we shall create such a storm that it is exceeding questionable if we shall be able to retain it if erected . . . The Bishop must see and approve before it is put up. If you could have given some other subject than the crucifixion it would of course be wholly different.[20]

The crucifix was at this time associated in the minds of many with the Roman Church, especially when it was placed on or near the communion table. The next day Morrell wrote that he had conferred with the vicar and Montagu Burrows and that 'we have not courage to admit the erection of what will amount in fact to a crucifix'. They suggested several other subjects and Street chose a Gethsemane.

Even after St Philip and St James was established there was controversy over the sort of services held at the church. The Rev William Acworth was moved by what he heard about the services to write a pamphlet entitled *The Acts of Uniformity Set at Nought in the Diocese of Oxford*. The occasion which led to Acworth's ire was the Good Friday service of 1866, and he registered his protest in a letter to the Archdeacon 28 April 1866: 'It is said, too, that the Service was not a mere fancy one, but an imitation of the Romanish service of "The Reproaches". It is certain that the Communion-table, by its shape, its drapery, and the metal cross with a crown of thorns hanging on it, bore a studied resemblance to a Romish altar.'[21] The old church of St Giles's continued with a plainer, more Evangelical liturgy, while St Philip and St James established itself as the Anglo-Catholic church in North Oxford.

Whether the sort of Anglicanism practised at St Philip and St James drew people to the suburb of North Oxford is difficult to determine. It was true that High Church practice prevailed in most of the suburban churches of Oxford. Besides St Philip and St James, St Paul's in Walton Street, for example, had been a centre for the followers of the Tractarians since 1844, and when St Barnabas was built in Jericho in 1868, it too was dedicated to High Church principles. It has been claimed that by 1860 the Evangelicals had reached the height of their influence, but their experience in North Oxford may have been a indication that their influence was beginning to wane.[22] In 1874 E.A. Knox, fellow of Merton College and staunch Evangelical, wrote to the president of St John's offering to build a church on some part of the College's North Oxford estate, in or near Norham Manor.[23] Knox was prepared to build the church on condition the patronage would rest in the hands of Evangelical trustees, thus ensuring a likeminded incumbent. The College was favourably disposed to the proposal, but there was a reservation about vesting the patronage of the church in private hands, and so began a ten-year struggle by Knox to establish his church.

In 1879, when the College was considering additional church accommodation in the now much expanded suburb of North Oxford, Knox again put forth his proposal. Once more his offer to build a church was accepted and a site 'at the bottom of Norham Manor' was reserved 'until further notice', but again the College baulked on the question of patronage.[24] The next time Knox and his Evangelical colleagues applied to build their church was in April 1881, and now they seemed to have the support of the College, but had to deal with the objections of E.C. Dermer, the incumbent of St Philip and St James, and the Bishop of Oxford.[25] The College had provisionally assigned some land on the east side of Banbury Road north of Park Town for Knox's church, but in the meantime in 1882 they authorised the building of St Margaret's Church at the corner of Kingston Road and Rackham Lane, later St Margaret's Road.[26] This was a chapel of ease within the district of St Philip and and St James, and was similarly High Church (Plate 85). It was designed by H.G.W. Drinkwater, the architect responsible for the design of the vicarage for St Philip and St James at 68 Woodstock Road and the parish school in Leckford Road. By the summer of 1883 Knox had still not been able to persuade the Bishop to agree to his proposal and the bursar of St John's wrote to say that the College was on the point of letting the land on the Banbury Road for house building.[27] In 1884 Knox left Oxford on being appointed rector of Kibworth Beauchamp in Leicestershire and the scheme for an Evangelical church in North Oxford fell into abeyance.

The Evangelicals may have been at a disadvantage because their chief support during the 1870s and 80s lay outside North Oxford, and what support they did have became diluted when the members of the colleges were increasingly able to move out to the suburb. As the vicar of St Philip and St James remarked in 1903, the population of his parish was 'unusually "churchy" in its tone, so many houses in the residential part being occupied by retired clergymen or the relatives of deceased clergy . . .'.[28] By the time the Evangelicals tried once more to build a church in North Oxford in 1899, they were better represented in the suburb than they had been. For one thing

85 St Margaret's, H.G.W. Drinkwater, 1883, porch by G.F. Bodley, 1898–9.

Wycliffe Hall, the Evangelical theological college, had become well established in the Banbury Road and its director, Rev F.G. Chavasse, and his colleagues offered £10,000 for a church in a new ecclesiastical district north of the one formed for St Margaret's in 1896.[29] This proposal was accompanied by a petition sent by Col F.A. LeMesurier of 31 St Margaret's Road and signed by many residents of the adjacent streets.

E.C. Dermer had now moved on to Wolvercote from St Philip and St James, but the Rev Mr Hartley, vicar of St Margaret's, was sensitive to any alteration to the boundaries of his recently established district, especially since his income was so poor. Whereas the permanent fixed income of St Philip and St James was £178 with a house, the income for St Margaret's was £90 without a house.[30] What Hartley feared was that the addition of the new district would make his own unviable. He believed that what was needed was the extension of his district as far as the Cherwell on the east, and any new district should come out of the one formed by Summertown. There was some logic in this suggestion, since when the supporters of Hartley and St Margaret's district produced a petition of their own, most of the signatories gave their addresses as those streets within St John's estate which would be affected by the change in the boundaries of the district.[31] Many of those signing Col LeMesurier's petition lived north of the College's estate in the streets between Rawlinson Road and Summertown.

In 1903 a diocesan commission was set up to inquire into the religious needs of the people of North Oxford. Some of the commissioners reiterated the doubts about the wisdom of assigning the patronage of a new church to private patronage.

> The principle of providing churches stringently and permanently attached to a particular school of doctrine and ceremonial seems to be opposed to

any true idea of a church open and common to all members of the Church of England, whatever may be their doctrinal stand-point. Such a principle, we conceive, is calculated to accentuate and perpetuate our unhappy divisions in a way much to be deprecated.[32]

These commissioners were concerned that a change in the population of the area could lead to 'an excess of Evangelicalism in the parish'. This was cold comfort for those Evangelicals who found an 'excess' of ritualism in North Oxford, and there was support even among some High Churchmen for a church which would serve the adherents of the so-called Low Church in the suburb.[33] The commissioners' report recommended a compromise by which the new church and district would be accepted and at the same time the district of St Margaret's would be extended as far as the Cherwell. In 1905 the Bishop of Oxford finally gave permission for the district of St Andrews to be formed and the College agreed to release a site on the corner of Linton and Northmoor Roads. Because the trustees of the new church intended initially to erect a temporary church of iron, the College made a condition that a permanent church would be started on the site before 1 October 1906.[34] The end result was a church in the Norman style designed by A.R.G. Fenning who continued his association with the Evangelicals when he designed the dining hall for Wycliffe Hall in 1913.

The churches built in North Oxford were institutions for the use of the inhabitants, but many of the other institutions which soon made their appearance in the suburb were there because they were marginal to the University and North Oxford provided a convenient space for their activities. As always the College's main concern was the long-term success of their suburb, so that every application to establish an institution in North Oxford had to be weighed up against its effect on the College's leaseholders and their tenants. If the trustees of a proposed institution were able to purchase the freehold of a piece of land on the estate, they could proceed to develop their site without any interference on the part of the College. This happened in only a very few instances, and usually the trustees had to make application to the bursar who then consulted with the leaseholders of the properties adjacent to the site before recommending the College to accept the proposal. Subsequent changes to the buildings also had to be sent for approval and in such cases the bursar could find himself acting as arbitrator between the leaseholders. It was essential for the College to maintain the residential character of the suburb especially in the early days of development, and all the institutions to establish themselves in North Oxford at this time had a strong residential character whatever else their purpose might be.

One of the first requests St John's received was for land to build a college intended for students of modest means who would otherwise be unable to afford an Oxford education. A constant theme in the discussions about University reform during the nineteenth century was the high expense of college life.[25] The radicals who wanted to see the power of the colleges diminished argued that the increased wealth of the colleges meant that even scholars and fellows of moderate means could enjoy a life not less opulent than that of the wealthy commoners, and as a result the cost of living in the colleges had become inflated beyond the reach of the ordinary middle class. The scale of indebtedness became cause for serious alarm as social pressure drove inexperienced undergraduates to outdo each other in expensive entertaining.[36] One suggested solution to the problem was to allow students to live outside the colleges, and even to enable them to take their degrees without belonging to a college. By living in lodgings, it was thought, the student would be better able to regulate his life by, for instance, drinking beer rather than wine. Such a solution was unacceptable for those members of the University who valued the religious influence the colleges could exert, expecially on those aspiring to enter the Church.[37] They proposed to build a new college which would be run in such a way that even poor students could afford to attend.

The idea for a new college had been discussed as early as 1845 by a group of Tractarians, including John Keble, E.B. Pusey, and Charles Marriott, and over the next twenty years this idea gained many influential friends. When St John's decided in October 1864 on a plan to develop the southernmost section of North Oxford, they quickly received enquiries about establishing a college there since the land provided a good site, situated as it was so close to the already existing colleges. When the first proposals were made to St John's in November 1864, the College reacted with their usual caution. They were not 'indisposed' to the proposal, but they wanted to know who the backers were.[38] In May 1865 an application from a Mr Abbott on behalf of a joint-stock company to take a lease for ninety-nine years on the land opposite the Parks was submitted, but St John's was still not satisfied with the standing of the backers, and they were understandably concerned about the extent and appearance of the new buildings. A letter from Dr Pusey in December 1865 received a more positive though still cautious response.[39] This letter was the result of a meeting in the hall of Oriel College held in November to consider the needs of poorer students who wished to study for the Church. In March 1866, John Keble, regarded by many as the father of the Tractarian movement, died, and those gathered for his funeral decided to make the proposed college his memorial. This put them in a stronger position since they were now able to establish a memorial fund to finance their scheme.

In April 1866 Dr Pusey formerly applied to the College to purchase the site opposite the Museum.[40] This the College was willing to do, but unlike a leasehold agreement a contract to sell meant that they would no longer have any control over what was built nor how the college was run. They therefore drew up conditions for the sale. Most of the conditions were of a practical nature and ensured that the surrounding houses on the College's estate would not be inconvenienced by the sewage from the new establishment. There was also a request that the side of the new buildings abutting what was to become Keble Road would be of an 'ornamental character' so that the College's tenants across the street would not be faced with a blank brick wall. The most important condition, however, was the first which included this covenant:

that if at any time hereafter the buildings to be erected thereon shall cease to be used as a College or Hall for the promotion of the object originally contemplated by the purchasers, they will reconvey to the vendors, if the vendors shall give them notice to do so, the site of the said College or Hall at the price which the same shall now be sold and the buildings thereon at a valuation, such valuation to be made on the principle of the worth of the buildings to be pulled down and sold.[41]

This covenant would presumably come into effect if the new college were to slip over the edge into the Church of Rome. Such a large institution with Tractarian leanings could be an asset to the new estate, but if it should come into the hands of the Roman Catholics, given the religious politics of the day, a cloud would descend over that part of the estate which the College had reserved for the most prestigious houses. The contract for sale was sealed 13 August 1867 and E.S. Talbot, the first warden of Keble College, remembered standing among the vegetable fields for the stone-laying ceremony in April 1868.[42]

For a serious undertaking the trustees chose a serious architect, William Butterfield. He was an associate of the founders of Keble through the Athanasian Creed Committee and his work was known to Sir John Taylor Coleridge, friend of Keble and of the proposed college, by his restoration of the church of Ottery St Mary, and he had done work for Keble at Hursley.[43] The layout of the residential buildings reflected the purpose of the college by providing rooms along a corridor rather than around individual staircases. Whereas the students of the other colleges could live an autonomous life if they wished, served by the college servants, life at Keble was to be more communal. The students' rooms were reserved for private study and no meals were to be served there. In this way it was hoped to cut the running expenses and to eliminate the elaborate entertaining which made life so dear in the other colleges. It was Walter Gray's task as first steward of Keble, to ensure the economical running of the college on which its early reputation depended.

Although Butterfield kept the quadrangle as the basic form he arranged his buildings to give a feeling of generous space on the limited 4 acre site. For the facades of his residential blocks he drew upon the domestic gothic he had developed previously in his parsonages, and Paul Thompson quotes Butterfield that he had decided 'to use in the buildings of Keble College materials such as the nineteenth century and modern Oxford provides'.[44] This decision may have been forced on him by the lack of money as Talbot suggested when he described the materials 'not the deep-red brick which (but for want of money) Mr Butterfield would have liked to employ – but the pale, dull brick of the modern builder's work'.[45] Most critics seemed as bemused by the effect as this one writing in *Building News*:

Red brick and white stone are the materials used, and their startlingly-contrasted colours are arranged in bands and zig-zag patterns covering the whole of the walls and destroying all breadth and repose. A 'holy zebra' of such collegiate dimensions is, however, so rare a phenomenon that we feel

86 Keble College
Chapel, William
Butterfield, 1876.

quite without sufficient precedent to enable us to speak positively as to the genus, and we await its completion with much curiosity, if but with comparatively little hope.[46]

Generally the Oxford colleges are characterised by their fine stonework, but Keble displays a virtuoso treatment of the humble suburban brick, identifying the college all the more with its North Oxford setting.

Butterfield's chapel dominates the college and can be seen right across the University Parks. It filled the gap on the north side of the site and before the engineering buildings were built on the other side of Keble Road, it made a striking presence in the southeast corner of North Oxford (Plate 86). The chapel is bolder than Street's St Philip and St James, and whereas the variety of colour and texture suggests movement, the extent of the brickwork with only small openings in the lower half of the building, gives a sense of substance. The scale and boldness of the gothic designs of both Keble College and the University Museum across the road marked them as monuments of the mid-nineteenth century, representing progressive science and religious renewal. Together they lent a contemporary, up-to-date character to the suburb of North Oxford.

Another institution which came to occupy a prominent site in North Oxford, the Convent of the Most Holy and Undivided Trinity, might seem a long way from the male world of Keble or the sceptical science of the new

University Science Museum, but of the convent's trustees one was Dr Acland, a promoter of the museum and another was Frederick Lygon, Earl Beauchamp, a strong supporter of Keble.[47] During the 1860s an Anglican convent for many people was not necessarily a welcome neighbour, an attitude to which the College was sensitive in their dealings with the sisters. The whole question of religious orders was a thorny one within the Anglican Church, and even High Churchmen could disapprove strongly of such societies, especially for women. The foremost exponent of religious communities within the Anglican communion was Dr Pusey, who gave encouragement to a number of women attempting to set up religious orders, including Marion Hughes in Oxford. In 1838 Miss Hughes had met Charles Seager, a protégé of Pusey, and he had introduced her to the Tractarians and their positive attitude to religious communities. She stayed with Seager and his wife in their house in St John Street when she made her religious vows in 1841,[48] but through family responsibilities in Gloucestershire she was prevented from establishing a community until 1849. Then she returned to Oxford and took a house in St John Street for her sisterhood. About fifteen years later in December 1864, at the same time the supporters of the new college were applying to build opposite the Parks, Miss Hughes made an application to St John's for land in North Oxford to erect a new convent.

The site that St John's saw themselves able to offer the sisterhood was one on the east side of Woodstock Road, immediately opposite the Horse and Jockey public house.[49] The College was prepared to lease the site for ninety-nine years, and as lessors they took a keen interest in what was built, requiring their approval of the plans before the final agreement was made. They were perhaps more concerned that the sisterhood might convert to Roman Catholicism than they were that Keble College would. Anglo-Catholics who adopted extremes of Roman practice had a reputation of defecting. In order to avoid an unpleasant situation, the College tried to insert a clause into the agreement which would prevent the sisters continuing on the site if they should convert to Rome: '. . . in the event of the sisterhood ceasing to be in communion with the church of England, as by law established, the lease of the land and buildings be at once forfeited to the College.'[50] Shortly after the form of words was modified to something more like the convenant made with Keble, but the anxiety was a serious one when selling houses depended on maintaining a suitable character in the neighbourhood.

The new convent was designed by Charles Buckeridge, a local architect trained by Scott and responsible for several houses on the North Oxford estate.[51] An elaborate design for a building which would have expressed in its tripartite form the Holy Trinity was given up for a more conventional scheme which is nonetheless impressive because of its size and the fact that amidst the red and yellow brick of North Oxford it is built in grey, hammer-dressed stone without the relief of the red stripes in Street's nearby St Philip and St James (Plate 87). What the inhabitants of North Oxford would have been aware of mostly was the high stone wall around the site, broken at the front only by the convent's entrance which was flush with the

87   Convent of the Most Holy and Undivided Trinity in 1929, Charles Buckeridge, 1866, chapel by J.L. Pearson, 1891–4, now St Antony's College (Local Studies Library, Oxford Central Library).

street and connected to the building through a short entrance passage. The result was to emphasise the enclosed character of the convent.

The sisters immediately installed in their new building the orphanage and the senior school for the daughters of professional families from their house in St John Street. In 1857 they had also established a school for the children of 'college servants and small tradesmen' which occupied premises at 10 St Giles's. In order to obtain the government grant after the 1870 Education Act, they were required to find a more suitable location for this school, and so they applied to the College for an additional piece of land to build a new school.[52] The problem for the College was to decide if a school of this sort was compatible with the surrounding area of their estate, and by their delaying tactics it would appear they had grave doubts.

The area of North Oxford where the sisters built their convent was sparsely occupied in 1870. There were ten houses on the south side of Bevington Road and three on the north, while further up Woodstock Road St Philip and St James was now completed. Almost directly to the east of the church was the earlier enclave of North Parade and building land had been taken on Banbury Road where another ten houses were going up. The rest of the property remained ripe for developers to take plots along the newly laid out Winchester and Canterbury Roads. Because the houses were not yet built the area was in a particularly volatile state, and any establishment, like a school, could affect the class of people willing to live in the area.

The sisters, because of their slim resources were not always consistent in what they requested. In 1870 they applied for a piece of land on the east side of the new Winchester Road to build a house for use as an infirmary. Then in 1872 they tried to exchange this land for a site on the west side of the road, directly north of their convent grounds for both the infirmary and the school.[53] The phrase the College used to describe the sisters' plans was 'inconsistent with the other designs of the College' and although another attempt in the spring of 1873 succeeded in getting approval for the infirmary, the College refused to accept the school, as it was 'inexpedient for the interest of the College to permit a Middle Class School'.[54] Instead they offered a site next to the new parochial school for St Philip and St James in Leckford Road.

From the tone of the letters from the bursar to Miss Hughes, it seems the College wished the sisters would drop their plans altogether. St John's was now receiving offers from builders to put up houses in the area. William Cross from London put in an application for the land on the east side of Winchester Road in April 1873 and Dorn and Galpin were after the land to the north of the convent site in November of that year.[55] The bursar was blunt about the reluctance of the College to allow the school to go ahead in his letter to Miss Hughes: 'We are advised that if the School proposed by you be placed near to the Woodstock Road the value of the land to the North of your present site would be greatly deteriorated.'[56] Nonetheless, perhaps aware that uncertainty was also detrimental to the College's interest, he offered the sisters the opportunity to build their school and infirmary on their present site with access from Winchester Road. The sisters would then be allowed to add about 66 feet to the northern end of their property as a buffer between the school and the surrounding houses. In August 1875 the plans for the school by J.L. Pearson, Buckeridge's successor, were approved, and at the same time tacit approval was given to the siting of the school which turned out to be in the northeast corner of the extended site, in fact in the buffer zone the College had intended be left free. By the time the oversight was recognised it was too late to rescind the approval.[57] In April 1876, while the school was building, the bursar received a complaint probably from John Dorn, the lessee of the property to the north of the school, which he passed on to Miss Hughes: 'I am very sorry to inform you that a serious complaint has been made to me by the Lessee of the land to the north of your boundary wall that the outbuildings connected with the School are so placed as to be a serious inconvenience to the future tenants of the houses adjoining . . .'[58] Since neither the school nor the houses were occupied, this complaint seems somewhat premature and perhaps revealed the nervousness of the developer in the face of a contracting market with houses next to what appeared to him an establishment detrimental to the tone of the neighbourhood. In June the partially built school was seriously damaged by fire, but it was nonetheless able to open in November of that year and subsequently flourished as St Denys's school.

Pusey was both one of the promoters of Keble College and a friend of Miss Hughes's convent. He was even more intimately connected with the work of Lydia Sellon who came to Oxford to consult him when she was in the process of setting up her own religious order in 1848. One of the

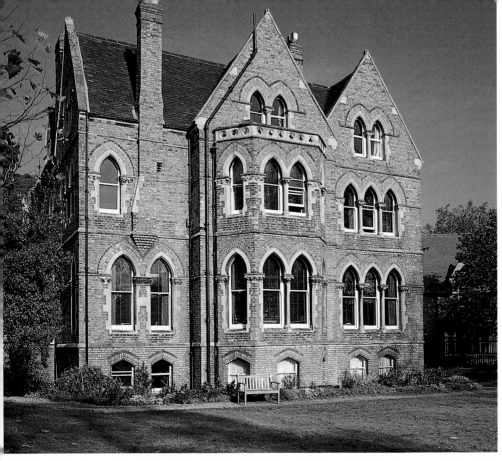

88 No 52 Banbury Road, Frederick Codd, 1870, from 1870 to 1883 the Convent of the Holy Rood.

activities of Miss Sellon's sisterhood was a printing school where young women could learn the printing trade as an alternative to domestic work. The young apprentices printed all Dr Pusey's work from 1855 and it was probably through his good offices that the printing press moved from the order's convent in Devonport to 52 Banbury Road, renamed Holy Rood Convent.[59] This house was a fine example of those elements characteristic of Frederick Codd's work, and held a prominent position at the entrance to Norham Gardens (Plate 88). Miss Sellon bought the leasehold at the beginning of November 1870 and very soon she asked the College through Dr Pusey if she could erect a wall around the property, perhaps similar to the one Miss Hughes was putting up around her convent.[60] This was another instance when the wishes of the institution came into conflict with the interests of the suburb as perceived by the College, and the bursar, conveying the fellows' rejection of the request to Dr Pusey, added these words:

I cannot say I am at all surprised at this, as the Leasehold in question is the key to one of the most important building properties belonging to the College; and although I can quite understand that the inhabitants of the house may be subjected to considerable inconvenience, this seems to be a necessary consequence of having an establishment of that kind located in what was intended, both by the College and by the original leaseholder, for an ordinary dwelling house.[61]

The house continued as a convent and printing establishment until the death of Pusey in September 1882. The order then sold the lease to the trustees of Wycliffe Hall in 1883, who added the house to No 54 which they already occupied.

Keble College and the convents reflected the growing influence of High Church sentiments in Oxford, but most of the fellows at St John's were probably more in sympathy with the strain of Anglicanism represented by the Evangelical trustees of Wycliffe Hall, the theological college, than they were with the Anglo-Catholicism of Dr Pusey and his sisterhoods. They were at least amenable to the new hall taking over the lease of 54 Banbury Road, one of the prestigious houses on the east side of the road. As noted in Chapter 5, No 54 had been designed by John Gibbs in 1866 for Thomas Arnold, the son of the famous headmaster of Rugby School. The house had fourteen bedrooms because it was Arnold's intention when he came to Oxford in 1865 to set himself up as a private tutor with some residential pupils. In 1876, however, Arnold decided he must return to the Roman Catholic Church to which he had belonged from 1856 to 1865, and the religious situation in Oxford was such that he had to seek work elsewhere after installing his family in a cheaper house in Church Walk.[62] A house with fourteen bedrooms was large, even in North Oxford, and by December Arnold was very anxious to conclude a sale, but luckily at this time the trustees of the new theological college were looking for just such a property.

Despite what appeared like a High Church hegemony, there was still a significant evangelical presence in Oxford, centred in the town Churches of St Aldate's, St Ebbe's and St Peter-le-Bailey.[63] Academics who subscribed to this branch of the Anglican Church saw a need in the 1870s for a theological college in the city which would offer candidates for ordination an Evangelical alternative to the High Church training given at Cuddesdon, the Oxford diocesan college. In November 1876 St John's received an enquiry from the trustees of the new college about whether they were prepared to allow 54 Banbury Road to be used as an educational institution.[64] The College had just been through their struggle with Miss Hughes over her school and in 1872 they had peremptorily refused an application by Codd on behalf of a potential lessee of 70 Woodstock Road for a licence to run a small school there. But by 1876 the area of North Oxford around Arnold's house was largely built-up so that it was not a question of establishing the character of the area, which was already acknowledged as one of the best in the suburb. Prince Leopold, the son of Queen Victoria, had occupied No 56, the house next door to Arnold's. A resident college for adult males was also a different propostion from a school for juvenile females, and the bursar answered the trustees that St John's did not object when leaseholders took pupils as residents into their houses, implying that they would probably not object in this case.

The only real doubt the bursar expressed was whether the neighbours would agree to the large additions the trustees were planning to make to the house. During his enquiries, the bursar found that the neighbours of No 54 were unhappy with the proposals as he reported to the trustees:

> It was thought right to consult the Lessees of the properties immediately contiguous and very strong objections have been made to which the College is bound to attend to the erection of any building of the size and height of that proposed and it would not be just to these Lessees to allow their comfort to be interferred with. The house itself is very high and a high building added thereto would be decidedly objectionable.[65]

The onus was on the house owner to obtain the permission of his neighbours, but in the end it often fell to the bursar of St John's to act as arbitrator and to suggest alternatives. The trustees of Wycliffe Hall wanted to add to the north side of No 54 and to replace a structure at the back of the house with a much bigger addition. The bursar tried to persuade the trustees to build to the south of the house since there was much more space on that side than on the north and an addition between Nos 54 and 52 would not interfere so much with the adjacent houses.[66] Finally in May 1877 the College and the trustees settled on a modest addition on the northeast corner of the house, which was greatly augmented in 1882 when Wilkinson and Moore designed the south wing of the hall in the same style as Gibbs's original house.

There is no doubt that the institutions which located in North Oxford were the result of social changes within the middle classes. The growing pluralism and tolerance within the Anglican Church was evident in the eventual establishment of churches of both High and Low ritual and colleges of Tractarian and Evangelical leanings. Keble College was a physical embodiment of the principle of university extension, whether it succeeded in its purpose or not. And however coersive they may have appeared to contemporaries, the women's religious orders gave their members the opportunity to administer people and property in a way denied most women.

Another sign that middle-class culture was changing appeared with the establishment in Oxford of the women's colleges, all of which except St Hilda's were located in North Oxford. The role of the suburb in fostering higher education for women will be dealt with more fully in the next chapter, but the relationship of the women's colleges with St John's as landowner is worth recording. The trustees of the first two women's halls, Lady Margaret and Somerville Halls, found property owned by St John's, but the difference was that the former remained lessees of the College while the latter were able to obtain the freehold of their site. The beginnings of Somerville may have seemed somewhat inauspicious to the trustees since they sub-let a house at the south end of Woodstock Road which had only five years left on its lease. Walton House had been built on St John's College property by Daniel Taunton in about 1829 and it was held on a twenty-year beneficial lease by him and later by his widow after his untimely death.[67] By October 1864 the house was in the hands of Charles Mostyn Owen, Chief

Constable of Oxfordshire, who renewed the lease for twenty years from that date. The property consisted of a substantial house and about 2 acres of land and by the 1860s it had occurred to the College that they would be advised to develop the site as building land when the lease fell in at the end of twenty years. For this reason they decided not to renew the lease at the usual seven-year intervals, but to allow it to run out in 1884.[68]

Capt Owen was unhappy with this arrangement, especially as the twenty years began to draw to a close. During 1879 he left Walton House, moved to Iffley, and tried to get the College to buy back the remainder of his lease. After a valuation, however, the College came to the conclusion that the price was too high, especially if by simply waiting for a further five years the property would revert to them anyway.[69] At this point Owen sublet the property to the trustees of Somerville Hall, and as the College was still thinking in terms of developing the property, they were not interested in negotiating a new lease with the trustees, nor were they willing to sell them the freehold which the trustees proposed buying in November 1879.[70]

The assumption lying behind the valuation of the property was that the site would be used for building, so when in April 1880 the Somerville trustees put in another offer of £7,000, although the fellows voted to negotiate with them, the bursar advised that the price was too low. There might have been a rumour that the College was trying to obstruct the establishment of the women's hall, but this the bursar assured the trustees was untrue:

> In my opinion which is of course derived from the data supplied by the professional advisers of the College it would be better for the College to hold the land over yet a while, with a view to eventually offering it as building land. The feeling of the Meeting, I may add, was in no sense adverse to the purchase of the freehold of Walton House by the Trustees, and it is simply in a commercial point of view, and as trustees of the College property, that they regard the proposal made by you today.[71]

The pressing financial situation of the College seems to have dictated that the fellows accept the money being offered them rather than wait for some hypothetical profit from future house building. In June the bursar wrote to accept the trustees offer, and on 23 April 1881 when the sale was complete Somerville had the security of owning the freehold of their premises.[72]

The trustees of Somerville soon set in train the building of an addition to Walton House, begun by T.G. Jackson in 1881, while not long after in 1886 Harry Wilkinson Moore designed a residence for them at the west end of the site. Jackson was the architectural man of the moment in Oxford, and he had just designed the High School for Girls at the south end of the suburb. The girls' school and the Acland Nursing Home were his only other buildings in North Oxford, but neither of these institutions were built on land owned by St John's. The red terracotta decoration of the school and its broad schoolhouse roof and belfry made it a landmark on its prominent site at the south end of Banbury Road. Basil Champneys in 1874 had set the style for women's colleges with his Queen Anne design for Newnham College,

154

Cambridge, and Jackson followed this trend, whether on his own initiative or at the request of the client.[73] Jackson's addition displayed the Dutch gable, the ball and cap, and window aprons of the style, but in deference to the stone of Walton House the new building was built in grey stone with red rubbed brick dressings which takes some of the lightness out of the Queen Anne style.[74] H. W. Moore's building was reminiscent of the houses he was designing in Banbury Road at this time, even to the little scrolls and garland motif.[75] As would become usual in women's colleges, the individual rooms of the students were arranged along a corridor, in this case pleasantly lit by windows on the north side. The single entrance into hall and staircase, and the drawing and dining rooms at the east end, gave the residence a domestic character thought particularly appropriate for a women's college while ensuring at the same time privacy and the opportunity for surveillance.

As freeholders the trustees of Somerville were at liberty to build as they chose, but the trustees of Lady Margaret Hall, although they had been able to take a house on a long lease, found that when they wanted to expand they had to contend with interference from St John's.

Miss Wordsworth, the principal of Lady Margaret Hall, went house hunting in May 1879, and after rejecting Cowley House on the other side of Magdalen Bridge, she turned to Norham Gardens where she and her trustees decided to take a ninety-nine year lease on No 21.[76] This was a large white brick house built by Pike and Messenger, and although it was obviously gothic in its external style, its white bricks set it off from the neighbouring houses. E.S. Talbot, warden of Keble College and chairman of the trustees, remembered it as 'the little ugly white villa' and Miss Wordsworth had some doubts about its design:

> The chief thing I remember about the house was thinking the passages were rather mean and narrow (as they certainly are). The fact that there was no possible access from the kitchen to the dining-room except up some mean little stairs in the greenhouse and through the drawing room, quite unfitted it for a gentleman's residence, and I hope was considered in the price.[77]

When staff and students moved in they were to find other drawbacks as Miss Wordsworth recalled: 'the draughts were fearful; the doors and windows all over the house were made of unseasoned wood . . . The way the chimneys smoked was awful.' The price for the lease was £3,000 and the annual ground rent £20.10s.0d., which might have seemed excessive except the location of the house at the east end of Norham Gardens with no other houses between it and the Cherwell was ideal for privacy and for future expansion.[78]

In less than a year the trustees of Lady Margaret Hall started building a small addition designed by Basil Champneys. Unfortunately as leaseholders they had neglected to inform St John's of what they intended doing, nor had they sent Champneys' plans for approval. Building had already begun when Omond, the then bursar, wrote at the end of July 1880 to Talbot to express surprise that the College had not received an application to build.[79] When the fellows did see the plans they were not satisfied on two counts. It seems that St John's were not completely confident that the women's hall would continue in occupation of the house in Norham Gardens. Whether they anticipated the hall's failure or simply its removal elsewhere, the College did not want any difficulty in leasing their property again, a situation they foresaw if there was no way of separating the addition from the house. They really wanted two independent houses joined by a temporary linking structure which could be readily removed, and they asked that the stairs and WCs Champneys had neatly fitted into the link be placed in the main body of the addition. To complicate the matter further the linking structure was not only to be temporary, it must look temporary as well.[80]

The other objection the fellows had was to the conjunction of styles, one beside the other. The gothic of Pike and Messenger's house sat uneasily next to Champneys' Queen Anne, but the real problem lay in the incongruity of the curious white bricks of No 21 and the red bricks of its addition. In their consent to the addition the fellows asked 'whether the two blocks cannot be brought more into harmony in external appearance'. Omond had a difficult task to reconcile Champneys' obvious commitment to his design and the requirements of his clients with the prejudices of the fellows. In November 1880 with the problem still unresolved he wrote to Champneys thus:

> . . . I wish you could suggest something to mitigate the harshness of the contrast: I should be very sorry to ask you to stucco over your Reading brick, or paint the existing house red! But can nothing be done to soften or break the intolerable glare of the difference? . . . Cannot you break the junction by introducing some other material between the two colours, or suggest some treatment of both houses which may in some degree reduce the discrepancy?[81]

Champneys suggested a half-timber treatment for the linking structure, and this proposal seemed to satisfy both the objections about function and appearance. Omond, himself at this time in the throes of designing his own house with his brother-in-law, J.J. Stevenson, made some additional suggestions for the treatment of the linking structure, but he only succeeded in annoying Champneys. Without Champneys' side of the correspondence it is difficult to know exactly who won this dispute, especially since today the linking structure contains a very convincing 1880s staircase together with the WCs (Plate 89).

Lady Margaret Hall did not gain the freehold reversion of No 21 and its addition until 1923, but when they next added to their buildings with a block by Reginald Blomfield in 1896, the trustees were at liberty to build without applying to the College since they had obtained the freehold of the site from St John's. Miss Wordsworth, however, found herself involved again with the College when she set up St Hugh's Hall as her own personal project. The hall was supposed to provide accommodation for women of modest means, and with her own money Miss Wordsworth rented two houses at 24 and 25 Norham Road. In 1888 she took the lease of 17 Norham Gardens and in March 1892 applied to the College for permission to build an addition to the

89   Lady Margaret Hall, brick and render link between the original Old Hall and Champneys'
1880 extension.

house.[82] Eventually the trustees of St Hugh's were able to buy Hester's old
house, the Mount, on Banbury Road where they opened their new buildings
in 1916. St Anne's, the other women's college in the area, evolved from
the Society of Oxford Home Students which supervised women students
boarding in private houses, many of them in North Oxford. The society
began buying the freeholds of houses at the lower end of Banbury and
Woodstock Roads in the early 1930s and built their first building designed by
Sir Giles Gilbert Scott in 1938.[83]

Annie Rogers, a pioneer of women's education, claimed that the success of
the women's colleges and the eventual achievement of degrees for women
in 1920 was partly due to the location of the colleges in the suburbs of
Oxford.[84] What Annie Rogers said of the women's colleges could be
extended to the other institutions which found space in North Oxford. All
of them expressed aspects of change in middle-class life during the second
half of the nineteenth century, from the growing pluralism and tolerance
within the Anglican Church to the principle of university extension. Except
for religious tolerance, the time had not come when these changes could
enter into the mainstream of university life, but they could nevertheless find
room in North Oxford. The suburb became a sort of Forest of Arden where
what could not find space at that time in the colleges was allowed to flourish.
The North Oxford dinner table vied with the Senior Common Room as a
place of discussion and debate, and the fact that so many people who
fostered the women's colleges lived in North Oxford showed how influential
the suburb could be both in conceiving an idea and in carrying it through. St
John's, by permitting the institutions to locate in the suburb, encouraged the
alternative activities in their suburb, but by their concern for the residential
quality of the estate, the College were instrumental in determining which
institutions became established in North Oxford and how they conducted
themselves.

CHAPTER VII
Social Life in North Oxford

THE BELIEF PERSISTS that the suburb of North Oxford was built for college dons, newly released from the celibate state to enjoy the pleasures of family life. As usual such rumours prove groundless when the facts are examined, and yet there is a spark of truth in the conventional wisdom. Since the colleges were the greatest source of wealth in the town, they had disproportionate influence given the relatively small number of those living within their walls. To assume that during the nineteenth century there were large numbers of dons permanently resident in Oxford, ready to buy suburban villas if only they were allowed to marry, is mistaken, but the enduring success of North Oxford did in part depend on the eventual release into the town of a greater share of the colleges' wealth through the salaries they paid their tutors.

Both Park Town and North Oxford were started a good twenty years before the University reforms which eventually resulted in the increase in the number of career tutors permanently resident in Oxford. The number of fellows supported by each college was determined by the college statutes, but the number of fellows resident in Oxford before reform amounted to only about half of these. In 1858, of the approximately 160 fellows resident, only 115 were college officers, that is tutors and administrators.[1] Those fellows without office were free to pursue their own interests either in or outside Oxford as long as their income remained below £500 per annum and they refrained from marriage. Many curates, schoolmasters, and aspiring lawyers, were subsidised in their early years by what were called 'prize fellowships'. There was no time limit on these, but either financial success or marriage would eventually cause most fellows to resign their fellowships, thus giving place to younger men.

Many of the colleges still required that their fellows take Holy Orders, and among their endowments most colleges had church livings which were in their patronage and reserved for their own nominees.[2] When a living fell vacant, usually through the death of the incumbent, the next fellow in line would be offered the living, and if he accepted, he would resign his fellowship and so begin his real career in the Church. Teaching in the colleges was often undertaken by the fellows awaiting a living, and the suggestion that they might remain in Oxford as tutors would have been greeted in most cases with incredulity, since tutoring, far from being

158

considered a desirable occupation was a duty undertaken only temporarily until a college living became available.[3] The sights of the college dons were fixed on parsonages in other parts of the country, and with no commitment to stay in Oxford, their ties were only those of sentiment.

Despite their reliance on the colleges for the main source of their wealth, the Oxford tradesmen suffered from the fact that they did not have access to the family resources of the fellows. More than affection held the Victorian middle-class family together, and when occasion arose the accumulated family capital would be put to work for the benefit of its members. It has been mentioned already that capital would be taken from the family business by a senior member in order to finance his retirement to the suburbs with his wife and unmarried daughters, but there were many other instances when the money held by the extended family would be called upon. The education of a child, the professional training of a son, the marriage portion of a daughter, a house for a newly married couple, the support of a widow, might all require the combined resources of the family. It was through this distribution of family wealth that the tradesmen of a town could prosper beyond anything they might hope to do when wealth was held in only a few hands. For this process to work there needed to be within a locality enough middle-class families with capital to share among their members. Manufacturing and commerce generated sufficient profit for this purpose, but there was little manufacturing in Oxford and not a great deal of commercial activity. And because most members of the colleges looked beyond Oxford for their real careers, when the fellows married they almost inevitably moved away, and the money their families gave them to help set up their homes, was spent elsewhere.

At mid-century there was a consensus among many tradesmen that the expansion of the size and range of business in the city was constrained by overdependence on the seasonal trade with the colleges, and that drawing wealth in from outside the town was the best hope for continuing prosperity. This could be done by bringing in industry, which would provide year-round work, and by encouraging wealthy people who had made their money elsewhere to settle in the city. The most significant attempt to establish manufacturing in the town during the nineteenth century was condemned by members of the University, and its failure can be attributed in part to their objections. In May 1865 the Town Council invited the Great Western Railway Company to set up their carriage works in Cripley Meadow, a 22 acre site owned by the city on the west side of the Railway station.[4] That the site was covered with water for most of the winter did not seem to occur to anyone until long after the proposal had been made and accepted. It was anticipated that between 1,000 and 1,500 skilled workmen would be employed in the new works, drawing an estimated collective wage of £4,000 per week, most of which would be spent in the town. *The Oxford Chronicle* welcomed the proposed works:

> Should the Town Council succeed in making terms with the Company, there can be no doubt that a great boon will be conferred upon the citizens

by the establishment of these large and important works in Oxford, especially during the Long Vacation, when trade is well-nigh suspended, and many of the tradesmen and small shopkeepers suffer no inconsiderable loss from the cessation of business.[5]

As the tradesmen congratulated themselves on drawing to Oxford a reliable source of business, the implications gradually dawned on the members of the University.

In May 1865 the *Chronicle* printed a letter from 'A Citizen' expressing the dismay of some in the academic community at the prospect of the coming of the carriage works:

> But I can imagine nothing less conducive to the permanent and solid prosperity of Oxford than an addition which would give it the character of a manufacturing town. As an ancient academic city it has peculiar and unrivalled attractions, which, if I mistake not, are beginning to be more widely felt, and will probably draw hither in increasing numbers visitors and residents of the wealthier class. But give the city a manufacturing character, and its special charm for people of the wealthier class is gone.[6]

In other towns where industry had come into the centre, the middle classes had soon made the move out to suburbs which quickly sprang up for their benefit. Most of the middle classes in Oxford lived either in the colleges or in their vicinity, and the ancient buildings of the colleges would prevent their removal beyond the smoke and congestion which seemed to accompany any industrial enterprise. Goldwin Smith, Regius Professor of Modern History, led the protest on behalf of the University. He had just moved into the first house on St John's Norham Manor estate, 7 Norham Gardens, and so was perhaps aware of the dangers to the nascent suburb as well as to the colleges (Plate 90). Norham Manor was a mile and a half from the site of the proposed works, but St John's had already decided to build the cottages in Kingston Road on the western side of the estate, which would have brought the railway workers in their numbers into the suburb itself.

The issue was brought to the attention of the nation when in June letters appeared in *The Times*, and that sentiment, which many former undergraduates and fellows felt for Oxford, was aroused. The correspondents argued that Oxford belonged to the nation and for that reason should be saved from becoming a manufacturing town. One of them wrote:

> But, after all, the great argument is that Oxford turned into a semi-manufacturing town will no longer be Oxford. Everywhere the spirit of business and the clouds of smoke in which it delights are penetrating. It is well that it should be so; but surely, if there is one place which may justly ask to be protected from it, that place is Oxford. Do the scholastic quiet, the half-medieval repose, the harmonious surroundings which lead to thoughts the busy 19th century world is too apt to lose sight of, count for nothing in the education she offers?[7]

The Times leader for 8 June agreed and called Oxford 'a national possession'

90 No 7 Norham Gardens, William Wilkinson, 1862, the first house erected in Norham Manor and the residence of Goldwin Smith, Professor of Modern History.

which needed to be preserved from industrial development for the good of the country.[8] A deputation from the University went to the directors of the Great Western Company, but the directors pressed on with their plans until October when a change of chairman led to dropping the scheme altogether.[9] Although some members of the University spoke in favour of the projected carriage works, no new industry came to Oxford for the rest of the century, and the whole affair left a sourness between the town and the University.

While blocking industrial development in Oxford, the University, through the exclusiveness of its society, also discouraged the wealthy from making their home there. Oxford was in competition with many other towns around the country for the patronage of those able to afford to live on the income from their investments or on a generous pension. Those returning from the colonies were especially interested in a healthy location, and all, conscious of the strictures of class, would look for a social milieu in which they felt most comfortable. Although it was generally agreed that Oxford had much to offer in the way of ancient buildings and cultural amenities, it had to be admitted that the high water-table made it unhealthy and the peculiar social structure generated by the split between the University and the town, made it difficult for outsiders to find themselves socially. Florence Mostyn Gamlen, whose father was Chief Constable for the County, recalled life in Oxford during the 1860s when her parents first came to the town: 'There was then scarcely any intercourse between the University and professional families. Credentials which were a good enough passport to the County were not valid in the University.'[10] She could recollect only one family in her youth who settled in Oxford because it was an agreeable place. From the *Census Enumerators' Returns* it is clear that there were other families who chose to spend some time in the city, and by the 1890s social intercourse between the dons and local professionals at least was easier. But as Thomas Arnold's daughter noted in 1890: 'As late as the 1870s it was reckoned to be impossible for outsiders to get a footing in university society, and it was only as an increasing number of academic families settled in the suburbs of North Oxford that attitudes began to change, but then only slowly.'[11] Far from being built to cater for an already existing middle-class society in the town, these remarks suggest that North Oxford may have helped to create that society.

Not only was social life difficult for outsiders, but contemporary manifestations of family life were discouraged, as exemplified by the 'crusade against the perambulator'. A by-law of 1812 forbade wheeled vehicles from the pavements of the city and required that they be kept to the gutters in the main streets.[12] In the 1860s when the perambulator became a popular way of airing babies and small children, nursemaids would be sent out with their charges on errands in the town or for walks in the Parks. It was considered, however, that the 1812 by-law applied to perambulators as well as hand carts and wheelbarrows. The whole affair came to a head in 1862 when town councillors were said to have stalked nursemaids through the streets and to have called a police constable to apprehend them if they dared push the pram along a pavement.[13] Several parents were fined, but even in Oxford this situation was deemed to be absurd and the 'crusade' was quietly dropped. The perambulator for the mid-Victorians seemed to have symbolised all that was wrong with suburban life,[14] and there were those who deplored the coming of the suburbs to Oxford as a diminuation of the glories of the old university city. Gerard Manley Hopkins referred to the new suburbs in *Duns Scotus' Oxford* as 'a base and brickish skirt'. The suburbs may have been associated in the minds of their critics with unwelcome university reform, which eventually was to benefit North Oxford by providing a larger middle-class market.

The demand for academic reform led to the organisational changes gradually introduced into the University during the 1870s and 1880s. Despite the claim by the colleges that the education they offered under the tutorial system was superior to that of the rival professorial system, the claim was being challenged more and more.[15] Because the ultimate destiny of most tutors was a church living outside Oxford they came and went with little reference to the teaching needs of the colleges. Specialisation was discouraged and just as the position of bursar at St John's rotated among the senior fellows each year, so did the positions of tutor in classics, law, theology, etc. This situation proved frustrating for serious-minded young dons who were asked to teach subjects for which they had little interest and even less expertise. Since tutoring was part of the fellows' duties, the stipend was small, compared by one fellow at St John's in 1869 'to that of an Usher in a third rate school'.[16] As can be expected, the results were less than brilliant, and it was generally accepted that if a student wished to do well in the examinations, he would need private tuition outside the colleges.

During the 1850s and 1860s a new generation of tutors, influenced by Dr Arnold at Rugby School, brought a more earnest attitude to their teaching. This coincided with the general fear that the amateur approach of British scholarship was no match for German and American professionalism. The result was that in the debate over University reform the voice of the tutors was heard when they asked for a lifelong career, studying and teaching the subjects of their choice, without the expectation that they would necessarily take up a college living. From these demands naturally followed the request that the rule of celibacy be adjusted so that career tutors could enjoy family life while retaining the decision-making powers in college affairs conferred on them by their fellowships.

Both the rule which enforced membership of the Anglican Church on members of the Universities and the rule of celibacy for fellows were seen to be part of the clerical domination of the universities, and agitation for their abolition tended to go together. The Universities Tests Act of 1871 removed subscription to the Anglican Church as a prerequisite for the taking of degrees or the holding of most university and college offices.[17] The act which dealt with celibacy, the Universities of Oxford and Cambridge Act of 1877, was intended to open the way for colleges to reform their statutes over the next five years, and as such was an enabling act and not a prescriptive one.[18] Nowhere did it state that fellows were to be allowed to marry, but the act simply gave to each college the power, at its own discretion, to change its statutes relating to the appointment of its fellows.

Even while believing married life was right for them, there were those who did not want to see celibacy abandoned altogether. Omond's letter to Bellamy in 1885, concerning the false position he felt he held as the College's bursar, debarred by his marriage from a fellowship, indicated that he believed that the College should keep the tradition of celibacy for their teaching fellows. At the time of the 1877 Act, he said, married fellowships were 'in the air' at St John's, but not demanded:

I do not think any of us contemplated a wholesale marrying and destruction of College life, of which Merton was then the great example. What we looked to was more after the pattern of Lincoln, two or perhaps three married fellowships out of 18 or 20. Had we known there were to be only seven resident fellowships, I doubt whether any of us would have sanctioned marrying.[19]

Every college took their own position on the issue. There was a powerful clique within St John's which held out against married fellows, but Merton College allowed four married fellowships as early as 1871, at the risk of appearing ridiculous in the eyes of the more conservative, as Mandell Creighton, one of their fellows, pointed out at the time: 'Merton always has been regarded as the most advanced and maddest College in Oxford; but the spectacle of all its Fellows rushing headlong into matrimony at once will make everyone in Oxford die with laughter.'[20] Whether their attitude was liberal or conservative, all the colleges had to face eventually the financial implications of the change, and how they would redistribute resources from communal consumption in the colleges to the individual members and their dependents in the town.

As has been shown the average fellowship at St John's in the 1870s was worth about £200 a year, and from the Report of the Commissioners appointed to inquire into the income of the universities this seems to have been comparable to payments made to the fellows in other colleges, although the specific amount depended on each college's endowment and the number of fellows stipulated in the college's statutes. Additional payments were made for tutorial duties, and it was up to the discretion of the college to make up the stipend of a tutor or lecturer who was not a fellow. Pressure on the colleges to provide the necessary undergraduate teaching within their walls led them to employ supplementary tutors and lecturers not fellows of the colleges. The scale of payment for tutors at St John's in 1880 was as follows:

Payment for tutors St John's College, 1880

	£
First tutor	550
Second tutor	500
Third tutor	350

The eight lecturers received an average of £135 in addition to their fellowships, and if they were not fellows, £100 was added to their lecturer's fee. By 1905 the old system of sharing out the College's profits had been replaced by a salary scale which included payment of the fellowships:

Payments★ for tutors St John's College, 1905[22]

	£	
Senior Classical tutor	720	
First Junior Classical tutor	600	
Second Junior Classical tutor	600	
History tutor	650	★Includes payment of fellowship

The average lecturer's salary was about £382. When it is remembered that these sums included the fellowship, it is clear that the fellows were not much better off than they had been twenty-five years before. One advantage they did enjoy over the 1880s was a college pension scheme, now generally considered necessary, especially if tutors were to marry and live outside the college.

The average middle-class income in 1869 was thought to range from £300 to £1,000 per year.[23] Inflation stayed low during the agricultural depression, so these figures are applicable up to the end of the nineteenth century. During this time college lecturers would have found themselves at the bottom of the range, while most tutors would be somewhere in the middle. Professors of whom there were an increasing number would have enjoyed the top of the range, as would have heads of the colleges. The president of St John's received £1,600 in 1887.[24] Middle-class houses in North Oxford, especially during the first twenty years of development varied in price from £1,000 to £3,000, and it is doubtful that anyone below the level of a professor could have afforded to buy one of these houses without some resources beyond their stipend. Professor Max Muller was delighted to be able to buy Goldwin Smith's house in Norham Gardens in 1867, and took pleasure in the fact that he had accomplished this through his own hard work.[25] For most tutors, however, some financial help from their families would be almost essential for the purchase of a North Oxford house.

Thomas Dallin, fellow of Queen's College and as has been noted, Wilkinson's client for 13 Norham Gardens, became tutor and lecturer at his college in 1866. The year before, his father, perpetual curate of Shooter's Hill, Plumstead, had died, leaving in the region of £3,000.[26] Dallin's house cost £3,150, and although he may already have been engaged to be married in 1869 when he began building, it seems that the house was also intended to be the home of his mother who came to live with him. He married in August 1870,[27] and despite having to relinquish his fellowship he continued at Queen's as tutor, later becoming Public Orator in 1877. The house was far grander than a tutor might be expected to afford, but in giving a home to his mother, Dallin would have had the use of the money left by his father.

There were a variety of ways families could provide money for houses. E.B. Poulton, fellow of Keble College and tutor in natural sciences, married in 1881 into the Palmer family, the successful Reading biscuit manufacturers, and his North Oxford house was part of the marriage settlement.[28] The Palmers were the trustees of the settlement, and they bought Wykeham House, 56 Banbury Road, the one John Gibbs had designed for Henry Hatch, the draper. In another instance, Charlotte Green, after T.H. Green's untimely death, mortgaged their newly built house at 27 Banbury Road to, among others, her brother, John Addington Symonds.[29] Many other family transactions would have been of a private and informal nature, but without this help most college members who hoped to move to a house in North Oxford would have found it impossible.

Some colleges built accommodation for their tutors in order to keep the most talented of them, even after their marriages. For example Scott built the first tutor's house for New College in 1875–7 and H.W. Moore designed one for University College which was erected in 1887. After the fellows of St John's refused to allow Sidney Ball to retain his fellowship on his marriage in December 1891, there was talk of building a tutor's house for him.[30] Ball's interpretation of the 1882 statutes had led him to believe that he could continue with his fellowship, but the other fellows were split on the issue, and in the end reaction prevailed. Although Ball was a radical, he was recognised as such an asset to the College that a house was promised. For Ball and his wife a large house in North Oxford was out of the question and their housing problem became acute when the older fellows blocked the building of the tutor's house. One of the elderly fellows was reported as saying that 'he wasn't going to have Mrs Ball trundling her perambulator in the quad'.[31] The house was finally built in Museum Road eight years later to designs by H.W. Moore, but in the interval the Balls lived in a 'dark and pokey' house in Alfred Street, now Pusey Street, off St Giles's.

So who was it that came to live in the suburb of North Oxford? Since Park Town was built with the expectation that it would fill a need, it is instructive to begin with this fragment of suburbia in 1861, the first year it appears in the *Census Enumerators' Returns*. The population in this year was only 317 in 48 households, while the total population of the parish of St Giles's was 5,025, but when St John's was taking the first steps towards developing their North Oxford property, Park Town was the only indication of who would want to live there. Of the forty-eight households, forty-four heads were in residence, and from the information on the heads it can be seen which occupations were represented.[32] Four groups emerge: those belonging to the professions; those living on private income; those involved in trade; and those in the military.

There were 20 heads who could be considered as professionals of one sort or another. Of these, 6 were Anglican clergymen. With such a close affiliation between the established Church and the members of the University it is not surprising that 3 of these were engaged in University work. One was the Taylorian teacher of Spanish, one the sub-librarian of the Bodleian, and the third, a private tutor. These 3 could be considered the first incursion of the University into North Oxford, and besides 2 other private tutors, they were the only evidence of it. The rest of the group of professionals included a Baptist minister, a solicitor, 2 doctors, a surveyor, an architect, an Indian civil servant and 3 schoolteachers.

That only 7 of the heads were engaged in trade is surprising, given the importance of the retail business to the economy of Oxford. The range of trades represented was rather narrow, including 2 drapers, a wine merchant, a grocer, an ironmonger, a cabinetmaker, and a print seller. They were, however, consistent with the sort of demand to be expected in unreformed Oxford where business depended to such a large extent on the colleges. The other surprise was that 6 heads had a military connection. Oxford does not spring to mind as a military town, although there were barracks and later a military college at Cowley. When it is realised that 4 out of the 6 were retired, then this group becomes more understandable as being allied to those living on income. The group of 9 living on private income were significant because these were just the people whom the developers were hoping to attract. At this stage most of them were from Oxford and the surrounding areas, and it is noteworthy that 6 out of the 9 were women.

In 1871 Park Town was complete and there were 55 heads of household in residence.[33] The same groups were represented, but some interesting changes had taken place. Within the professional group of 23, 8 could be easily identified with the University. There were 2 professors, a vice-principal, 2 tutors, an undergraduate, and 2 librarians.[34] The number of clergy was reduced by 1 to 6, and the other professions had shrunk to 5. During the ten years from 1861 to 1871 those engaged in University work had become a recognisable group. More people in trade had settled on the estate, and those living on private income had continued to come to Park Town, now from other parts of the country as well as from Oxford and its surroundings. There was still a preponderance of women in this last group.

Park Town, with its very limited numbers, could only indicate the categories of occupations which might be expected to be found in the new suburb of North Oxford. Proportionately the figures can be represented thus:

Park Town, occupations of heads of household as a % of total resident heads

	1861	1871
Professions	45.4	41.8
Private Income	20.5	27.2
Trade	15.9	21.8
Military	13.6	3.6
Other	4.5	5.4

By 1871 St John's North Oxford estate was making an appearance in the *Census Enumerators' Returns*, and an evaluation can be made about those who were taking houses in the new suburb. It becomes evident from a first glance at the returns that the College's intended segregation of the classes in the suburb is reflected in the Census, and the figures for the suburb have to be divided by location: first the central area where the villas were built; and second the Kingston Road area of artisan houses (including the western end of Leckford Road).

There were 97 heads of households resident in the central area of North Oxford in 1871, and their occupations were those of their close neighbours in Park Town.[35] The professions were represented by 44, of whom 10 were clergy, 15 were connected to the University, and 19 belonged to a variety of other professions, including 6 schoolteachers. Trade formed the next largest group with 30, and 20 heads depended on private means. Of this latter group 17 were women, and increasingly women of independent means were coming from outside the area to live in North Oxford.

By 1881 the first phase of the North Oxford development was complete, and some effects from the early attempts at University reform might be expected. Out of a total of 266 heads of households in the central area whose occupations are known, 101 were professionals, and of these 17 were clergy,

7 were schoolteachers, no fewer than 49 were engaged in University work, and 28 belonged to the other professions.[36] The next largest group was the one embracing those living on private income, and from the evidence of the previous years it is not surprising to find that of the 83 with private means, 77 were women. Trade provided a livelihood for 58 heads and there were 6 military men. The 18 heads engaged in 'other' occupations were mostly college servants or lodginghouse keepers. Put proportionately the two census years for this central area of North Oxford can be represented thus:

North Oxford central area, occupations of heads of households as a % of total heads resident

	1871	1881
Professions	45.3	37.9
Private Income	20.6	31.2
Trade	30.9	21.8
Military	1.0	2.2
Other	2.0	6.7

The 1881 *Census* indicated that the population of North Oxford was becoming more evenly distributed. While the proportion of those in the professions and trade dropped, the proportion of those living on income rose, and the 77 female heads living on their investments formed a considerable group on their own, easily outnumbering those engaged in trade and in the constituent professions. The women themselves would probably have made their own differentiation between those who had acquired their money from land or trade and those who considered themselves belonging to the Church, the University, or the other professions, still it cannot be denied that 29 per cent of all household heads were women of independent means.

As early as the 1861 *Census*, it was apparent that Park Town was a female domain. The number of female heads of household in 1861 was not especially high, 8 out of 44, but for every male in the population there were 2.5 females, and this ratio was still the same ten years later. It has already been suggested that a high ratio of females to males characterised middle-class areas in the nineteenth century.[37] While the ratio in the parishes of central Oxford in 1841 was 1.03, in St John's Beaumont Street development the ratio was 1.55, higher in Beaumont Street itself. The greater proportion of females to males in middle-class areas can easily be attributed to the number of female servants living in the households, but one of the effects of a general increase in wealth was the number of women who could afford to live independently, whether they were widows or spinsters. The ratio of females to males in North Oxford in 1871 was 1.9, and in 1881, it had risen to 2.9. A ratio of nearly 3 to 1 suggests that North Oxford, more than just another middle-class suburb, was at this time satisfying some unfilled need for a female presence in a town dominated by the male influence of the colleges.

One reason for the 75 per cent female population in the central area of

North Oxford in 1881 was that a third of the heads of household were women, and they tended to preside over predominantly female households. Indeed 20 per cent of all households were entirely female in composition. Two other groups contributed to the female character of the suburb. One was, of course, the servants, but there were also those who were not part of a nuclear family and yet were members of a household, that is relatives, visiting friends, and boarders.

There were 538 servants living in 246 households, giving an average of 2.1 per family. Overwhelmingly the servants were female, with only 15 male. They were also for the most part young, although those under 17 accounted for only 16 per cent. Along with the high ratio of females to males, a soldily middle-class suburb could be recognised by the age of its servants. Families of small means could afford only very young girls, while the better off could employ servants in their prime, between the ages of eighteen and thirty-five, and in North Oxford 70 per cent of servants fell into this age group. It is interesting to consider that 30 per cent of the population in this middle-class suburb was made up of young working-class women.

Those household members who belonged neither to the nuclear family nor to the servant class numbered 304 in the central area of North Oxford in 1881, and together with the servants formed nearly 50 per cent of the total population. Of this group 81 per cent were female, 108 relations or visitors and 138 boarders. The female boarders were mostly schoolgirls, resident at the convent, at one of the small private schools, or boarding in private houses while they attended the newly established Girls' High School. This meant that most of the boarders were young as well as being female.

The households in this solidly middle-class area of North Oxford revealed different characteristics according to whether they were headed by a male or a female, and there was a difference too between families dependent on the University and those supported by trade or the other professions. The different structure of these households affected the composition of the suburb as a whole. The figure of 60 per cent seems low for the proportion of households where children were resident until it is discovered that while 70 per cent of households headed by men had children living at home, they were present in only 42 per cent of households headed by women. One reason for this was that 40 per cent of female heads were unmarried and so childless, but the other 60 per cent were widows, and the maturity of their families meant that it was more likely that their children had grown up and left home. The maturity of the female-headed families also meant that well over half the daughters in these households were 18 years and older, compared to 19 per cent of the daughters in the University families and over a quarter in other families.

If maturity marked the families headed by women, University families tended to be relatively young with nearly two-thirds of the heads between the ages of twenty-six and forty-five. Most of the other male heads of household tended to fall within the age range of thirty-six to sixty-five. The age of the families may account for a discrepancy between the two groups with regard to daughters living at home. In the University families there was no difference between the number of daughters and sons at home, but in the other group 61 per cent of children in residence were daughters. Before children reached an age when the sexes were educated separately, they lived together at home, so that a population of young families might be expected to be more equally divided than one where the sons had left for education and a career, while the daughters remained at home, or even if they had been away to school, returned to await marriage. Another difference between these two groups was that the University families had a higher than average number of servants, another consequence, perhaps, of young families, who generated work and required nursery staff along with the usual cook and housemaid.

Noticeable differences in the structure of households in North Oxford had probably more to do with the marital status of the heads and the maturity of the families than with any marked social differences, but subtle divisions in the population were reflected in the geographic location of its inhabitants. Whereas those involved in trade and the other professions lived in houses right across the suburb, those working in the University clustered in the Norham Manor area and around the Church of St Philip and St James, along the eastern side of Woodstock Road and in Canterbury Road. Wealthy tradesmen such as James Hughes, the grocer, and Thomas Cousins, the chemist, had large houses on the east side of Banbury Road, and the banker, John Parsons, lived in Norham Gardens, but most families in trade were to be found to the west of Banbury Road, and especially on the other side of Woodstock Road in the area around Leckford and Warnborough Roads. Households headed by women also had their preferred areas in North Oxford. The houses women chose were for the most part in Norham Manor and between Banbury and Woodstock Roads, and they were more likely to live in the smaller houses in streets like Museum, Norham, Bevington, and Winchester Roads. These houses were in those areas of the suburb favoured by University families, and the perceived shortage of suitable houses experienced by young tutors may have been because they were in competition with female heads who would also have been looking for the smaller, less expensive houses.[38]

As has been suggested above, there was very little overlap between the central section of North Oxford where the villas were being built, and Kingston Road, where the College had ensured the building of cottages and small houses suited to artisans, clerks, and small shopkeepers. It is not often that such clearly defined areas of different classes are found side by side, and it is instructive to compare the characteristics of both. In 1881 the people resident in Kingston Road and the western end of Leckford Road were not poor. Nearly all the 167 heads of household were employed as were most children over fourteen years, but their occupations varied from those of their neighbours to the east. By far the greatest number of heads of household, 68 of them, were employed as artisans, making things or running machinery. Many worked for the University Press as compositors or for the Great Western Railway as drivers. Lucy's Iron Foundry provided work for some but most of the others were either in the building trades or tailoring. Shop-

Kingston Road area, occupations of heads of household as a % of the total resident heads, 1881

Artisan	40.7
Trade	18.5
Service	16.1
Clerical	10.7
Income	9.5
Other	4.1

keepers and traders were the next largest group with 31, selling food, clothes, and coal, some in the town market and others in Walton Street. This connected Kingston Road with the rest of Oxford and was the shopping street for working-class Jericho. About the same number, 27, were involved in service of some sort, from college cooks and laundresses to lodginghouse keepers and gardeners. Clerical work accounted for 18 and those living on income, mostly widows, 16. The remaining 7 were involved in a variety of occupations such as the police or farming.

When the *Census Returns* for this area are examined, the main difference between here and the central area was that the sexes were much more evenly balanced. The ratio of females to males was 1.1 which was closer to that prevalent in the parish generally. Of the heads of household 80 per cent were male, and 94.6 per cent of these were married. The proportion of households with children living at home was 76.4 per cent, slightly higher than the one for male-headed households in the central area. Both boys and girls were working at fourteen years, and only 13 per cent were over eighteen years and still resident at home, with little difference between daughters and sons.

There was nothing in the composition of the nuclear families to increase the ratio of females over males, nor did the other members of the households contribute to this. While there were more female relatives and visitors than male in the households, there were more male than female boarders and lodgers, so that these two groups cancelled each other out. Only 36 households had servants of which there were 36, 1 per household. Such a small number of servants, 4.3 per cent of the population, was not going to effect the overall number of females. As might be expected over half these servants were under the age of eighteen.

The families in the Kingston Road area were more often from Oxford and its environs than those of the families living in the central part of the suburb. Of the heads of household in the Kingston Road area 57 per cent were born in Oxford or the county of Oxfordshire, while of those in the central area 28 per cent had been born in the locality. Like today the middle classes in the nineteenth century were notoriously mobile, and at first glance the difference between the two parts of the estate seems simply to reflect the difference between the artisans and shopkeepers in the Kingston Road area and the middle class living in the North Oxford villas. However, those various groups already identified in the centre had diverse origins. It is no surprise that of the heads of families engaged in University work only 6.25 per cent came from Oxford. Since the University drew students in from every part of the country and it was mostly graduates of the University who came to teach there, this section of the population could be expected to come from elsewhere in the country. Perhaps more unexpected was that of the female heads, only 22.4 per cent came from the city or the surrounding areas. Among the rest of the inhabitants of the central area, 40 per cent of the heads of household came from Oxford, and of those from outside, many had become well established in the city through years of residence. These different groups suggest that the new suburb of North Oxford had various functions. First, it fulfilled the need of the local tradesmen and professionals to move out of the centre of the city to a middle-class suburb. Second, it seems to have succeeded in attracting people with private means, particularly women, from the town, but also from further afield. And third, parts of the suburb became home for families formed by those brought from all parts of the country to Oxford through their work in the University.

Among the middle-class groups in North Oxford, it is the voice of the University families that is heard. In reminiscences of academic life the snippets of information about domestic matters reveal how they found their houses and how they lived in them. Other professionals and tradesmen were dumb, as were the widows and spinsters, and what the suburb meant to them can only be pieced together through various fragments. There is, however, a value in the academic memoirs because they bear witness to the formation of a new group within the middle class, the salaried professionals.[39] These people were more like the clergy who had previously done their work than they were like businessmen who made profits or other professionals who collected fees. And like the clergy, although they might have status, they usually had only a moderate income. From their situation developed a way of living which made virtue out of necessity, and was characterised by a strong anti-materialism. These were the people for whom plain food and long-lasting tweeds enabled them to afford what they really valued, books, travel in the vacations, and a full complement of servants.

By 1881, as the *Census* reveals, the University families were by no means dominant, but their influence was beginning to be felt. In its obituary of F.J. Morrell in 1883, *The Oxford Chronicle* acknowleged his achievement in initiating the suburb of North Oxford in these words: 'There are now several hundred gentlemen's houses erected upon the ground, inhabited by senior members of the University, chiefly Professors and Tutors, all of whom have votes for the University and City, and they are a great bond of union between the two bodies.'[40] In the early years of the suburb, the transition from the life within the colleges to that outside as a married tutor could cause some painful personal adjustment, which sometimes was not worth the struggle. Once Mandell Creighton had been elected to a married fellowship at Merton in December 1871, his problems were far from over.[41] He and his wife were able to find a newly built house on the west side of Banbury Road, and although North Oxford was so close to the centre of the town and the college, it was almost impossible to combine the life of the two. The suburb depended on a separation of work and home, but the college was a rival home, and Creighton found himself toing and froing throughout the day starting with morning chapel at the college first thing, followed by breakfast with the other fellows. After two years he gave up the house in Banbury Road and moved to one opposite Merton, but even so the uncertainty of his position as a married fellow and the drudgery of the teaching load without any chance to do any study of his own led him to accept the college living of Embleton in Northumberland. Creighton returned to academic life by accepting the Dixie professorship of ecclesiastical history at Cambridge in 1884 and went on to conclude his career as Bishop of Peterborough and subsequently of London.

Once the married tutor became more common, a way of life began to evolve which reconciled the demands of the college and those of family life. The wives recalled the simplicity of their young domestic lives, circumscribed as they were by the modest incomes of the tutors. Louise Creighton remembered those early days as a wife in North Oxford thus:

> If the college dinners were sometimes luxurious, the dinners given by the young married people were very simple. We were all comparatively poor, we were acquainted with one another's pecuniary position, and there was no desire for pretence, to do everything as prettily and simply as possible, and at the moderate cost, was our common ambition.[42]

Mrs Humphry Ward the novelist and wife of a tutor at Brasenose College had a similar recollection:

> Professors possessed as much as a thousand a year. The average income of the new race of married tutors was not much more than half that sum. Yet we all gave dinner-parties and furnished our houses with Morris papers, old chests and cabinets, and blue pots. The dinner parties were simple and short. At our own early efforts of the kind, there certainly was not enough to eat. But we all improved with time; and on the whole I think we were very fair housekeepers and competent mothers.[43]

This was all done of course with four servants: a cook, a parlourmaid, a nurse, and a housemaid.

North Oxford, as revealed by the *Census*, had a predominantly female population. The female character of the suburb was acknowledged by the inhabitants of the colleges, even feared, as it was by Charles Oman when he returned to Oxford to take up a fellowship at All Souls:

> 'North Oxford' had already come into existence, and for those who liked them there was plenty of opportunity for mixing with its ladies young and old. Such joys were not for me! I had a perfect horror of dances, collegiate or private, and always refused invitions to them. To say the truth, the sight of girls *en masse*, in their best frocks, conversational, restless, sometimes a little skittish, and always self-centred was a terror to me. Dances were, no doubt, the worst possibility, but I avoided with equal care mixed lawn-tennis and boating parties: croquet was still in vogue, and picnics not unknown.[44]

Oman would have seen the North Oxford women only at play, and he may not have realised how self-improving they could be. As Mary Ward commented, 'Most of us were very anxious to be up-to-date, and in the fashion, whether in aesthetics, in house-keeping, or education.'[45] The energy they put into the latter cause helped to establish women's higher education at Oxford. Women's colleges would have had to come to Oxford sometime, but that they came when they did may have had not a little to do with the appearance of North Oxford and the support they were to get from the women living there.

After a series of lectures by Ruskin in 1873, a group of women led by Louise Creighton organised a series of their own for the women of Oxford. In 1866 Miss Eleanor Smith, the sister of the Savilian Professor of Geometry, had attempted to set up lectures for women, but these had not proved popular. The new ingredient in 1873 was North Oxford, where there were enough interested women to make this new venture succeed. Mrs Creighton had the assistance of Georgina Max Muller, Mary Ward, Charlotte Green, Clara Pater, Lavinia Talbot, and Bertha Johnson.[46] All these women were the wives or sisters of University professors and tutors living in the suburb. Bertha Johnson recalled how they would send out the advertising circulars from the Creightons' house in Banbury Road where she was impressed by 'the care and interruptions of the one-year old baby being shared, turn about, by the mother, and her friends, and the father in his study'.[47] The first lectures were given by the Rev A.H. Johnson in the old Clarendon Building and an examination was set at the end of the course.

Although the women were enthusiastic for the lecture series, the establishment of women's education in Oxford required a more formal organisation. Annie Rogers acknowledged the North Oxford women's strength and their weakness: 'Some of them were full of energy and of interest in women's education and other public matters, and their husbands were generally in sympathy with them ... They had, however, little knowledge of the University, or of educational movements in the country, and could not have effected much by themselves.'[48] At Cambridge, the women's colleges of Newnham and Girton were being established, and outside interest in setting up a similar institution in Oxford stimulated those involved in the women's lecture programme to forestall any action which would prejudice the University against women's education by establishing their own hall of study.

The women's colleges began not as places of instruction, but only as halls of residence. Although women could not receive Oxford degrees until 1920, in 1875 the University set separate examinations for women in what were considered suitable subjects, but since women found it difficult to obtain the instruction necessary to pass the examinations, the gesture was somewhat empty. On 4 June 1878 a meeting of both men and women interested in women's education was held at Keble College, to consider the possibility of establishing a hall of residence which under the auspices of the Church of England would allow women to come to Oxford to study and attend chaperoned lectures.[49] At a second meeting at Jesus three weeks later the

174

same group decided to establish the Association for the Education of Women which would sponsor classes and arrange for women to attend lectures in the University and colleges. The proposed hall would in the first instance only provide a suitable place for the women to live while they worked for their examinations. It was decided to call the new hall after Lady Margaret Beaufort, the mother of Henry VII, and a principal was found in Elizabeth Wordsworth, the daughter of the Bishop of Lincoln.

Lady Margaret Hall was intended to provide a 'Christian family' under the auspices of the Church of England, in which the women could live while they studied and attended lectures. This arrangement satisfied Talbot, the warden of Keble, who with his wife Lavinia, had organised the initial meeting. Among the North Oxford supporters of women's education was a more secularly minded group, including the T.H. Greens and the Humphrey Wards, who found themselves out of sympathy with a hall of such a strong Anglican affiliation. At a meeting on 7 February 1879, this group decided to set up a non-denominational hall, not in rivalry to Lady Margaret Hall, but complementary to it.[50] The name chosen for this hall was Somerville, after Mary Somerville the distinguished mathematician.[51] The 'English family' was to be the model for Somerville, shorn of any specific religious significance, but upholding those virtues associated with the middle-class family of the period.

As has been shown, both these institutions along with the later colleges of St Hugh's and St Anne's, found that the villas of North Oxford suited their purpose very well. But the early emphasis on the 'family' reveals that the suburb supplied more than just the necessary houses, and indeed those notions attached to the suburb of retreat and the female domain made it easier for both the women's colleges and the University to co-exist without having to deal with serious questions like what the women were to do after they were educated. Annie Rogers believed that the suburban setting of the women's colleges allowed them to develop without interference from the University:

> The colleges were fortunate in the sites they secured. They were all within a mile and a half of Carfax, which was, at that time, the limit for keeping residence . . . [They] were not too far from the University quarter for their own convenience nor so near it as to occupy land which the University or the men's colleges might want for themsleves. They were within easy reach if you wished to visit them or to keep an observant eye upon them, and yet they did not thrust themselves upon you. No one could possibly suppose that such modest establishments could rival the men's colleges.[52]

For some time the administration of women's education in Oxford was in the hands of inhabitants of North Oxford, both men and women. Bertha Johnson was secretary of the Association for the Education of Women from 1883 to 1894 and secretary of Lady Margaret Hall from 1880 to 1914. Charlotte Toynbee, the widow of Arnold Toynbee, was treasurer of Lady Margaret Hall from 1883 to 1920. A Delegacy for Women was set up by the University in 1910, and after women could receive the BA in 1920, the

91   No 19 Norham Gardens, Frederick Codd, 1876, left by Miss Jephson to Elizabeth Wordsworth, principal of Lady Margaret Hall, for use by the Hall.

association was no longer needed. There must have been many women in North Oxford who did not approve of higher education for women, and there were certainly a majority for whom it could have no significance, but because the suburb was predominantly female, there was a freedom there for women to initiate first their own lecture series, and then with the help of husbands and friends the women's colleges. The other side of this was that the women's colleges were circumscribed at first by the suburban ethos from which they eventually had to struggle free (Plate 91).

Whatever else they thought about the women's colleges, the townspeople viewed them along with the rest of the University as a source of business. A commentor in *Jackson's Oxford Journal* in 1886 hoped that the presence of the women would enliven the trade in female attire even if it meant supplying the 'aesthetic' fashion:

> Tradesmen also who do their best to gratify the caprices of the fair sex will have reason to grumble if they are not well patronised by Somerville Hall. The aesthetic greens, and drabs, and blues, if they can never gratify our sense of beauty either in colour or shape, may nevertheless help to replenish the empty exchequer, and keep Oxford trade on its feet.[53]

North Oxford provided the town with new markets in clothing for women and children, in furniture, draperies, and china. The profits from this trade made it possible for more people to live in the suburb, but also enabled more to buy property as an investment, and this was particularly so in the streets in the west and the north, such as Southmoor, Polstead, Chalfont, and Frenchay Roads.

The people living in these streets had their own concerns which, while not the same as those in Norham Manor, reflected their desire for the establishment of a proper suburban order. In 1884 a group of residents applied to St John's to build a Wesleyan chapel in Upper Walton Street. The interested residents included Alfred Boffin, the confectioner, who lived in Winchester Road, John Dorn, the builder, from the Parks Road, James Nix, who worked in the Post Office and lived in Warnborough Road, and the schoolmaster, Joseph Richardson of Blackhall Road.[54] These men were forwarding the interests of the non-conformists of North Oxford just as Morrell and his friends had worked to establish St Philip and St James thirty years before.

Sometimes the battles to establish or maintain the suburban quality of the less exalted areas of North Oxford were far more difficult than those faced by the villa residents. For example, John Peattie of 16 Kingston Road discovered in 1886 that the College had authorised a slaughter-house behind the butcher's shop at No 14. In protest he wrote to the College:

> My position is this: On the recommendation of my doctor and in consequence of my wife's delicate health, I purchased this property – If a Slaughter house is established it will be absolutely necessary for me to leave the house as my wife's health is such that she could not possibly live near such a place . . . This would not only affect one in the shape of inconvenience in being obliged to remove but it means that the value of this property will be decreased by the proximity of a Slaughter house and I should not be able to let the house at anything like its present value.[55]

Problems could arise when a better class of house was built in proximity to already existing houses, as happened when the west side of Chalfont Road was built during the 1890s so that its gardens backed onto those of Hayfield Road. The Chalfont Road tenants soon discovered that their neighbours kept pigs as W.T. Walker of No 37 reported to the College in 1896. And as he pointed out: 'It is not only the keeping of pigs that is a nuisance, but also the killing, two were killed last year, close to my garden, a pleasant sort of thing to have close to you!'[56] These sorts of conflicts were a long way from the difficulties experienced by the Creightons, trying to juggle college and suburban life in the early days of the married don.

The houses of North Oxford, particularly in the working-class streets on the west side of the suburb, could provide their inhabitants with a source of income if they chose to let out rooms to lodgers or boarders. St John's did not have any objection in principle to the tenants of North Oxford letting rooms, since this did not contravene the covenant that the houses be reserved for residential purposes. The social implications of allowing tenants to let off house room were, however, unpredictable, since in other suburbs the presence of lodgers was the prelude to multiple occupancy and the resulting downward spiral of property values. North Oxford had an advantage over other suburbs in that the proximity of the colleges and other educational institutions meant that a large number of those seeking lodgings were middle class, and if they were undergraduates, not only their lodgings but their behaviour was monitored by the University.

In 1868 the regulations were altered so that undergraduates were allowed to live outside their colleges in order to relieve the overcrowding that came in the wake of an increase in numbers after the reforms of the 1850s. At the same time, in a move to make the University more accessible to those of modest means, undergraduates were allowed to come to Oxford and study unattached to a college, since it was thought that the expense of college life deterred many from attending University. Both these groups needed accommodation in the town and the University set up a Lodging House Delegacy to oversee and regulate their lodgings.[57] Householders who wanted to provide rooms had to apply to the Delegacy who then sent inspectors to evaluate the standard of hygiene in the house and whether the circumstances of the household were acceptable. Kingston Road and later Southmoor Road, on the west side of North Oxford, came to supply many of the University's lodgings up to World War I.[58]

The Lodging House Delegacy required that each undergraduate have both a bedroom and a study-sitting room, called together a set. Two students could share a study as long as they had separate bedrooms. For families in modest sized houses, providing two rooms for each student could bring sacrifices. One family in Southmoor Road put their two eldest boys, aged sixteen and eleven, in a boxroom 6'10" × 5'8", and only 6'11" in height. In another family seven daughters, the eldest nineteen, slept in an attic with three beds.[59] There were many examples of families sending at least one child to sleep in a neighbouring house during term time, but what made these disruptions possible was that they occurred for only twenty or so weeks in the year while the undergraduates were up at University during the terms.

The houses in North Oxford registered with the Lodging House Delegacy were confined mostly to the streets on the western periphery of the suburb, with a very few houses also in Leckford, Warnborough, and Museum Roads. It was not until women began to attend the University in significant numbers that houses in the central area of North Oxford became available for undergraduate lodgings. In 1910, when the University Delegacy for

92 No 3
Norham
Gardens,
Charles
Buckeridge,
1868, with large
extension on the
west side.

Women was established, they set up their own system of inspection and approval of lodgings, which carried on until 1921 when it was amalgamated with the Lodging House Delegacy.[60] Even then, the lodgings suitable for women and men were kept carefully separated, with the houses in North Oxford almost exclusively catering for women undergraduates. After World War I the number of men's lodgings declined in the Kingston Road area while they increased in the east and south of the city, but the women's lodgings available in North Oxford continued, only tailing off after World War II.

The nineteenth-century suburb was expected to present an image of stability and permanence, but despite their solid appearance, the houses of North Oxford were subject to change almost from the start of building (Plate 92). While the suburb was still being developed, the earliest houses were being altered and expanded to suit the needs and tastes of successive tenants. As mentioned above, in 1867 the Max Mullers decided to bid for Goldwin Smith's 'bachelor's house' at 7 Norham Gardens once they had satisfied themselves that the house could easily the enlarged as Georgina Max Muller recalled: 'Directly the house was bought plans were made for adding a drawing room, and what Mr Goldwin Smith afterwards irreverently called a "baby-hutch", and the work was at once begun . . .'.[61] The year they bought the house there were three young daughters in the family, soon to be joined by a son, and in 1871 the *Census* records six servants in the household.[62] Extra space was needed for a household of twelve, expecially

179

when it was still important to keep separate the different aspects of domestic and family life.

Not long after the Poultons moved into 56 Banbury Road they built an addition, the plans for which were approved by the College in March 1884. The family had five children, and a couple of years after the youngest was born in 1892, the then Professor Poulton added another extension to the house.[63] St John's received a steady stream of requests for alterations from around 1880 to about 1905. Many of the extensions fit so well into the irregular gothic of the original houses that it is difficult to distinguish the additions from the original, particularly as stone continued to be used in the detailing. In 1874 Codd added a wing containing a large dining room to 14 Norham Gardens for the Hon. W.E. Sackville West, bursar of Keble, and in 1903 J.L. Myres added a dining room to his house, 1 Norham Gardens.[64] The desire for new dining rooms suggests that some formal entertaining was moving out of the colleges and into the suburb.

Since permission to extend a house depended on the agreement of the neighbours, not all the requests were automatically granted. One of the most idiosyncratic requests for an addition was from Dr James Murray the editor of the *Oxford English Dictionary*. When he began working on the dictionary at his house in Mill Hill, he built a temporary structure to house his reference books and the endless pieces of paper needed to prepare the entries for each word. On his removal to Oxford in 1885 he needed a similar 'scriptorium' or 'scrippy' at his new house, 78 Banbury Road.[65] The bursar of St John's was very anxious to accommodate Dr Murray and his work in North Oxford, and as if to anticipate any objections from Murray's neighbour, Professor Dicey at No 80, Omond wrote to Dicey asking him to make his objections known:

> Dr Murray . . . is anxious to erect a building in his garden, temporary indeed, but likely to last ten or twelve years at least. You are the only neighbour whom it could annoy, and I should be glad to know if you think it likely to be productive of any annoyance. I do not know myself that it will be, and of course one would be glad to help on a great work like this as far as possible.[66]

At first Murray wanted to put the scriptorium in front of the house, but this was rejected immediately by Omond, and the bursar suggested that it be erected at the end of the garden. Murray then wanted to place it close to his house with access from the kitchen, which would put it immediately opposite Dicey's drawing room windows and 'prejudice his outlook'. The solution found was to lower the structure between 2 and 4 feet below ground level, with the loss of wall space for windows made up by a glass roof on the north side. The result was that the scriptorium was notoriously badly ventilated, very hot in summer and extremely cold in winter.[67]

When the Canadian Sir William Osler was appointed Regius Professor of Medicine in 1905, it was to be expected that he and his American wife would come to live in North Oxford. For their first year they stayed in Mrs Max

93 No 13 Norham Gardens, William Wilkinson, 1869, built for Thomas Dallin and extended for Sir William Osler, Regius Professor of Medicine by N.W. Harrison, 1905.

Muller's house, and Mrs Osler reported a very favourable impression of the suburb to her mother shortly after their arrival:

> Mrs Max Muller has been most kind in every way. The house is comfortable. There is a little lawn with broad flower-beds and shrubs and lovely trees. It looks into the Parks, and nothing could be more wonderful than the lilacs, laburnam and hawthorn. It is one huge mass – up and down every street and in every garden, hanging from the roofs. It is really wonderful.[68]

A year later the Oslers were house hunting in the area, and finally settled on 13 Norham Gardens, the house Dallin had built in 1869. Osler wrote to a friend that though they liked the location on the Parks and the large garden, they felt the house needed 'many changes' which included additional bathrooms and central heating. N.W. Harrison was given the job of designing the additions to the Oslers' house, which included a substantial extension of the south-facing garden front and an entirely new bay on the southwest side, containing a drawing room of 540 square feet and a master bedroom.[69] Perhaps as significant as the increase in space, was the change in the style, represented by classical interiors and a move away from the pointed gables of Wilkinson's gothic to an overhanging hipped roof (Plate 93).

While the suburb was in a state of physical flux, institutions grew up which gave a sense of stability, and the ones most successful at providing continuity were those started by the occupants of the suburb. St Philip and St James, proposed so many years past by Morrell and the few inhabitants of North Oxford in the 1850s, became a focal point in the suburb for those who liked a mildly ritualist Anglicanism. In 1868 a critical eye-witness report of the services at the church commented that most of the congregation were women, and the ritualists did indeed seem to attract female support.[70] As early as 1872 a parochial school was built in Leckford Road for the children of the suburb and E.C. Dermer, who continued as vicar from 1872 to 1896, took an interest in secular as well as spiritual matters in the parish. As a fellow of St John's he could act as advocate for the less wealthy inhabitants of the suburb in their dealings with the College. When in 1879 J.G. Blencowe wanted to set up a shop for selling beer in Kingston Road, he sought the approval of Dermer before approaching the College with his proposal.[71]

Middle-class families were always concerned with the education of their children and a community consisting of a relatively high number of University families could be expected to have strong views about suitable schools. Most boys would have gone to public school, but there was a need in the suburb for a preparatory school for boys and a High School for girls. This latter was provided in part by the Girls' Public Day School Trust who opened their first school in 1875 in one of St John's houses, 16 St Giles's. The initiative to establish the school lay with the North Oxford parents who intended it to serve every family in the suburb, whether University or trade. As Mararget Fletcher remembered, this approach caused some confusion among the young who still held to the tribal differences between town and gown.[72] In 1879 the school moved to the new building designed by T.G. Jackson in Banbury Road.

The Misses Mardon started a boys preparatory school first in St Giles's Road and then at 3 and 4 Bradmore Road, but it was the parents of the suburb who initiated the most famous of Oxford preparatory schools, the Dragon School. This began in 1877 in two rooms in a house known as 'Balliol Hall' at 26 St Giles's under the headship of A.E. Clarke, a young graduate of Magdalen College.[73] He moved the school to 17 Crick Road in 1879, but his plans for the school came to an abrupt end in 1886 with his sudden death, and in the next year the school was taken over by his assistant, C.C. Lynam. Under Clarke the school had been successful in training boys for entrance to public school, but Lynam, or 'the Skipper' to his pupils, seemed to have been able to combine the rigours of Latin grammar with an imaginative approach to education.

Lynam took a building lease in 1893 on land at the southeast corner of Bardwell Road, and from that base was able over the years to develop his school. Educational institutions came and went in North Oxford, and it was unusual for them to last beyond the lifetime of their proprietor, but arrangements were made in 1894 for Lynam's Oxford Preparatory School to be run by a company made up of the pupils' parents, past and present. The school's bursar pointed out this new status to St John's at the end of 1894 when he applied for more land in Bardwell Road:

> Under the building scheme The Oxford Preparatory School passes from the ownership of Mr C.C. Lynam and becomes the property of the Oxford parents and others, who have had or now have boys at the school . . . The aim of the new Company will be to provide suitable premises for the education of present and future generations of sons of Oxford graduates. The enterprise is therefore quite removed from the platform of a private speculation and becomes (tho' of course in quite a minor but important degree) a question of general interest to the University.[74]

This argument did not move the College at this time, but there is evidence that the school attracted the support of many in the suburb. Professor Poulton was an enthusiast for the school and helped provide the school's mortgage, while Mrs Haldane chose their North Oxford house so that her daughter, Naomi, could attend the school, which she did in 1904. On the other hand Charles Oman did not approve of Lynam's attitude to religion and sent his children elsewhere.[75]

Lynam's choice of site at the extreme end of Bardwell Road and the eastern boundary of the estate was a wise one, since the position allowed expansion of the school over the years without arousing the hostility of its neighbours. The line between taking pupils for tuition and running a school was a fine one, and occasionally complaints would be made to the College that a house was being used as a school in contravention of the covenant ensuring that the suburb's houses be reserved for residential use only. Even the women's halls did not escape criticism. Although St Hugh's Hall had been running for twenty-five years in 1909, James Walker of 30 Norham Gardens charged that houses around him were being used by the hall for other than residential purposes.[76] About the same time, in Bradmore Road at the other end of Norham Manor, the neighbours of the Misses Mardon faced an even more alarming prospect, when the sisters, now resident in Winchester Road, sub-let Nos 3 and 4 to the breakaway students from Ruskin College.

Ruskin Hall had been set up in 1899 to offer further education for working-class men and had gained support from not a few in the University, since it was seen as a means of bridging the gulf between the classes. In 1907 St John's agreed to sell the hall premises in Walton Street close to Worcester College.[77] However, a group within the hall, who called themselves 'the Plebs', came to believe that the University was trying to subvert the purpose of the education offered there by insinuating its influence into the running of the hall. The result was the students' strike of 1909, and the decision of a rebel group to set up their own college to be called 'the Labour College'.[78] For the people in Bradmore Road who had no doubt been following the events at Ruskin in the press, the news that the breakaway college was to set up in their road must have come as a grave shock. This was a time when a rising working-class consciousness was causing a great deal of labour unrest and consequently fear among the middle classes.

St John's received a number of letters in protest at the imminent arrival of the Labour College in Bradmore Road. Their neighbour to the north, Professor Sidney Owen, first heard about the college from his wife whose weak health led her to despair of the change: 'I really doubt if we could live next door to them. They will be about the road and in the garden, over-looking what we are doing – It would not be nice for our young maids.'[79] Professor Owen foresaw a continuous disturbance from the presence of the working men whom he was sure would join forces with those destroyers of the peace, the itinerant musicians:

> The Band threatened to be a great nuisance to me and to my girls when teaching. I succeeded in staving them off on the ground that our road was occupied much with Professors and Tutors, whose work was seriously interrupted by it. But these people would probably enjoy and encourage the band and collect a mob of sympathetic auditors, I need not enlarge on the various particular forms of nuisance, as their whole style would constitute them an indescribable nuisance. And the desirableness and value of the property in their neighbourhood, and of the whole region would certainly be much deteriorated by their presence.[80]

It was difficult to use the argument that the Labour College would change the use of the houses from residential to educational, since the Misses Mardon had run a school there for many years, and even Professor Owen's daughter had taught at No 5 next door.

St John's sought Counsel's Opinion, and it was thought that it would be possible to remove the Labour College by an injunction from the Court of Chancery.[81] In the end it was agreed that the College should leave Bradmore Road by September 1911. During the spring of that year other premises were sought in North Oxford, and St John's had to inform the lessees of 30 and 32 Bardwell Road, next door to the Dragon School, that they would not be permitted to sub-let the houses to the college.[82] As the women's colleges had found, the most suitable premises for educational institutions were in North Oxford, but the antipathy to the Labour College made it difficult for them to find a house to rent there. In 1911 they moved to London, where they were able to establish themselves in Earls Court, and discovered a constituency of working people and trade unions which suited them better than the inhabitants of middle-class North Oxford. Whereas the suburb had actually helped the womens' colleges to develop almost unnoticed, the Labour College had been only too conspicuous.

The incident of the Labour College must have made the occupants of Bradmore Road realise how vulnerable the social character of their area had become. It was the irony of the suburbs that, while they exuded solidity and continuity, they were themselves subject to the capricious flux of economic fortune and of fashion. Although James Walker was unable to specify any grievance he had against the women of St Hugh's boarding in the houses around him, he sensed that even this subtle change of use could affect the neighbourhood adversely. The fear of a reduction in the value of property was ever present, whether among the leaseholders of the large villas in the centre of the estate or among those of the smaller houses in the west. St John's, as the ground landlords, received reproachful letters of complaint that the College, in not preventing some personally perceived transgression of the covenants, was somehow failing the suburb as a whole. Like a neglectful parent, it was implied, the College had let their tenants down.

The eventual success of North Oxford was a tribute to the foresight of those who advised St John's to go ahead with the development. In the 1850s and early 1860s, it was local professional men and tradesmen who formed most of the market for the new houses, and only very slowly did the University, as reform took effect, provide leaseholders and tenants. One factor which may have encouraged the early developers was that under the Universities Act of 1854, the Congregation of the University was limited to those MAs resident within a one and a half mile radius of Carfax, the centre of the town.[83] This gave voting rights in the legislative body of the University to any resident member of Convocation, whether engaged in academic work or not, and eventually it encouraged the retired to seek houses in North Oxford so they could occupy their last years with University affairs.[84] The one and half mile rule also worked against the dispersal of University society once married fellowships became more common. The concentration of University families around the centre of Oxford began to change in 1913 when the rule was altered. The residential requirement was abolished and voting rights in the Congregation were reserved for the academic and administrative staff of the University. Now there was no particular advantage to living within the one and a half mile limit, and with the help of the motor car and the bus, University society along with the rest of middle-class Oxford began to move out beyond North Oxford to Foxcombe, Headington, and Boar's Hills. Even before World War I change in North Oxford had been set in train.

CHAPTER VIII

The End of St John's North Oxford Estate

THE APPEARANCE OF stability in North Oxford was belied by the actual changes that took place in its physical fabric and in its social composition. Although North Oxford could be described in 1968 as 'a unique example of a well preserved Victorian suburb', it was not inevitable that this should be so, especially as the forces for change had long been working in Oxford and the University. The drift of the senior members of the University from North Oxford to the hills around the town, mentioned at the end of the previous chapter left many of the larger villas to be taken over during the inter-war period for academic purposes. The women's colleges leased a number of the larger houses whose freeholds they were eventually able to buy. After World War II the men's colleges found that houses in the suburb could provide them with much-needed additional accommodation. During the 1950s and 1960s, the function of the suburb remained residential, but its original social composition had altered, and its strong association with the University, instead of insulating it from physical change as it had before the war, now made it vulnerable to plans for University expansion.

The most dramatic change in the city after World War I was the development of the car works at Cowley. As a result of the influx of workers, the population of Oxford rose by 20 per cent between 1921 and 1931. The full impact of this sudden expansion was felt to the east of Magdalen Bridge, but the effects of the resulting increase in traffic eventually reached North Oxford. Every scheme for dealing with the Oxford traffic problem involved driving relief roads through the residential streets of the suburb.

St John's as always had to look to its long-term revenues. Trying to adjust to the shifting pressures placed on the Oxford properties would have been taxing enough, but the College also had to deal with the maturing of the ninety-nine-year leases which began in the early 1960s. Many of the houses were unsuited to modern living and would require such a large expenditure to bring them up to date that redevelopment seemed in many cases inevitable. Whether this course should be taken and if so how it should be implemented, were questions obscured by the Leasehold Reform Act of 1967 and the emergence of the conservation lobby.

Immediately after World War I it would seem that the management of the

94   Bainton Road, north end, 1924–30, T.H. Kingerlee, builder.

North Oxford estate did not make many demands on the College. The leases of the earliest houses still had forty-five or fifty years left to run, while only Blackhall Farm on the Bardwell estate and the top end of Bainton Road were left to be developed. However, after the war there was a backlog of repairs needed on the fabric of the rack-rented property and a new economic climate in which to manage the College's revenues. In October 1919 Bidder, the bursar of St John's since Glasson's resignation in 1896, announced his retirement at Michaelmas 1920. By April the committee set up to find a new bursar had to be urged to look outside the College for a successor, and in June 1920 they appointed Ronald Hart-Synnot. The new bursar had an army and agricultural background, and came to the College from University College, Reading, where he was Dean of the Faculty of Agriculture and Horticulture. It made sense to appoint someone with agricultural knowledge since, despite the changes brought about by the war, the College's fortunes still lay with its endowment lands. Hart-Synnot put the energy of the bursary into managing the College's rural properties, but he also oversaw the completion of the suburban development.

Building had tapered off in North Oxford during the war as materials and labour disappeared, so that by 1915 all work had ceased on those areas of the estate still left incomplete. When the building industry recovered after the war, it was time to consider the unbuilt areas of the suburb. In June 1922 the tenant of Blackhall Farm was given notice in order to free the land for building, and proposals were accepted for plots on the unfinished sections of Northmoor and Charlbury Roads.[1] When the lease on the farm expired, a new road was built from Banbury Road to Charlbury Road and named Belbroughton Road in 1924. This was the area of the estate where the architect Christopher Wright was active and after 1927, when Garford Road was started to the south of the farm land, he became involved there as well. The other unfinished section of the College's estate was the top of Bainton Road to the west of Woodstock Road, which was taken on building leases by Messrs Wooldridge and Simpson in 1923 (Plate 94).[2] By 1930 St John's North Oxford estate was virtually complete.

The only other large-scale building in North Oxford was Belsyre Court, a block of service flats and shops built in 1934 on a site where Observatory Street and St John's (now St Bernard's) Road converge on Woodstock Road. At first, in February 1932, the site was considered for a theatre, but by October of that year a scheme by J.C. Leed for shops and flats was being considered.[3] Leed had collaborated with F. Matcham & Co on the Oxford Picture House in 1924, but St John's Estates Committee were unhappy with his design and went to E.R. Barrow, an architect who had designed college rooms and flats for Sidney Sussex College, Cambridge.[4] In his design, Barrow combined a classical colonnade at street level with Jacobean mullions and gables above in a style which did nothing to challenge Wilkinson and Moore's houses in Woodstock Road. The total estimated cost of the scheme was £45,500 and the College took precautions to ensure a return on their investment. The bursar negotiated with the Inland Revenue to take the offices which were included in the scheme and care was taken to test the market for the type of flats to be provided. In January 1937 the Estates Committee decided to request the City Council to zone areas north and south of Belsyre Court for shops and flats in case it was perceived that there was a call for these, but this did not come about before the outbreak of war in 1939.[5]

That the Estates Committee was asking the City Council to change the zoning for part of the St John's estate shows the extent to which the new ideas about town planning had penetrated, even into Oxford. Since 1876 house plans had to be approved by the city engineer and permission from the Local Board and later the City Council was necessary before a new road could be laid out, but the power to zone areas of the town for different purposes gave the city a more strategic influence over Oxford's development. The enthusiasm for town planning had emerged before World War I when cheaper transport offered the possibility of regulating urban growth by means of working-class suburbs. The 1909 Housing Act included the provision for local authorities to formulate a town-planning policy, although there were few at the time who took advantage of this. After the war the Chamberlain Report recommended a planning approach to urban problems which would encourage the co-ordination of the location of industry, transport, and housing.[6] Enthusiasm for planning was undoubted and it affected a cross-section of people with many different interests. Those concerned for the countryside as much as those interested in the efficient running of the towns became caught up in the pros and cons of planning in its broadest sense.

Unease at the way Oxford was developing appeared sporadically and the suburbs, which had been the pride of the town in the 1850s and 1860s, were regarded increasingly with disfavour, especially by those who had spent their youth among the colleges. The undergraduate years coincide with that time of life when emotions are heightened and vivid impressions are engraved in the mind, and not a few judges, bishops, and members of parliament were jealous of any changes which would disturb their memories of Oxford. By World War I North Oxford was built up to Summertown, as the owners of the land just to the north of St John's followed the example of the College by laying out streets of villas and semi-detached houses. After the war the vast extension of Cowley transformed the eastern approaches to the city from sleepy villages into what seemed like endless suburbs. Gradually the 'brickish skirt' that Gerard Manley Hopkins had disliked so much was growing longer.

Because of its site Oxford had for a long time remained in glorious isolation, so that the traveller approaching the city was first aware of the spires floating in the air. The river and the water meadows had prevented the spread of suburbs, and the social concentration of the city around the colleges worked against that centrifugal force which had burst the bounds of so many towns. It is supposed that it was Copleston, provost of Oriel in the nineteenth century, who confided to the young John Henry Newman his ideas for the improvement of Oxford:

> He considered it was worth the consideration of the Government whether Oxford should not stand in a domain of its own. An ample range, say four miles in diameter, should be turned into wood and meadow, and the University should be approached on all sides by a magnificent park, with fine trees in groups and groves and avenues, and with glimpses and views of the fair city, as the traveller drew near it. There is nothing surely absurd in the idea, though it would cost a round sum to realize it.[7]

This picturesque ideal for Oxford was the one which came to be accepted and applied as the standard when judging change and the measures proposed for its control. A.C. Headlam DD, the distinguished Professor of Dogmatic Theology at King's College, London, used the vehicle of a review of Aymer Vallance's *Old Colleges of Oxford* in the *Burlington Magazine* in 1913 to plead that such as ideal should be kept in mind when further development was undertaken in the city, whether by the University, the colleges, or the ordinary citizen. He called for some kind of planned control for the whole Oxford area:

> The time has come for a great and far-reaching scheme for dealing with the city of Oxford, the valleys of the Isis and the Cherwell, and the woods and hills that surround them. As year by year our favourite haunts and walks are seized on by the builder we feel some restraint and control is necessary . . . The married tutor must have his home, and the professor will want to live on the slope of the hills, but let roads and houses and gardens be wisely planned.[8]

Dr Headlam put forth the same argument used by the opponents to the carriage works in 1865 that Oxford, as a 'priceless possession' of the nation, must be guarded against unthinking development which would destroy its character, and he called on both the University and the city to unite 'in promoting a great town-planning scheme for Oxford and its surroundings'.

There were two forces which were acting for change in Oxford: one was the expansion of the University; and the other was the introduction to the city of the Cowley Motor Works. William Morris, later Lord Nuffield, had begun building handmade cars before World War I, and in 1922 he set up the factory in the southeast suburb of Cowley. Industry was a long time coming to Oxford, and when it did arrive it came in the form of a so-called 'new' industry, that is one which was expanding while so many others were contracting during the slump and depression of the 1920s and 1930s. The result was that Oxford had to deal with the effects of industrialisation long after other towns had come to terms with the disruption that manufacturing brought and were coping with the problems of decline. Another example of Oxford being 'always a century behind other towns'.[9] Between 1921 and 1931, while the population of the city as a whole rose by 20 per cent that of Cowley and Iffley increased by 112 per cent.[10]

Because the car works were built on the periphery in what became an industrial suburb, the centre of Oxford was at first unaffected. However, as Cowley became the home of a large working-class population, in regular, well-paid employment, the tradesmen of the town began to benefit. No longer did they have to shut up shop during the Long Vacation, but enjoyed trade for the whole year round. The drawback to this increase in business was that traffic in the centre of Oxford also increased, with a constant flow over Magdalen Bridge and up the High Street. If the centre of Oxford was not defaced by the new industry, it began to be strangled by its traffic, and yet no one could seriously consider returning to the old days.

The other force for change, the expansion of the University, began before World War I, but quickened after the war when the funding for the University's activities was put on a firmer basis. The sciences benefited most from the increase in financial resources, and the site around the Museum, to the south of the Parks, became established as the science area of Oxford. All this activity also generated traffic, and any spare space around the colleges was used for parking. Even St John's, on the northern edge of the city, but close to the science area, was subjected to parking in St Giles's, the broad thoroughfare just outside their door. In 1923 the College registered their alarm at the traffic in St Giles's by urging the City Council to impose a 10-mile-an-hour speed limit in the street.[11]

An early response to what was seen as the planning needs of Oxford was the Town Planning Scheme drawn up in 1925, the year of the Town Planning Act.[12] The City Council decided to deal with the historic centre separately from the surrounding areas which were zoned according to their functions. Cowley and the area along the railway line and the canal were zoned for industrial use while North Oxford was designated for residential purposes. One trend which had developed from the war was for an increasing number of goods to be carried by road rather than by rail, and Oxford had assumed again its importance at the convergence of a number of main routes, with heavy traffic passing up the High Street and up and down Cornmarket. This led the City Council to include in their scheme a ring road well beyond the centre of the town, which was thought would deal with the cause of the congestion in the centre.

Traffic in Oxford was recognised as a problem early on, and even the Town Planning Scheme of 1925 suggested that drivers should be encouraged to leave their cars outside the centre. A car park was established in St Giles's with a paid attendant.[13] The suggested by-pass was started, but remained incomplete and as time went on traffic congestion became more acute. In 1936 R.F. Bretherton of Wadham College in *A Social Survey of the Oxford District* reported that Oxford's chief architectural problem was 'to prevent her ancient buildings from being hammered to pieces by the vibration of traffic, which was not local at all but that of half England'.[14] Eventually proposals began appearing which their supporters claimed would solve the traffic problems of the city. T. Lawrence Dale is remembered today because he was the first to propose a road that would run from the Iffley Road in the east across Christ Church Meadow to St Aldates just above Folly Bridge.[15] This 'Christ Church Mall' as he called it, would take through traffic away from the High Street, thus freeing the centre of the town of unnecessary congestion, but at the expense of the peace of Christ Church Meadow.

The idea of the mall was taken up by Thomas Sharp when he was requested by the City Council in 1945 to prepare a report on the planning and development of the city. In *Oxford Replanned* Sharp not only put forward a scheme for a road across Christ Church Meadow, he also suggested that the mall should be placed much further up the Meadow, closer to Christ Church and Merton College.[16] He proposed a wide avenue that would run from the east side of Magdalen Bridge across the Meadow to St Aldates, with limited access to the High Street. The negative reaction of Christ Church to Sharp's proposal and their appeal to the House of Lords could have been predicted. What followed was twenty years of controversy punctuated by a series of public enquiries. St John's and North Oxford might seem a long way from the High Street and Christ Church, but the Woodstock and Banbury Roads formed the main northern route out of the city and every traffic scheme proposed had implications for St Giles's and North Oxford. For example, Sharp's proposed road layout would have funnelled heavy traffic up St Giles's, past St John's and through the suburb.

In their amended Development Plan of 1955 the City Council included two relief roads, one to the south of the town between Iffley and Abingdon Roads and another to the north which would have crossed through a section of the Parks and have entered St Giles's just north of St John's College on the site of the Lamb and Flag public house.[17] This road would not only have been an inconvenience for the College, it would have had a detrimental affect on the Science Area in the Parks, possibly disturbing delicate instruments through traffic vibrations. For the enquiry that was held in February 1956 St John's asked Sir Patrick Abercrombie to present an alternative road plan which would spare them the proximity of two main roads, St Giles's and the proposed Lamb and Flag relief road. The Abercrombie scheme was an inner ring road which on its northern arm followed a line through Leckford Road, Church Walk, and Norham Road with a return through Bevington Road (Plate 95).[18] The line was similar to the one proposed for the railway in 1851 before the suburb had appeared, but the difference now was that North

95   No 13 Bevington Road, built by John
Dorn in 1870, and one of the houses to be
disturbed by the proposed scheme intended to
conduct traffic through North Oxford.

Oxford was very much a physical presence, and still its integrity could be
threatened by agencies beyond the control of the College.

None of the grandiose road schemes was built. In 1963 Colin Buchanan
put forward in *Traffic in Towns* the idea of traffic control as the solution to
congested roads, and although enquiries continued for another five years,
they came to an end in 1968 with Wilson and Womersley's *Oxford Central
Area Study* which suggested an acceptable scheme of traffic management and
restricted parking.[19] North Oxford was saved the disruption that large-scale
road building would have made to its coherence, but not through its own
merits. The vulnerability of the suburb was that, certainly after World War I
and for a very long time to come, it was considered to be ugly beyond
measure. When buildings are to be defended on their value apart from their
function, the judgment as to their value depends to a large extent on taste,
and the style of North Oxford suffered a severe eclipse up to the mid-1960s.

During the winter and spring terms of 1935 and 1936 H.S. Goodhart-
Rendel devoted three of his Slade lectures to North Oxford.[20] These lectures
were novel since they took the architecture of the suburb seriously, but
although he found much to praise in the individual houses, he could not
refrain from speaking of the 'stupid villas'. More sinister was that those who
began to put forward radical ideas for the development of Oxford seemed to
regard the area north of St Giles's as totally without merit. T. Lawrence Dale
in his discussions about post-war rebuilding wrote thus about the North

192

Oxford houses: 'Tall, shapeless, uncouth, the roofs of machine-made tiles combined the hipped form with many gables that were neither acutely pointed nor obtuse; that followed neither the Gothic nor the classic tradition but effected a 'rational' compromise and achieved utter ugliness'.[21] And he continued:

> The literary men had taught them [the college dons] to look through their ears and by the best literary standards the houses were admirable. To the eye, however, they affronted heaven and when in due course trees grew and hid them, no further persuasion was necessary to demonstrate that nature was preferable to art.[22]

Thomas Sharp in his influential *Oxford Replanned* followed the same line as Dale. The trees of North Oxford were magnificent and must be saved, while the houses were to be tolerated only for the sake of the trees:

> Indeed the inner parts of North Oxford are saved by their trees: their arid and gloomy Victorian-Gothic villas are mercifully hidden for most of the year and at least veiled for the rest. Thus the Banbury Road, with the great trees in the gardens fronting it, looks like a two-mile-long drive through a forest: without its trees it would be two miles of architectural nightmare.[23]

In 1956 Marcus Dick could write about the 'jungle of Victorian Gothic' and expect his phrase to be received with approval. This attitude to the architecture of North Oxford, especially by those who had influence in planning circles, did not bode well for a time when other functions would claim priority over the residential character of the suburb, since then the perceived intrinsic value of the houses would not be enough to save them from redevelopment. If the city could contemplate driving a road through such a beloved landscape as Christ Church Meadow, it is not surprising that it could also consider widening existing roads in North Oxford to carry heavy traffic despite a commitment to the residential character of the suburb in the *Oxford Redevelopment Plan*. During the 1950s and 1960s there seems to have been an underlying assumption that parts, at least, of North Oxford could be sacrificed to other apparently more pressing needs, whether traffic routes or University expansion.

Despite these external pressures, St John's had to ensure the value of their North Oxford property, and as the century advanced and the leases of the houses reached maturity, the College had to decide what course they would take to maintain the income from the estate. The leasehold system by which North Oxford was developed had been a useful tool in the nineteenth century to make building land available by guaranteeing the ground landlord a return with little risk to himself. Most people at the beginning of the lease had no concern for the date of termination since it was so far in the future, but as the leases from the nineteenth-century building booms began to approach full term, the ground landlords were faced with the problems of first, how to maintain the value of the property as the value of the lease rapidly declined, and second, what to do with the property when the lease finally fell in. Many houses, especially in a suburb like North Oxford, were unsuited to modern living and required a great deal of capital expenditure if they were to be divided successfully into smaller units with the appropriate services. Only by allowing some houses to be used as lodgings or as offices could the College hope to see their leases reach the full ninety-nine years.

In 1949 Hart-Synnot retired as bursar, and was replaced by Arthur Garrard. Hart-Synnot had concentrated on the agricultural interests of the College at a time when this was a very difficult task. During the depression years he had helped establish a College farm at Long Wittenham in conjunction with the School of Rural Economy, and in the course of World War II St John's had accommodated a branch of the Ministry of Food.[24] Garrard came to the College from managing the estates of the Duchy of Lancaster in Cheshire and Yorkshire, and he had had extensive experience in housing management as well as in agriculture. This coloured his approach to the College's property, with a great deal more interest being taken in the Oxford houses.

Before the ninety-nine-year leases started falling in the College had to deal with those properties that had been built before North Oxford was developed – the Beaumont Street area and the streets in what was formerly Tagg's Gardens, just to the north of the Observatory. Even before Garrard took over as bursar, the Estates Committee had considered what to do with the houses in Beaumont Street.[25] At least these houses did not pose any problem as far as their aesthetic value was concerned. Although the street had been criticised in 1849 for being straight and charmless, one hundred years later its gentle curve down to Worcester College from St Giles's was much admired.[26] T. Dale Lawrence in 1944 regarded Beaumont Street as a fleeting glimpse of what might have been residential Oxford and praised its 'variety of uniformity' as opposed to the monotony of North Oxford's 'unvarying variety'. Hart-Synnot regarded Beaumont Street as a 'property of outstanding importance' as did Garrard who described it, St John Street, and 45 to 55 Woodstock Road as 'houses which I consider worth preserving at almost any cost, regardless of their age and condition'.[27] In order to preserve these houses new functions had to be found for them, and Hart-Synnot had adopted the practice of converting the houses in Beaumont Street and some of the better ones in St John Street into offices and flats to accommodate doctors and dentists who found that high rents in Cornmarket and surrounding streets were pushing them out of the commercial centre. Professional men had long been established in Beaumont Street so that turning over the houses to offices in this instance did not radically change their use.

Another concern at this time was the cheaper property the College owned, not just in Tagg's Gardens, but in the Walton Street area, Jericho, and in Kingston Road. Many of these properties had been leased on sixty-six-year leases, and were now rack rented. In his reorganisation of the management of the Oxford properties in 1950, Garrard suggested drawing up a plan of redevelopment whereby houses in very poor condition would be left unlet until a block of houses became available for replacement by flats or new houses.[28] In the meantime he proposed appointing a woman housing manager, in the tradition of Octavia Hill, to collect rents and compile a list of necessary repairs. He was careful not to criticise the previous regime in the bursary, but he found a trace of neglect in the relations between the tenants and the College:

> There does not appear to have been any serious attempt to reproduce here the spirit of partnership which has been developed so successfully with the farm tenants and I have found, on the few occasions when I have gone into small houses, a rather moving pleasure at having the Bursar himself come to the house. I attach immense importance to ownership being regarded as a social service, and there is no reason why an artisan should not react just as agreeably as a countryman.[29]

As the pace of events quickened in the housing market during the 1950s and 1960s, it was not always so easy to take such a benevolent view of the relations between tenant and landlord.

By the early 1950s it became apparent that the post-war demands on the College would require a change in the way it financed its activities. The bursar reported in 1952 that St John's was operating at a deficit and that in 1953 they would have to find an additional £2,800 in new money.[30] An increase in College tuition fees was immediately instituted, but it was also suggested that more profit could be secured from the College's estates, although it was recognised that this was not such a sure source of revenue as it had been. One reason for the uncertainty about the future profits expected from house property was that the private rented sector, from being the dominant type of tenure up until 1939, had fallen out of favour with the public and the politicians. Owner occupation and municipal housing were the two types of tenure being put forward as desirable means of overcoming the perceived post-war housing shortage. Although housing legislation was intended to protect the tenant from exploitation by the landlord, the effect was to make rented property less attractive as an investment.

The 1954 Landlord and Tenant Act was meant to provide security for tenants and sub-tenants in low-rented houses, but it would also make it more difficult for landlords to manage rack-rented property. This was especially unwelcome with regard to the College's property in Tagg's Gardens, the area bounded by Observatory Street and Leckford Road, because it had assumed a settled and mixed character compared by the bursar to London's Chelsea.[31] It was here that the College traditionally housed their own staff. The 1954 Act did, however, allow landlords to take properties in hand if they had prepared a redevelopment plan which was approved by the local authority, and in September the Estates Committee recommended that the College ask Lionel Brett (later Lord Esher) to prepare a redevelopment plan for what came to be called 'Walton Manor'.[32] The eventual plan, including flats, shops, and refurbishment, was never fully carried out, but it continued to be an important part of the College's strategy for their Oxford houses.

Although a Committee on the Financial Prospects of the College

96 Nos 39–40 Leckford Road, Charles Williams, builder, 1875–81, two of the houses considered 'ripe for redevelopment' in 1960.

recommended that more effort be put into increasing the profitability of the College's estates, it came to be realised that the dependence on property for most of the external income was not realistic. In October 1959 one fellow prepared a memorandum which laid out the case for diversifying the College's investments.[33] In 1958 house property, both leasehold and rack rented, accounted for 70 per cent of the external income. Only 8.8 per cent of income came from gilt-edge investments and 1.2 per cent from equities. One reason that the College depended to such a extent on property, a form of investment which had come to be seen as vulnerable and old fashioned, was that under the Universities and Colleges Estates Act of 1925, they were restricted in how they managed their endowment. Capital was deposited with the Ministry of Agriculture which had taken over from the Land Commission as the guardians of the colleges' property. If a college sold property, they were not free to use the purchase money in any way they thought best, but had to deposit it with the Minister and to seek his approval either to buy more property or to put the money into alternative investments. This situation lasted until the Universities and Colleges Estates Act 1964, when the capital of the colleges was transferred from the Minister into their own hands, and most of the restrictions on their financial affairs were lifted.

In the meantime the fellows turned their attention to how they could diversify the investments of the College, and the bursar started the process in

January 1960 by initiating a review of the future of the North Oxford properties.[34] He reminded the fellows that there was a move, particularly among Labour politicians, to reform the rules governing leasehold which would give tenants the right to buy the freehold of their houses. If the Labour party were to form the government in the near future, the College could find that they would be forced to sell their properties whether or not it appeared to be in their interest. By selling a substantial number of North Oxford houses, the College could both forestall a future forced sale and diversify its investments.

The bursar's Memorandum which he prepared with the assistance of Messrs Dulake, a local firm of chartered surveyors, recommended that the suburb of North Oxford be divided into different areas according to the types of houses to be dealt with. The rack-rented and leasehold houses in the Beaumont Street area ought to be kept as should those in Walton Manor. Because they were of a 'more expensive type' the houses north of Bardwell Road also were considered worth keeping for their reversionary value when the leases fell in. The bursar anticipated that the City Council would eventually allow the very large houses in Banbury Road to be used for offices and these should be sold for that purpose. Those houses not already in the freehold possession of St Antony's and St Anne's Colleges in the Bevington and Winchester Roads would no doubt be bought by them. East of Banbury Road and south of Bardwell Road had been scheduled for University expansion on the Town Plan. This area covered what was known as Norham Manor, where many of the large houses had been poorly converted into flats and had not been well maintained. Rather than sell these off to individuals it was thought that the houses in this area should be sold in blocks for redevelopment when their leases fell in. The rest of North Oxford, most of which lay west of Woodstock Road, ought to be sold.

There were approximately 620 North Oxford houses, plus another 100 or so in the Walton Street and Jericho areas, which came under the category for sale. Some of the houses were in hand and could be sold freehold with vacant possession, but most were leasehold. It was estimated that the freeholds of the leasehold properties could be sold for between £500 and £2,000, depending on the size of the house, while those houses with vacant possession could fetch up to £3,000. Altogether it was estimated that the sale of the Oxford property would yield about £950,000. One reason for selling the leasehold property was that the lessees on the termination of the leases were liable for dilapidations, but most of the leaseholders were not in a position to pay the substantial amounts needed for basic repairs. It was noted in the Warnborough Road area that: 'The majority of properties in this block are three-storey basement houses without garage space; many are in a poor state of repair and will deteriorate rapidly, partly due to the type of occupier and partly to the height and general construction of the buildings, which make repair work exceptionally expensive.'[35] If the College waited for the leases to fall in they would find themselves in possession of a very poor stock of houses, requiring large amounts of capital to bring them up to acceptable modern standards (Plate 96).

Two chartered surveyors from the two firms, Messrs Dulake and Messrs Cluttons, were asked to collaborate with the bursar in preparing a *Joint Report on the Future of the North Oxford Estate* which was ready by June 1960. Once the report was circulated among the experts for comment, the fellows found themselves in a confusing situation of conflicting advice. That the College should reduce its dependence on the type of property it then held was not questioned, but that this should be done by simply selling the freehold of large numbers of houses was considered unwise by most of their consultants. The property was bound to appreciate in value in future, and the College ought to ensure it benefited from the increase.

It was a short step from a planned strategy for disposing of property to a redevelopment plan, and Lord Harcourt, chairman of the Oxford Preservation Trust, took the line that North Oxford was 'ripe for development' and recommended that the College consider a redevelopment plan for the whole of North Oxford.[36] The Trust's main purpose from its institution in 1927 had been to campaign for the preservation of the open space around the city, so it had an interest in the redevelopment of Norh Oxford at a higher density in order to forestall any further urban sprawl. In the minutes of a meeting of the College's Finance Committee held in December 1961 Lord Harcourt was reported as saying: 'He disliked garden cities and did not believe that most working class people wanted to live in semi-detached houses. He felt strongly that the solution of Oxford's problem must be a highly urbanised town, with the surrounding country undeveloped.'[37] Lord Harcourt claimed that the execution of a redevelopment plan could be carried out by a joint development company formed by the College and a group of insurance companies. Consultation with the Ministry made it doubtful that the College would be allowed under the act to sell its freeholds in exchange for a shareholding in a development consortium. The Ministry also pointed out that the College might come in for local opprobrium if it gave over the control of redevelopment in North Oxford to outside interests.[38] A rent rise in 1960 had already caused a great deal of resentment and the articulate North Oxford tenants could be expected to put up resistance to redevelopment which disregarded the tradition and amenity of the area.

Doubt was also cast on the judgment that North Oxford was 'ripe for development'. A representative from Wates, the building firm, pointed out in June 1961 that the state of the housing market in Oxford meant that houses as they stood were more valuable than vacant sites would be.[39] An example of this was Bradmore Road, part of the Norham Manor estate which had been considered ready for redevelopment in the bursar's memorandum of January 1960. By November 1961 the situation was perceived differently. As a development site the street was valued at £53,000 and the bursar gave the following evaluation of the area as it stood:

> The houses are generally large: most of them are structurally sound and many appear to have been converted into what are assuredly flats with a good deal of accommodation. The unexpired terms of the leases range

from 6 to 15 years, and their value to the College in November 1961 we believe to be not less than £117,385. Or double the site value.[40]

Another consideration was that redevelopment could be contemplated only when the College were in a position to take possession of their property within two or three years. Many leases throughout the suburb still had fifteen to twenty years before maturing, and buying these in with so many years still to run would be very expensive. The Universities and Colleges Estates Act required that when leaseholds were bought back the shortfall on rent to the date of expiry had to be made up through a sinking fund, which had the effect of tying up yet more of the College's capital.

Although all the experts were agreed that the College was 'sitting on a gold-mine', it seemed that they would not be able to benefit from it for a good many years. In March 1962 the bursar suggested that the College accept a policy of postponing plans for redevelopment for twenty years until a sufficient number of leases were bought in, and there seems to have been a general sense of relief that no radical change was therefore contemplated for a long time yet.[41] The Estates Committee made their recommendation in October:

> Since it is unlikely that redevelopment on the North Oxford Estate will be economic for 10/20 years, the College should adopt a policy of buying-in leases, primarily to facilitate redevelopment when the time is ripe, but not as a rule to obtain an increase in income ... Should the college decide, however, to reduce their holding of bricks and mortar, then sales should be restricted to poorer property on the periphery of the estate, and to blocks of property rather than individual houses.[42]

The only area which continued to be considered for imminent redevelopment was Walton Manor and in 1964 the College, in order to maintain some control in the face of any prospective legislation, set up a housing association to manage their rented property there.[43]

One suggestion from 1960 that the College acted upon after some discussion among the fellows was the disposal of their property in Jericho, the working-class suburb southwest of North Oxford (Plate 97). Houses in the area were offered to Worcester College, the University Press, and Lucy's Ironworks. For some time the City Council had been considering the possible redevelopment of Jericho, but when the College was ready to sell their houses in Cranham Street at the beginning of 1961, the city baulked at the prospect of re-housing the tenants.[44] In the event a property company, Ashdale Land and Property Company, bought the houses at auction, and after submitting some inappropriate schemes for redevelopment, the Ashdale Company were able to sell a cleared section of their property in 1966 to the city with outline planning permission for 107 dwellings.[45]

In 1965 and 1967 the legislation that the bursar had come to fear was passed. The Rent Restrictions Act 1965 added another constraint to the College's management of their property. Many of their houses let on low rents were already regulated under previous Rent Acts so that they could

97   Cranham Street, Jericho 1961 (SJC Muniments).

raise rents only on a change of tenancy. These acts dated from World War I when rent strikes had threatened war production, but they had continued afterwards in order to keep rents low and social unrest at bay. The result of the restrictions in an area like North Oxford in the 1950s and 1960s was that many elderly people refused to move from a house which had become inappropriate to their needs because on leaving the tenancy they would lose their regulated rent, and it was unlikely that they could afford the rent of even a small flat if its rent were unregulated.[46] A partial deregulation under the Rent Act of 1957 had badly affected elderly landladies. Providing rooms for undergraduates had become an important means of making a living for a number of women tenants, particularly in St John Street. By now, however, many of them were elderly and when the level of the rateable value for regulated rents was lowered, they were unable to cover the resulting higher rents from what they received from their lodgers. Their accommodation was their sole means of support, and as their plight became known, the College was attacked in the local press for raising their rents.[47] One reason the College wished to keep control of Walton Manor was that their redevelopment plan included low-rent flats suitable for such people. In fact the only part of their scheme which was carried out was the building of fourteen old-peoples' flats in Adelaide Street.[48]

200

Under the 1965 Rent Act even the unregulated rents were to be subject to the control of a local rent officer who was to set rents regardless of the scarcity value in the area. Although there was provision for rent adjustments to be made from time to time, this act was a further disincentive for landlords to rent property for profit, and it dimmed the prospect of the College increasing their income by letting their houses at whatever rent the market would bear.

The Leasehold Reform Act was passed in 1967 and came into force on 1 January 1968. The White Paper on Leasehold Reform was published in February 1966, and although it had been long expected, when it came it at last threw the College into action. Under the Act tenants in houses below the rateable value of £200 and with long leases of over twenty-one years, would be able to opt either to buy the freehold of their property or to extend their leases to fifty years after the expiry date.[49] The point of the Act was to prevent unscrupulous speculators from buying for very little money the freehold reversion of leasehold properties with only a few years left to run, and then turning out the tenants without compensation when the leases fell in.[50] The limit on rateable value meant that the big ground landlords in London like the Bedford and Portland Estates would not be affected too adversely. The decline in property as a desirable long-term investment had been in evidence for some time, and it was one of the factors which had opened the way for speculation. As responsible landlords moved their capital into investments which provided a better return, those left holding leasehold property were often the economically vulnerable who could not sustain the value of their investment with their limited resources, and fell prey to unscrupulous developers looking for bargains. The College was out of step with the times by relying so heavily on leasehold house property for their external income, but they could also point out that they had taken a consistently responsible approach to the management of their property and should not be penalised along with the speculators.

After the appearance of the White Paper the bursar pressed for an aggressive sales policy of both the rack-rented and leasehold houses and he anticipated that the bulk of the houses could be sold within three years.[51] Such a sell off would reduce the workload of the bursary and the bursar suggested that what property remained in the College's hands could be managed by independent firms of chartered surveyors. He recommended too that the Beaumont Street area and Walton Manor be excluded from the sale, the latter because, in his words, the area '. . . provides a wide variety of accommodation; it has considerable character, and above all, tranquillity. And we have, over the years, taken much trouble to secure its future.'[52] It was thought that a housing association, as a non-profit organisation, would be immune from both the Acts, and it was decided to sell the freehold of the houses in Walton Manor to the housing association set up to manage the properties in that area. By this means it was hoped that redevelopment could take place, but it was important to make the plans public as soon as possible to forestall any attempt by the tenants to buy their own freeholds. Application for planning approval was made to the City Council and an announcement of the scheme was made in *The Times* on 3 January 1967 in which Lord Esher was quoted as saying: 'Like the mews and cottage dwellings of central London, its small houses now have a wider appeal and there is no reason why its present miniature domestic scale should not be retained indefinitely.'[53] This suggests that the project was now being seen in terms of conservation. Subsequently it was discovered that a housing association was not exempt from the Rent Restriction Act and that the amount of compensation necessary to pay to leaseholders in a redevelopment area would make the redevelopment of Walton Manor uneconomic for the College, and the scheme was dropped.

In the spring of 1966, after the White Paper appeared, a committee was set up by St John's to deal with the effects of the Leasehold Reform Act and to work out the implications of the Act for the finances of the College. The committee went back to the report of 1960 and it was decided in the first instance to begin selling off the rack-rented houses in the streets along the west side of the estate by putting up for sale immediately seventy-eight houses in Kingston Road.[54] If tenants had difficulty in raising the capital to buy, the College offered loans at a fixed rate of interest, slightly below the rate charged by the building societies. This was to be a pilot scheme, and if it worked it was to be applied to other parts of the estate.

Another reason for selling the freeholds of the North Oxford houses arose during the spring of 1966, when the fellows of St John's considered building substantial new accommodation within the College. In response to the Robbins Report on higher education, the Franks Report recommended that the Oxford colleges accept more graduate students as well as an increased number of undergraduates. The report also suggested that the number of fellows be augmented to ensure that the ratio between tutors and students be maintained.[55] St John's had these recommendations in mind when they planned their new accommodation, but they were also aware that a large building programme would be a drain on the College's finances, especially if there was no appeal to outside sources. The proceeds of the sale of the North Oxford properties, therefore, were earmarked for the building fund and the new building was named after the founder, Sir Thomas White, in recognition that construction had been made possible by the sale of part of the College's original endowment. The profits from the sale not only provided the new building which increased the College's competitive edge in attracting well-qualified undergraduates, they also provided enough additional income to double the number of teaching fellows.[56] As a result the standing of St John's among the other colleges improved and its academic reputation was enhanced.

In December 1967 the committee appointed to deal with leasehold reform reported that, out of the College's leasehold estate, 661 houses were rated below the limit under the Act of £200.[57] It was not at all clear how many leaseholders would want to enfranchise. Absentee landlords did not qualify, but if a landlord sold the lease to an owner-occupier, the status of the house would change. Most of the houses falling within the limit were situated to the west of Woodstock Road, but there were enough qualifying houses scattered throughout the estate to make any idea of a planned redevelopment of North Oxford completely out of the question. By October 1968 there had been 165 applications from eligible leaseholders, but also 85 from those who came outside the terms of the Act by occupying houses of a higher rateable value.[58] There was no point in collecting very low ground rents for years without the expectation of high reversionary values, and when the College decided in January 1968 to sell houses above the £200 limit, they in effect brought their controlling influence in North Oxford to an end.

Up to September 1969 the College had had applications to buy their freeholds from 480 leaseholders of houses outside the £200 limit.[59] It may seem surprising that so many people wanted to buy the more expensive houses, because it had been supposed that these houses would require more money to modernise than most people would be able to raise. However, domestic technology had recently improved to such an extent, that adapting an old house to modern living was not beyond the means of the middle-class householder. A combination of small bore central heating pipes and gasfired boilers solved the problem of heating draughty houses, and space heating meant that the contemporary desire for open planning could be achieved through taking down the walls between rooms.[60] Local authority improvement grants contributed to the upgrading of the housing stock, but the responsibility for rehabilitation came to lie with the individual householder and the process which became known as 'gentrification'.

In November 1968 St John's passed the management of their remaining North Oxford property into the hands of the chartered surveyors, Messrs Cluttons. While the day to day running of the estate passed beyond the bursary, the bursar did not give up all decisions, nor did the College turn away entirely from new development in the suburb. After Clutton's report on Walton Manor in July 1969, the fellows decided that a site on the north of St Bernard's Road should be developed as houses for letting to College servants and junior research fellows.[61] A cul-de-sac of houses designed by the Oxford Architects Partnership was ready for occupation by the autumn of 1973, and named after the late bursar, Arthur Garrard. However, much of the College's autonomy had already been eroded by the planning powers of the City Council, and by selling the bulk of their leaseholds, the guardianship of the interests of North Oxford had passed to the individual residents.

The reason that the Oxford Preservation Trust had been keen for the College to take on the task of redevelopment in 1960 was that under one landlord schemes could be co-ordinated and piecemeal and inappropriate development be avoided. Now it lay entirely with the City Council to decide what form the suburb would assume in future, and to many residents of North Oxford it was becoming obvious that there needed to be some new criteria for judging the merits of proposed developments. The University, experiencing a period of expansion, was perhaps the greatest threat to the continuation of the suburb as a residential area, and although there were attempts to encourage building on the east side of Magdalen bridge, the University looked to North Oxford as the natural area for expansion.

With the sciences well established around the Museum on the edge of the

98 The corner of Banbury and Keble Roads during the building of the Nuclear Physics Laboratory. It was scenes such as this which aroused the concern of the preservationists (Local Studies Library, Oxford Central Library).

Parks, parts of North Oxford were designated as potential sites for the extension of the University in Sir William Holford's study published in 1963. As long ago as January 1913 a request was made to St John's that they sell the land at the corner of Banbury and the Parks Roads for an engineering laboratory.[62] The site was occupied by Filsell's house and florist business and was larger than the usual suburban plot. The consensus among the members of the College at that time was that if the site was required for 'University purposes' no objection should be made. The laboratory was built in 1914 to the designs of W.C. Marshall in a prominent position at the entrance to the suburb.

In 1934 the University were interested in several North Oxford properties including the houses at the back of Keble College in Museum and Blackhall Roads, and those in what became known as the 'Keble Triangle', the island site bounded on the south by Keble Road and on the other two sides by Banbury and the Parks Roads. The apex of the triangle was already occupied by the engineering laboratory, so a further development of this area by the University would seem logical. The College offered the site to the University for £50,000, but refused to sell the houses in the Museum Road area.[63]

No further redevelopment occurred in the Keble Triangle until the mid-1950s when Basil Ward was asked to plan the site for new science buildings. A renewed confidence in scientific research was reflected in Ward's plan for a collection of buildings of a style and scale unfamiliar in Oxford. *The Builder* reported that instead of the usual traditional building materials 'Steel or reinforced concrete frames are suggested, with such sheet materials as glass, metal and plastics for exterior cladding'.[64] Since drawing up their Town Planning Scheme in 1925 the City Council had adopted a policy of building height control in the historic centre, and yet they approved tall structures on

204

this site. Ward's scheme was not fully implemented, but the appearance of the buildings that were erected during the 1960s, the Department of Engineering and the Nuclear Physics Laboratory, were evidence of an aggressive and to some an unwelcome penetration of the University science area into North Oxford (Plate 98).

The city's Development Plan designated North Oxford as a residential area, but St John's supported the University's application in June 1962 to have sites in Banbury Road zoned for 'University purposes' in the city's new Town Plan. Perhaps mindful of the developments in the Keble Triangle, when they sold a site on the east side of Banbury Road to the University in January 1965, the College insisted that the site be developed in a manner 'compatible with the residential character of the neighbouring area'.[65] The houses involved were 56 to 64 Banbury Road and 1 to 11 Bradmore Road and the site was part of the area identified by Sir William Holford as suitable for the expansion of the science area. The University decided to devote the site to the new Pitt-Rivers Museum. Although the museum introduced a departure from the provisions of the City's Development Plan, the Planning Committee were satisfied that it fitted well enough into the council's intentions. However, since the proposed development was on such a large scale, the committee decided to hear any local objections, although they seem already, before the hearing, to have made their decision to give planning permission.[66]

The eventual design by the Italian master of concrete, Pier Luigi Nervi in collaboration with Powell and Moya, included a large concrete rotunda in the centre of which was placed a latticed dome which would contain sub-tropical plants. The walls of the circular structure were to be 35 feet high, and the apex of the dome 90 feet above the pavement level, and, as the *Architects' Journal* pointed out, the rotunda was 'in direct contrast to neighbouring Victorian buildings'.[67] Despite the intrusive character of the design, it was generally admired,[68] but it is instructive to listen to the objections which were made at the Planning Committee hearing in July 1966, before details of the design were known.

One of the objectors found that the scale of the proposed museum would interfere with the amenities of the neighbourhood, especially increasing the amount of traffic and the need for parking in a residential area.[69] The Oxford Architectural and Historical Society disagreed with the Planning Committee that the museum could be reconciled with the Development Plan which specified for the site buildings 'appropriate for a special type of University use compatible with a residential area'. The society suggested that the houses on the site be given over to University residential or hostel accommodation. This suggestion applied particularly to Nos 60 and 62, and in her submission Councillor Miss Ann Spokes made the point that these houses had been included in the provisional list of buildings of special architectural or historic interest under Section 32 of the 1962 Town and Country Planning Act. No 60 was one of Wilkinson's more gracious houses and No 62 was by E.G. Bruton with a carved tympanum over the front door whose design was attributed to Hungerford Pollen (Plate 99).[70] No 64, another Bruton house,

99 No 62 Banbury Road, E.G. Bruton, 1865, one of the houses threatened by the proposed Pitt-Rivers Museum in 1966.

and John Gibbs' Nos 56 and 58, would also have had to be demolished along with Nos 60 and 62, but because the latter two had provisional listing, Miss Spokes argued, they ought to be preserved.

The Planning Committee overrode the objections and proposed to give outline planning permission for the museum, but this was temporarily delayed by a vote of the City Council. The decision provoked wide interest and the debate was reported in *The Times*:

> Alderman D.N. Chester, Warden of Nuffield College, said the siting of the museum between Banbury Road and Bradmore Road would widen the 'dead area' at the centre of Oxford. The residential fringes would be become narrower and narrower . . . Councillor Peter Spokes, Sheriff of Oxford, said the museum would be too large for its surrounding. It was a preposterous overloading of the four acre site.[71]

Although the council finally gave outline planning permission, in the end lack of funds defeated the scheme. However, the appeal to the Town and Country Planning Act to preserve the North Oxford houses revealed an attitude to the houses and the suburb far removed from the scorn in which they had been so recently held.

There were earlier indications that the domestic architecture of Victoria's reign might at least be worth reconsidering. That Goodhart-Rendel, as noted in chapter five, chose to devote three of his Slade lectures in 1935 and 1936 to the serious analysis of the architecture of North Oxford was significant, although his purpose was pedagogical in order to show the student that discrimination was possible in any style. In 1948 John Summerson published in *The Architectural Review* an article on middle-class speculative houses of the nineteenth century.[72] In this article he set out the design characteristics of the 'lower school of designers', not as debased versions derived from works by bigger names, but as worth consideration in their own right. By the 1950s Victorian architecture was beginning to be rehabilitated. Kenneth Clark's book of 1928, *The Gothic Revival*, was republished in 1950, but perhaps it was thanks chiefly to John Betjeman that the public came to appreciate Victorian architecture through the associations that it was his genius to bestow on previously unloved buildings. In *An Oxford University Chest* he included an appreciation of North Oxford, and this was published as early as 1938.[73]

The renewed interest in Victorian houses coincided with a period of general redevelopment in the country as nineteenth-century leases fell in, and the preservation lobby was forged in the struggle to keep something of the past intact. It came to be accepted that attempting to save individual buildings which could not be considered outstanding of their kind was best achieved through conservation areas. In 1967 the Oxford City Council considered a scheme for the protection of North Oxford which would include Canterbury Road, Church Walk, North Parade Avenue, Park Town, Norham Gardens, Norham Road, and Winchester Road. The thinking behind the scheme was explained in the Planning Committee minutes:

> This area includes some of the best Victorian buildings in the City, a number of which are already listed under Section 32 of the Town and Country Planning Act, 1962, as being of special architectural or historical interest, but the Committee feels that it is important to preserve the character of the whole of the area and that it is not enough to protect individual buildings.[74]

When the Civic Amenities Act was passed in 1967 the committee decided to designate their North Oxford area a conservation area, which they did in 1968, and in 1972 the area was extended to take in the whole of Norham Manor, including Bradmore, Crick, and Fyfield Roads. The reasons for declaring at least part of North Oxford a conservation area were set out by the City's Architect: 'From the planning point of view this is a well integrated housing area, with its own church (St Philip and St James') and its own shopping centre (North Parade) – a probably unique example of a well preserved Victorian suburb still largely unspoiled by subsequent development.'[75] Since so many houses had already changed from their original residential use and since the freeholds of the houses in the central area of North Oxford were now being sold, it was considered that there was a real need for the sort of control that a conservation area could give. This was a long way from the planning commonplaces of twenty years before when the suburb was thought a desert, and Thomas Sharp regarded even the 'grandeur' of the scale of North Oxford misplaced.

During the 1950s and 1960s North Oxford was in a situation not dissimilar to a hundred years before when as a working suburb its various functions began to be stripped away. It has been seen that while it was in that stage of transition between agriculture and building, the suburb was considered available for any number of purposes. A cemetery was laid out on its land and attempts were made to build a workhouse there and to lay a railway line. Thanks to F.J. Morrell and Dr Adams the most disruptive proposals were discouraged and the residential suburb was allowed to develop. Since the houses of North Oxford depended so much on individual taste it was to be expected that they would soon be changed by successive owners who, however, carried out their extensions and additions under the watchful eye of the College. Social change was more difficult to control, and change in the University and the town had its effect, but as long as the suburb retained its function as a residential suburb, its integrity remained unquestioned. Although its basic function remained residential even in the 1960s, other functions had begun to make inroads on houses no longer suited to the inhabitants' needs or tastes. At this point the suburb again became vulnerable to radical change, made more so by the various pieces of legislation, intended to protect tenants, but which made it impossible for St John's to retain the estate as an entity. By keeping control of North Oxford for so long, the College had ensured that despite changes in the function of many of the houses, the suburb had maintained much of its character. When the College relinquished their control and so abandoned the possibility of planned redevelopment, the conservation lobby was able to convince the City Council to take some responsbility at least for the general character of North Oxford.

CONCLUSION

THE WAY NORTH Oxford developed had much to do with the sort of institution St John's College was during the nineteenth century. The long term interest the College took in their endowment property meant that they could develop their estate slowly, holding out for the sort of suburb they believed would retain its value over the longest period. In this way St John's was like the aristocratic landlords described by David Cannadine in *Lords and Landlords* who relied on the continuity of their family when they first granted long building leases on their land.[1] But the College was perhaps even more like the Foundling Hospital in London which, as Donald Olsen has pointed out, was vitally concerned with its Bloomsbury estate because it lay in such close proximity to the hospital's own establishment, and the quality of the estate and its management reflected on the Foundling Hospital itself.[2] Likewise North Oxford was on the doorstep of St John's in the very town where it was most important for the College to enjoy prestige and approval.

The Beaumont Street development showed the College interested in building around Oxford at least by the 1820s and probably before. As pressure was put on St Giles's Fields by various nineteenth-century needs such as the municipal cemetery, railway lines, and the proposed new workhouse, the pasture land and nursery gardens there began to take on value as a potential development area. The intention of the College to profit from the coherent development of their North Oxford property seems to have been formulated at least by the early 1850s when they began vigorously to fight off the schemes proposed by the railway companies and the Board of Guardians. However, the College was circumscribed by legislation which hindered them from developing their land as they would wish.

But for the combined efforts of the College's steward, F.J. Morrell, and the senior fellow, Dr Adams, both of whom made sure that the building initiative did not falter, it would have been possible for the College to have been defeated by the difficulties presented by such obstacles as the short-term beneficial leases. Even when the first lots to be let in Woodstock Road failed to attract interest, Morrell and Adams did not give up the project. Besides the difficulties placed in the way of the College by virtue of its quasi-ecclesiastical status, it had also to wait on the maturing of financial structures in Oxford. Seckham had resorted to a tontine to raise the capital for Park

Town, and development may have been slow at first on the North Oxford estate because there was not yet in place a sufficient network of borrowers and lenders.

Capital for house building was provided by individual investors, and Morrell himself made loans to a number of builders and leaseholders. Those leaseholders who were able to draw on family money from outside the city spread the net wider. However, many of the smaller builders depended on building societies and organisations like the Oxford Building and Investment Company. These financial institutions were nonetheless still primitive instruments of saving and borrowing, and they were vulnerable to slumps in the market. It was also argued at the time that they artificially sustained the market when demand dropped, so that builders and lenders were encouraged to engage in a market which was no longer viable. In 1883 the demise of the Oxford Building and Investment Company broke up a local, but extensive network of lenders and borrowers, and when building began again in North Oxford, the suburb was more or less under the control of one developer, Walter Gray.

Although North Oxford is now considered a fine example of the Victorian suburb, it shows no innovation in terms of its layout. The physical success of suburbs like North Oxford seems to have resided in the union of two models; the inner suburb with its economical division into lots, and the picturesque arrangement found in the suburban village. The layout of North Oxford is very straightforward, following roughly a north-south grid. The Norham Manor area was the only one in which any kind of picturesque layout was attempted and that was soon lost in the practical task of getting the houses built. Nevertheless, the generous plot sizes, the judicious position of the most striking houses, the encouragement to retain mature trees, and to plant front as well as back gardens, resulted in a satisfying, picturesque effect.

The layout suited well the sort of development St John's was interested in undertaking. Unlike many private landlords, the College could afford to take their time to release land, waiting on the market when it was down and responding to it when it rose again. Their interests did not always mesh with the more short-term interests of their builders, and men like Frederick Codd could be squeezed between the slump in the market and the demand by the College to maintain the high value of the houses. The College could also contribute to an already existing slump by refusing to release land as they did at the end of the 1870s. Since they relied at this time far more on their agricultural revenues, the College were more attuned to the slump in agricultural prices than they were to the requirements of the housing market, and when they found that they could not afford to supply the infrastructure required if they released additional suburban building land, they refrained from doing so.

The point when the College seriously considered developing North Oxford had little to do with the dons being allowed to marry, something which happened only gradually and started twenty years after the suburb was begun. The early residents of the suburb were drawn from the commercial and professional families of Oxford and gradually the town also gained a reputation, especially among women, as a pleasant place to which to retire. Eventually the suburb also became the domicile of many within the University and the colleges. The University at first supplied the professors and the rule requiring members of Congregation to reside within a mile and a half of Carfax guaranteed that they would find it convenient to cluster in North Oxford. When they were finally allowed to marry, the same rule led the college fellows to seek houses in the suburb, if their finances permitted. After World War I it was no longer necessary for members of Congregation to live within the one and a half mile limit and the incentive to reside so close to the centre lessened. However, the University and the colleges, by virtue of their attachment to their ancient buildings, remained in the centre, and North Oxford continued to be an attractive place in which to live.

Today the split between town and gown does not have as much resonance as it once had. The rise of the national retail chains has taken its toll among the local independent tradesmen, and the days when James Hughes, the grocer, and Henry Hatch, the bootmaker, could afford to buy and run prominent North Oxford houses are long since gone. There is now a greater interweaving of the interests of business and the University. For example, publishing, which in recent years has flourished in Oxford, depends to a large extent on the availability of a highly educated staff and a ready supply of manuscripts and expertise from the academic community.[3] The greatest split in North Oxford is now probably between permanent residents who own their own houses and those who reside in the suburb temporarily while they follow a course or work at fixed-term employment, usually in the University or the colleges.

During the twenty years since St John's began to sell its properties in North Oxford, a pattern of corporate and private ownership has emerged in the suburb. The College still owns approximately 200 dwellings, divided half and half between flats and houses. Some of these are occupied by the College's staff and tutors, while others are let on the open market. St John's has continued to sell houses, but since the 1988 Housing Act and the lifting of restrictions on the rents of new tenancies, the rented sector has become once more a viable option when the College decides how best to deal with what suburban properties remain in its possession. Those colleges, such as St Antony's, Lady Margaret Hall, and St Hugh's, whose main premises are located in the suburb, have taken the freehold of houses in their vicinity, and the older colleges have also bought houses to accommodate their tutors and students. Other institutions engaged in secretarial and language instruction have long found North Oxford conducive to their work, and the larger houses suit their needs for premises and accommodation.

Single families are still to be found in the smaller houses, while many of the larger ones have been turned into flats. Those streets such as Kingston and Southmoor Roads, intended by the College for artisans and clerks, have been colonised by University families, and the working classes have all but disappeared from the suburb. The social centre of gravity for single family occupancy has moved north from the large houses built in the early days of

North Oxford to the Polstead Road area on the northwest and the Bardwell estate on the east, but without Norham Manor and the streets around St Philip and St James, these northern districts would be the poorer. If there is conflict of interest in the suburb, it is between the private residents who especially appreciate the low density and mature planting, and the institutions, tempted as they are to expand into their generous front and back gardens, thus changing the character of the suburb. It is the responsibility of the City Council, under the provisions of the Conservation Area, to safeguard the character of North Oxford and to arbitrate between the various interests when they conflict.

Goodhart-Rendel predicted in 1936 that there would be a pendulum swing back to a taste for nineteenth-century gothic, and it was a new appreciation of the style in the 1960s which helped establish North Oxford as a Conservation Area.[4] The Conservation Area of North Oxford now very nearly coincides with the boundaries of St John's former estate, but this was achieved only after the piecemeal designation of different areas as they appeared under threat. Norham Manor and Park Town in the southeast were the first to be given Conservation Area status in 1968 and later were added the district around Rawlinson Road, Walton Manor and the Bardwell estate. Although the designation of a Conservation Area did not exclude new developments, it ensured that the City Council was given the opportunity of scrutinising any proposed changes to existing buildings and any schemes for development.[5] In recognition that planting was a vital part of the character of the suburb, permission was needed to remove existing trees and the 'characteristic vegetation' of the area was to be retained through replanting where necessary. One important aspect of the conservation procedure was the obligation on the part of the council to make known publicly any application for development which might affect the character or appearance of the areas. Any representations from the public were then to be taken into account when the applications were considered, and in this way it was believed that ample opportunity would be given to groups interested in the preservation of the suburb to make their views known.

North Oxford, to retain its character must remain identifiable as a picturesque suburban estate, and the concept behind 'the conservation area,' that it would ensure the retention of the general amenities of the area while allowing controlled changes to individual houses, was considered by some sufficient for this purpose. However, as has been shown some of the houses in the suburb are important examples of domestic architecture of their period, and as such should be preserved. This was the idea sustaining the attempt to ensure listed status under the 1962 Town and Country Planning Act of the houses in Banbury Road. Only Nos 60 and 62 were successfully listed, but as was seen in the previous chapter, when their site was required for the proposed Pitt-Rivers Museum, they were considered dispensible. Despite campaigning by the Victorian Group of the Oxford Architectural and Historical Society, set up in 1966 to defend Victorian architecture in Oxford and especially in North Oxford, the houses of North Oxford remain under-represented in the lists of buildings protected for their architectural

100 Spire of St Philip and St James.

value. During the 1960s and early 1970s a number of architecturally significant houses were lost, for example the house designed by Wilkinson at 31 Banbury Road and that by Edis at 80 Banbury Road. Latterly the conservation area has prevented demolition, but many houses of distinction have been given unsympathetic additions and their gardens have been eroded by infill building, and while change has been piecemeal, it has also been cumulative so that many important houses have now been transformed almost beyond recognition.

There is no doubt that the City Council and the conservation groups have had some success in retaining the character of North Oxford over the last twenty years, but saving the physical fabric of the suburb is different from preserving the suburb itself and this is apparent in the case of the church of St Philip and St James. A change of taste has favoured the smaller, more adaptable churches, and when the contraction in the number of North Oxford churchgoers led to an episcopal plan for pastoral re-organisation, the decision to close a church fell on St Philip and St James. Since it was acquired from the diocese by the Oxford Centre for Mission Studies the church is only rarely used for public worship, and the congregations of North Oxford are to be found at High Church St Margaret's and Evangelical St Andrew's. Although St Philip and St James was such a focal point of the estate, its physical presence is now its only immediate connection with the suburb. It may be that the high architectural quality of the church made it less adaptable to present day religious observance which often involves less liturgical formality (Plate 100).

The society which evolved in the suburb has given a meaning to the name 'North Oxford' which goes beyond the geographical location bounded by the old estate of St John's College. The social composition of North Oxford came to have a greater share of salaried professionals than had most suburbs, and the way of life which emerged under their influence is still enormously attractive and still emulated. A contemporary commentator claims that the 'North Oxford ladies' are still resident and that the social values of academic families hold sway, even among those who cannot claim academic credentials.[6] Thanks to its proximity to the University, North Oxford has gained affectionate notoriety among generations of undergraduates and academics, and there must have been many readers who smiled with recognition when they came across Barbara Pym's posthumously published novel, *Crampton Hodnet*. When the novel appeared in 1985 it was acknowledged as a cleverly observed description of North Oxford society despite the fact that the book had been written in 1940. But the fate of St Philip and St James illustrates that the social life of the suburb has changed, and there are indications that further changes are in the offing despite the preservation of the physical fabric of North Oxford.

There are differing opinions at present about the social composition of the suburb, even among the residents. The decline in academic salaries in comparison to those of other professions has put University families at a disadvantage when they seek to buy freehold houses in North Oxford. An important reason why the colleges hold property in the suburb is to ensure that some of their members, both staff and students, can still afford to live there. The unknown factor in North Oxford today is what will happen in the future as Oxford becomes more integrated into a larger economic region beyond its borders. The city is now within easy commuting distance of a number of expanding commercial centres from London to Bristol and as far away as Birmingham. Already there is a demand for substantial houses and newly converted luxury flats in North Oxford by those who work well outside the Oxford area and are able to pay the high house prices. But rather than wanting to redevelop their properties in a contemporary style, developers are anxious to maintain the character of the suburb through building neo-gothic additions to the original houses. Some of the larger houses are being reclaimed by the more affluent families, and the secretarial and language schools are finding themselves neighbours with people who have very different interests from their own. North Oxford may well be on the threshold of another phase in its history and the pressures of prosperity could bring about the changes that have been resisted for the past twenty years.

APPENDIX
Gazetter

IN THE COMPILATION of this gazetteer, the lease has been the basic source of information. Every house in North Oxford had a lease, whether for ninety-nine years or for sixty-six, and copies of these have been kept in the Muniments Room of St John's College. Although the lease indicated that the carcass of the house had been erected, it did not necessarily mean that the house was completed. However, of all the documents connected with the building of the houses in North Oxford the leases are the most consistent in their information and they also reveal who first owned the houses, although not always who lived in them since many were let to tenants by their lessees.

For each address in North Oxford the date of the first lease, the name of the leaseholder, and the leaseholder's occupation are given. When the first lessee was a builder or building society, and the lease was held for no more than three years, this lease has been regarded as part of the building process and the name of the second leaseholder has been given. Where the information is available, the name of the architect and the builder have been added. Supplementary information on the architects and builders has been derived from the Oxford City Engineer's Office *Register of Plans Deposited* and from the list of Victorian buildings, both held in the Local Studies Library of the Oxford Central Library. The *Oxford University Calendar* has supplied the identity of the colleges of those fellows who took leases.

For the purposes of the gazetteer North Oxford includes only those streets laid out from the beginning of the College's development in 1860. The southern boundary follows a crooked line from Walton Well Road in the west, along Leckford Road, Bevington Road, and Museum Road in the east. The small streets between Observatory Street and Plantation Road are not included, nor are Cranham and Juxon Streets in Jericho. Bainton, Rawlinson, and Marston Ferry Roads simply follow the northern boundary of the College's property. The houses in Banbury and Woodstock Roads included in the gazetteer do not fall neatly within the boundaries because the College owned some land bordering the turnpike roads north and south of the limits of their suburban estate. Obvious anomalies have been explained in the notes.

Address	Date of Lease	Architect	Builder	Leaseholder	Occupation
Bainton Rd					
1	1912			William Shelton	Upholsterer
3	1912			William Shelton	Upholsterer
5	1912			William Shelton	Upholsterer
7	1912			William Shelton	Upholsterer
9	1912			William Shelton	Upholsterer
11	1912			William Shelton	Upholsterer
19[1]	1928		Wooldridge	Elliston & Cavell	Draper
21	1928		Wooldridge	Fred C. Howard	College Servant
23	1909		Wooldridge	John Wooldridge	Builder
25	1909		Wooldridge	E. Northcote-Green	Not Known
27	1909		Wooldridge	Jane Wooldridge	Wife/Builder
29	1909		Wooldridge	Jane Wooldridge	Wife/Builder
31	1909		Wooldridge	John Wooldridge	Builder
33	1906		Wooldridge	William Hunt	Bookseller
35	1909		Hutchins	Samuel Hutchins	Builder
37	1908		Hutchins	Percival Aldridge	Rent Collector
39	1909		Hutchins	George Cooper	Baker
41	1910		Hutchins	Samuel Hutchins	Builder
43	1912		Hutchins	Samuel Hutchins	Builder
45	1912		Hutchins	Samuel Hutchins	Builder
47	1912		Hutchins	Samuel Hutchins	Builder
49	1912		Hutchins	Samuel Hutchins	Builder
51	1912		Hutchins	Emma Blencowe	Widow
53	1912		Hutchins	Clara Blencowe	Spinster
55	1911		Wooldridge	Percy Phipps	Organ Builder
57	1911		Wooldridge	Charles Exon	Baker
59	1912		Wooldridge	Sydney Hunt	Cashier
61	1911		Wooldridge	Percy Whitman	Clerk
63	1912		Wooldridge	John Pierce	Engineer
65	1912		Wooldridge	Louisa Judge	Spinster
67	1919		Wooldridge	Dorothy Ward	Spinster
69	1913		Wooldridge	A. Reginald Heath	Dentist
71	1924		Wooldridge	William Poynton	Tutor
73	1924		Wooldridge	Sarah Badcock	Spinster
75	1930		Wooldridge	Leonard Alden	Farmer
77	1930		Wooldridge	Louis Gardiner	Auctioneer
79	1931		Wooldridge	Wooldridge & Simpson	Builder
81	1931		Wooldridge	Harry Collins	Esquire
83	1931		Wooldridge	Wooldridge & Simpson	Builder
87	1930		Wooldridge	Ellen Dore	Widow
89	1929		Wooldridge	Julia Shepherd	Spinster
91	1930		Wooldridge	Percy Whitman	Clerk
93	1928		Wooldridge	Thomas Robinson	Esquire
95	1927		Simpson	Jane Lewis	Spinster
97	1925		Wooldridge	Herbert Quinton	Architect
2	1910		Simpson	George Simpson	Builder
4	1910		Simpson	George Simpson	Builder
6	1924		Wooldridge	Ellen Crocker	Spinster
8	1924		Wooldridge	Mary Hawkins	Spinster
10	1910		Inness	John Wooldridge	Builder
12	1910		Inness	John Wooldridge	Builder

Address	Date of Lease	Architect	Builder	Leaseholder	Occupation
Banbury Rd					
27	1882	J.J. Stevenson		Charlotte Green	Widow
29	1882	J.J. Stevenson		Thomas Omond	Bursar, SJC
31[2]	1866	Wilkinson		Geo Ward	Esquire
33	1867	E.G. Bruton		Rev J.V. Durell	Clergyman
35	1868	Codd		George Kitchen	Lecturer, ChCh
37	1866	Codd		Frances Norris	Spinster
39	1867	Codd	M. Gray	Frederick Codd	Architect
41	1867	Codd	M. Gray	Frederick Codd	Architect
43	1870	T.E. Collcutt	Honour & Castle	James Taylor	Organist, New Coll
45	1870	T.E. Collcutt	Honour & Castle	Margaretta Tyrwhitt	Widow
47	1870	Cross	Dorn	William Cross	Builder
49	1870	Cross	Dorn	William Cross	Builder
51	1872	Dorn	Dorn	John Dorn	Builder
53	1872	Dorn	Dorn	John Dorn	Builder
55	1870	Codd	M. Gray	William Nevell	Corndealer
57	1870	Codd	M. Gray	Charles Underhill	Grocer
59	1871	Codd	M. Gray	Frances Yorke	Spinster
61	1871	Codd	M. Gray	Thomas Brindley	Gentleman
61A[3]	1897	H.W. Moore	Sims	John Gee	Nurseryman
81[4]	1873	Codd		Charlotte Wyatt	Spinster
83	1873	Codd		Edward Bracher	Gentleman
85	1873	Codd		Capt George Elwes	Esquire
87	1873	Codd		George Mallam	Solicitor
99	1887	Pike & Mess.	Kingerlee	William Speer	Esquire
101	1886	H.W. Moore	Money	John Massie	Gentleman
103	1886	H.W. Moore		George Mallam	Solicitor
105	1886	Wilk. & Moore	Kingerlee	Maj Henry Adair	Army
107	1887	H.W. Moore	Money	Rev Thomas Gorman	Clergyman
109	1889	J.W. Messenger	Wilkins	J.W. Messenger	Auctioneer
111	1888	H.W. Moore	Money	Joseph Billiat	Gentleman
113	1888	H.W. Moore	Money	Robert Abbott	Tutor, Non-Coll
36	1869		Thos Jones	Samuel Pottage	Tailor
38	1869		Thos Jones	Mary Windle	Spinster
40	1869		Thos Jones	Rev Stephen Edwardes	Fellow Merton
42	1869		Thos Jones	Jane Blachford	Spinster
44	1868			Elizabeth Beaumont	Widow
46	1870		Thos Jones	Thomas Jones	Builder
48	1867			Emma Bates	Spinster
52	1870	Codd	Reynolds	Priscilla Sellon	Spinster
54	1866	John Gibbs	Selby	Thomas Arnold	Tutor
56	1867	John Gibbs	Young	Henry Hatch	Draper
58	1867	John Gibbs		William Walsh	Chemist
60	1869	Wilkinson		Thos Cousins	Chemist
62	1865	E.G. Bruton	Wyatt	Rev R. St J. Tyrwhitt	Clergyman
64	1873	E.G. Bruton	Symm	John Weaving	Corndealer
66	1874	Codd		Catherine Fry	Widow
66A	1863	Wilkinson		James Hughes	Grocer
72[5]	1885	Wilk. & Moore	Brucker	Rev Sir J Hawkins	Clergyman
74	1885	Wilk. & Moore		George Baker	Loc Ex Delegacy
76	1885	Pike & Mess.		Margaret Jeune	Widow
78	1885	Pike & Mess.		Dr James Murray	Editor

Address	Date of Lease	Architect	Builder	Leaseholder	Occupation
80	1886	R.W. Edis		Prof A.V. Dicey	Prof English Law
82	1896	H.W. Moore	Money	William B. Gamlen	Esquire
84	1896	H.W. Moore	Money	Edward Gay	Esquire
86	1895	H.W. Moore	Money	Bertha de lay Hey	Wife/Clergyman
88	1896	H.W. Moore	Money	Edward Gay	Esquire
90	1890	H.W. Moore		Alfred J. Butler	Fellow, BNC
92	1891	H.W. Moore		Harry Clarke	Merchant
94	1891	H.W. Moore	Money	Falconer Madan	Fellow, BNC
96	1892	H.W. Moore	Money	Walter Gray	Auctioneer
98	1892	H.W. Moore	Money	Rev Henry Hall	Clergyman
100	1893	H.W. Moore	Money	Rev Llewellyn Bebb	Fellow, BNC
102	1893	H.W. Moore	Money	Rev Joseph Maude	Fellow, Hertf
104	1894	H.W. Moore	Money	Sir Chas Aichison	Ind Civil Servant
106	1895	H.W. Moore	Money	Rev Louis Cockerell	Clergyman
108	1896	H.W. Moore	Money	Edmund Brooks	Auctioneer
110	1896	H.W. Moore	Money	Edward Wingfield	Esquire
112	1897	H.W. Moore	Money	Harry Cooper	Corndealer
114	1899	H.W. Moore	Money	Maria Waterman	Widow
116	1898	H.W. Moore	Money	Thomas Bullock	Prof Chinese
118	1904	H.W. Moore	Kingerlee	Charles Kingerlee	Builder
120	1904	H.W. Moore	Kingerlee	Henry Kingerlee	Builder
122	1923		Wooldridge	Henry Sarson	Esquire
160[6]	1903	Geo Gardiner	Pipkin	Geo Gardiner	Architect
162	1901	Geo Gardiner	Pipkin	Geo Gardiner	Architect
164	1901	Geo Gardiner	Pipkin	Geo Gardiner	Architect
166	1901	Geo Gardiner	Pipkin	Clifford Cunningham	Gentleman
168	1901	Geo Gardiner	Pipkin	Henry Abrams	Antique Dealer
170	1902	Geo Gardiner	Pipkin	Geo Gardiner	Architect
172	1902	Geo Gardiner	Pipkin	Geo Gardiner	Architect
174	1902	Geo Gardiner	Pipkin	Henry Abrams	Antique Dealer
176	1902	Geo Gardiner	Pipkin	Henry Abrams	Antique Dealer
178	1902	Geo Gardiner	Pipkin	Patty Gardiner	Wife/Architect
180	1902	Geo Gardiner	Pipkin	Patty Gardiner	Wife/Architect
218	1878			John Gardiner	Clerk
220	1878			John Gardiner	Clerk

Bardwell Rd

Address	Date of Lease	Architect	Builder	Leaseholder	Occupation
1	1891	H.W. Moore		Ernest Hardy	Esquire
3	1893	J.C. Gray		Robert Clifton	Prof Exp. Philosophy
5	1892	H. Quinton	Walker	Ada Mary Codner	Wife/Ironmonger
7	1892	H. Quinton	Walker	Frederick Hawkins	Gentleman
9	1894	H. Quinton	Sturman	Edmund Brooks	Auctioneer
11	1894	H. Quinton		Edmund Brooks	Auctioneer
13	1897	H.W. Moore	Buckingham	Catherine Phillips	Wife/Solicitor
15	1895	H.W. Moore	Buckingham	Jane Wilson	Wife/Clergyman
17	1898	H.W. Moore	Buckingham	Geo Hughes	Bank Manager
19	1895	H. Quinton	Wyatt	Caroline Carpenter	Widow
21	1898	H. Quinton	Wyatt	Arthur Pilkington	Esquire
2	1893	Radcl. Wat.	Jarvis	Richard Green	Esquire
4	1893	Radcl. Wat.	Jarvis	Edwin Elliott	Prof Mathematics
6	1894	Radcl. Wat.	Jarvis	Robert Buckell	Auctioneer

Address	Date of Lease	Architect	Builder	Leaseholder	Occupation
8	1894	Radcl. Wat.	Jarvis	Robert Buckell	Auctioneer
10	1894	Radcl. Wat.	Jarvis	Emmeline Wood	Wife/Clergyman
12	1894	Radcl. Wat.	Jarvis	Louisa Worner	Widow
14	1892	H. Quinton	Capel	Jane Emily Booker	Spinster
16	1894	H. Quinton	Capel	John Buckingham	Builder
18	1894	H.W. Moore	Buckingham	John Buckingham	Builder
20	1893	H.W. Moore	Buckingham	Henry Underhill	Merchant
22	1894	H.W. Moore	Buckingham	John Buckingham	Builder
24	1897	H.W. Moore	Buckingham	Alfred Boffin	Confectioner
26	1904	Radcl. Wat.	Jarvis	Julia Shepherd	Spinster
28	1921	Radcl. Wat.	Jarvis	Octavius Milman	Army, Retired
30	1895		Jarvis	Thomas Bell-Dixon	Gentleman
32	1895		Jarvis	Thomas Bell-Dixon	Gentleman
Dragon School	1896	C. Lynam	Kingerlee	Charles Lynam	Schoolmaster

Belbroughton Rd

Address	Date of Lease	Architect	Builder	Leaseholder	Occupation
1	1926	C. Wright	Organ	Marian Buchanan	Spinster
3	1927	C. Wright	Organ	Lois Gane-Wright	Wife/Ind Civil Servant
5	1927	C. Wright	Organ	Bertram Hodgson	Esquire
7	1927	C. Wright	Organ	Caroline Tyson	Spinster
9	1931	Fisher & Trubshaw	Hutchins	Gerald McMichael	Physician
11	1932	N.W. Harrison	Hutchins	Charles Hutchins	Builder
13	1927		Benfield & Loxley	Mary Macdonell	Wife/Esquire
15	1928	C. Wright	Organ	Robin Collingwood	Fellow, Pembroke
2	1938	Mills & Shepherd	Benfield & Loxley	Hester Shepherd	Spinster
4	1926	C. Wright	Organ	Marjory Scott	Widow
8	1925	T. Rayson	Hinkins & Frewin	Charles Alexander	Esquire
10	1925	C. Wright	Organ	Margaret Baird	Spinster

Bevington Rd

Address	Date of Lease	Architect	Builder	Leaseholder	Occupation
1	1869	Codd	M. Gray	John Townsend	Accountant
2	1869			Sara Whiting	Spinster
3	1868			Joseph Castle	Engineer
4	1868			Rowland Wheeler	Printer
5	1867			Sleeman Lovis	Commercial Traveller
6	1867			Sleeman Lovis	Commercial Traveller
7	1868		M. Gray	Standish Betteris	College Cook
8	1868	Codd		Anna Bertram	Spinster
9	1868	Codd		James Ryman	Print Seller
10	1868	Codd		James Ryman	Print Seller
11	1871	Wilkinson	Dorn	Sarah Venables	Widow
12	1874	Wilkinson	Dorn	James Lewis	Gentleman
13	1870	Wilkinson	Dorn	Maria Parsons	Spinster

Address	Date of Lease	Architect	Builder	Leaseholder	Occupation
Blackhall Rd					
1	1865			Moses Allnutt	College Servant
2	1865			Frederick Irwin	Hairdresser
3	1865			Frederick Irwin	Hairdresser
4	1866		Dorn	Joseph Richardson	Schoolmaster
5	1866		Dorn	Mrs M.A. Herbert	Widow
6	1867		Dorn	Edwin Elliott	Bootmaker
7	1867		Dorn	Edwin Elliott	Bootmaker
8	1873			Magdalen Turner	Spinster
9	1875			Richard Spiers	Alderman
Bradmore Rd					
1	1870	Codd	Hall	Emma Browell	Widow
2	1871	Codd	Hall	John Aldridge	House Steward
3	1871	Hall	Hall	Elizabeth Beaumont	Widow
4	1872	Hall	Hall	John Chillingworth	Farmer
5	1872		Reynolds	Sidney Owen	Fellow, ChCh
6	1873		Reynolds	Thomas Barclay	Esquire
7	1872	Galp. & Shir.	Dover	Thomas Barrett	Timber Merchant
8	1872	Galp. & Shir.	Dover	Thomas Barrett	Timber Merchant
9	1874	Galp. & Shir.	Dover	Thomas Arnall	Postmaster
10	1873	Galp. & Shir.	Dover	Rev William Bebb	Clergyman
11	1873	Galp. & Shir.	Dover	Rev Henry DeBrisay	Fellow, Univ
12	1873	Galp. & Shir.	Dover	John Galpin	Auctioneer
13	1874	Codd	M. Gray	William Esson	Fellow, Merton
14	1872	Codd	M. Gray	Charlotte Neate	Spinster
15	1872	Codd	M. Gray	Henry J. Sides	Librarian
16	1872	Codd	M. Gray	Charles Underhill	Grocer
17	1872	Codd	M. Gray	Thomas Humphrey Ward	Fellow, BNC
18	1873	Galp. & Shir.	Dover	Rev Anthony Mayhew	Clergyman
19	1873	Galp. & Shir.	Dover	Beatrice Harington	Spinster
20	1873	Galp. & Shir.	Dover	Dowager Lady Buxton	Widow
Canterbury Rd					
1	1873	Codd		John White	Fellow, New Coll
2	1873	Codd		Frederick Crow	Draper
3	1875	Codd		Robert Hills	Photographer
4	1874	Codd		William Baker	Upholsterer
5	1874	Codd		Rev Henry Pickard	Inspector of Schools
6	1884	Codd		Rev Edwin Hatch	V-P St Mary's
7	1876	Codd		Ann Ward	Widow
8	1874	Codd		William Sidgwick	Gentleman
9	1876	Codd		Frederick Codd	Architect
10	1874	Codd		Robert Hills	Photographer
11	1873	Codd		Mary Hammons	Spinster

Address	Date of Lease	Architect	Builder	Leaseholder	Occupation
12	1873	Codd		William Houldsworth	Clergyman
13	1873	Codd		Rev William Bliss	Fellow, Magdalen

Chadlington Rd

Address	Date of Lease	Architect	Builder	Leaseholder	Occupation
3	1917			W.H. Perkin	Prof Chemistry
5	1915	N.W. Harrison	Capel	Noah Capel	Builder
7	1915	N.W. Harrison	Capel	Noah Capel	Builder
9	1912	N.W. Harrison	Inness	George Inness	Builder
11	1910	F. Mountain	Inness	Edwin Cannan	MA
2	1913	N.W. Harrison	Organ	Sally Walker	Spinster
4	1915	N.W. Harrison	Grimsley	Thomas Grimsley	Builder
8	1911	N.W. Harrison	Grimsley	Francis Budd	Esquire
10	1912	N.W. Harrison	Grimsley	William Geldart	Prof English Law
12	1911	N.W. Harrison	Grimsley	Thomas Grimsley	Builder
14	1912	N.W. Harrison	Grimsley	Fred Blencowe	Builder
16	1912	N.W. Harrison	Grimsley	Fred Blencowe	Builder

Chalfont Rd

Address	Date of Lease	Architect	Builder	Leaseholder	Occupation
1	1890		White	Jessie Holloway	Spinster
3	1890		White	William White	Builder
5	1891		White	Alfred Walker	China Dealer
7	1892		White	William White	Builder
9	1892	H.W. Moore	G. Horne	Norman Smith	Bursar, Mansfld
11	1892	H.W. Moore	G. Horne	Mary Cousins	Wife/Missionary
13	1891	H.W. Moore	G. Horne	Emily Davis	Spinster
15	1893	H.W. Moore	G. Horne	Ernest Hardy	Gentleman
17	1892	H.W. Moore	G. Horne	Alice Pinnock	Spinster
19	1891	H.W. Moore	G. Horne	Sarah Bennett	Wife/Carpenter
21	1901	H.W. Moore	Payne	Edward Joy	Barrister
23	1900	H.W. Moore	Payne	Elizabeth Workman	Widow
25	1901	H.W. Moore	Blencowe	Thomas Pierce	Estate Agent
27	1901	H.W. Moore	Blencowe	Thomas Pierce	Estate Agent
29	1893	H.W. Moore	G. Horne	Frank Kelson	Tailor
31	1893	H.W. Moore	G. Horne	Ann Giles	Wife/Carpenter
33	1896	H.W. Moore	G. Horne	William Embling	Tailor
35	1896	H.W. Moore	G. Horne	William Embling	Tailor
37	1898	H.W. Moore	G. Horne	William White	Engineer's Assistant
39	1895	H.W. Moore	G. Horne	Charles Jollands	Gentleman
41	1896	H.W. Moore	G. Horne	William White	Engineer's Assistant
43	1897	H.W. Moore	G. Horne	William White	Builder's Manager
45	1897	H.W. Moore	G. Horne	Ernest White	Accountant
47	1897	H.W. Moore		Hannah Way	Widow
49	1897	H.W. Moore		Hannah Way	Widow
51	1902	H.W. Moore		Eliza Kelson	Widow
53	1902	H.W. Moore		Eliza Kelson	Widow
55	1898	H.W. Moore		Florence Hedges	Spinster
57	1898	H.W. Moore		Florence Hedges	Spinster
59	1898	H.W. Moore		Hortense Mowbray	Widow

Address	Date of Lease	Architect	Builder	Leaseholder	Occupation
61	1898	H.W. Moore		Hortense Mowbray	Widow
63	1897	H.W. Moore		Frederic Taylor	Physician
65	1897	H.W. Moore		Frederic Taylor	Physician
67	1897	H.W. Moore		Frances Bull	Spinster
69	1897	H.W. Moore		Thomas Hodges	Law Clerk
2	1898	H.W. Moore	Hutchins	Samuel Hutchins	Builder
4	1898	H.W. Moore	Hutchins	Samuel Hutchins	Builder
6	1899	H.W. Moore	Hutchins	Elizabeth Pannell	Spinster
8	1897	H.W. Moore	Hutchins	Fanny Pannell	Spinster
10	1896	H.W. Moore	Hutchins	Fanny Pannell	Spinster
12	1896	H.W. Moore	Hutchins	Agnes Kidd	Wife/Clergyman
14	1898	H.W. Moore	Capel	Frances Peyton	Spinster
16	1898	H.W. Moore	Capel	Gertrude Brown	Wife/Gentleman
18	1899	H.W. Moore	Capel	James Nix	Gentleman
20	1899	H.W. Moore	Capel	James Nix	Gentleman
22	1900	H.W. Moore	Capel	Josiah Nix	Gentleman
24	1900	H.W. Moore	Capel	Alfred Boffin	Confectioner
26	1899	H.W. Moore	G. Horne	William Embling	Tailor
28	1898	H.W. Moore	G. Horne	Lilian Kelson	Wife//Tailor
30	1904	H.W. Moore	G. Horne	Florence Price	Wife/Gentleman
32	1902	H.W. Moore	G. Horne	Caleb Bolton	Gentleman
34	1900	H.W. Moore	G. Horne	Edgar Dickeson	Bootmaker
36	1900	H.W. Moore	G. Horne	Ernest White	Accountant
38	1899	H.W. Moore	G. Horne	Ernest White	Accountant
40	1899	H.W. Moore	G. Horne	Ernest White	Accountant
42	1899	H.W. Moore	Buckingham	George Phillips	Gentleman
44	1899	H.W. Moore	Buckingham	Rev James Carter	Clergyman

Charlbury Rd

Address	Date of Lease	Architect	Builder	Leaseholder	Occupation
1	1909	N.W. Harrison	Capel	Rev Henry Hilton	Clergyman
3	1909	N.W. Harrison	Capel	Noah Capel	Builder
5	1909	A.I. Rowley	Wild	Henry Wild	Builder
9	1915	N.W. Harrison	Wyatt	William Wyatt	Builder
11	1907	N.W. Harrison	Organ	Thomas Tims	Boat Bldr
13	1908	Hart & Waterhouse	Wooldridge	Amy Mallam	Spinster
15	1907	N.W. Harrison	Hutchins	William Craigie	Esquire
17	1908	N.W. Harrison	Grimsley	James Huxley	Esquire
23	1927			Frederick Penny	Esquire
25	1912	N.W. Harrison	Grimsley	Thomas Grimsley	Builder
27	1914	N.W. Harrison	Grimsley	Elinor Eckford	Widow
29	1915	N.W. Harrison	Fisher	Emily Walker	Wife/Doctor
31	1926		Kingerlee	Emily Geldart	Widow
2	1910	Stephen Salter	Wild	Henry Wild	Builder
4	1910	Stephen Salter	Wild	Henry Wild	Builder
6	1910		Wild	William Ross	Fellow, Oriel
8	1908	A.I. Rowley	Wild	Henry Gillett	MD
10	1907	N.W. Harrison	Symm	R.J. Axtell	Builder
12	1906	J.R. Symm	Symm	R.J. Axtell	Builder
14	1905	J.R. Symm	Symm	Sydney Acott	Music Seller
16	1906	N.W. Harrison	Symm	Jane Abbott	Widow
20	1911		Fisher	Samuel Scott	Esquire
22	1912	N.W. Harrison	Symm	R.J. Axtell	Builder

Address	Date of Lease	Architect	Builder	Leaseholder	Occupation
24	1912		Symm	R.J. Axtell	Builder
26	1924		Symm	Chas Henry Harper	Esquire
28	1924	C. Wright	Wooldridge	Edmund Molony	Esquire
30	1921	N.W. Harrison	Benfield & Loxley	Charlotte Adair	Widow
32	1924	C. Wright	Wooldridge	Mary Hodgkin	Widow
34	1924	C. Wright	Wooldridge	Winifred Van Oss	Wife/Gentleman

Church Walk

Address	Date of Lease	Architect	Builder	Leaseholder	Occupation
1	1876	Codd		Frederick Codd	Architect
2	1876	Codd		Frederick Codd	Architect
3	1878	Wilkinson	Dorn	Elizabeth Beaumont	Widow
4	1877	Wilkinson	Dorn	John Guy	Esquire
5	1877	Wilkinson	Dorn		

Crick Rd

Address	Date of Lease	Architect	Builder	Leaseholder	Occupation
1	1874		Reynolds	Elizabeth Stephens	Widow
2	1873		Reynolds	William Sendall	Gentleman
3	1874		Reynolds	William Beaufort	Gentleman
4	1877		Reynolds	Oxford Building Co.	Building Society
5	1880	Codd	Reynolds	Oxford Building Co.	Building Society
6	1880	Codd	Reynolds	Oxford Building Co.	Building Society
7	1879	Willson Beasley	H. Castle	A.L. Smith	Fellow, Trinity
8	1879	Willson Beasley	H. Castle	William Brain	Gentleman
9	1886	Willson Beasley		Edward Bartrum	Clergyman
10	1878	Codd		Sibella Roxburgh	Spinster
11	1876	Codd		Henry Harper	Gentleman
12	1877	Codd		William Roxburgh	MD
13	1875	Codd		William Flint	Clergyman
14	1878	Pike		George Pinhorn	Clergyman
15	1879	Pike		Henry Bazely	Clergyman
16	1873	Galp. & Shir.	Dover	John Dover	Builder
17	1873	Galp. & Shir.	Dover	John Dover	Builder

Farndon Rd

Address	Date of Lease	Architect	Builder	Leaseholder	Occupation
1	1880	Galp. & Shir.	Dover	John Dover	Builder
2	1880	Galp. & Shir.	Dover	John Dover	Builder
3	1880	Galp. & Shir.	Dover	John Dover	Builder
4	1880	Galp. & Shir.	Dover	John Dover	Builder
5	1887	Galp. & Shir.	Dover	John Green	College Servant
6	1888		Groom	James Nix	PO Clerk
7	1888		Groom	James Nix	PO Clerk
8	1883		Groom	Francis Nix	Clerk
9	1882		Groom	Alfred Bayliss	Gentleman
10	1879	Wilkinson	Martin & Hutchins	William Willis	Harness Maker
11	1879	Wilkinson	Martin & Hutchins	William Willis	Harness Maker
12	1879		Martin & Hutchins	Rev E.S. Talbot	Warden, Keble
13	1879		Martin & Hutchins	Isaac Stevens	Gardener
14	1879		Martin & Hutchins	Elizabeth Pannell	Spinster

Address	Date of Lease	Architect	Builder	Leaseholder	Occupation
15	1879		Martin & Hutchins	Elizabeth Pannell	Spinster
16	1879		Martin & Hutchins	Richard Bishop	Gentleman
17	1879		Martin & Hutchins	Richard Bishop	Gentleman
18	1884	Wilk. & Moore	Money	John Green	College Servant
19	1884	Wilk. & Moore	Money	Annie Andrews	Spinster
20	1884	Wilk. & Moore	Money	Joseph Green	Coal Merchant
21	1883	Wilk. & Moore	Money	Frederick Dolley	Clerk
22	1883	Wilk. & Moore	Money	Frederick Dolley	Clerk
23	1883	Wilk. & Moore		Elizabeth Hurst	Wife/Gentleman
24	1883	Wilk. & Moore		Elizabeth Hurst	Wife/Gentleman
25	1881	Wilkinson	Money	Joseph Faulkner	Gentleman
26	1881	Wilkinson	Money	John Money	Builder
27	1880			Philip Tyrwhitt	RN Retired

Frenchay Rd

Address	Date of Lease	Architect	Builder	Leaseholder	Occupation
1	1898	H.W. Moore	Buckingham	William Duck	MA
3	1897	H.W. Moore	Buckingham	Ernest Alden	Butcher
5	1898	H.W. Moore	Buckingham	Edwin Smith	Ironmonger
7	1898	H.W. Moore	Buckingham	William Goundry	Ironmonger
9	1898	H.W. Moore	Buckingham	Frank Townsend	Cashier
11	1898	H.W. Moore	Buckingham	Ellen Martin	Wife/Licensee
13	1906	H.W. Moore	Money	Walter Gray	Auctioneer
15	1906	H.W. Moore	Money	Walter Gray	Auctioneer
17	1906	H.W. Moore	Money	Walter Gray	Auctioneer
19	1906	H.W. Moore	Money	Walter Gray	Auctioneer
21	1906	H.W. Moore	Money	Walter Gray	Auctioneer
23	1906	H.W. Moore	Money	Walter Gray	Auctioneer
25	1900	H.W. Moore	Wooldridge	John Wooldridge	Builder
27	1900	H.W. Moore	Wooldridge	John Wooldridge	Builder
2	1900	H.W. Moore	Brucker	Alfred Hill	Clerk
4	1897	H.W. Moore	Money	Francis Andrews	Secretary
6	1897	H.W. Moore	Money	Francis Andrews	Secretary
8	1897	H.W. Moore	Money	James Kimber	Farmer
10	1897	H.W. Moore	Money	James Kimber	Farmer
12	1897	H.W. Moore	Money	W.F. Buckell	Auctioneer
14	1897	H.W. Moore	Money	W.F. Buckell	Auctioneer
16	1897	H.W. Moore	Money	Edward Giles	Draper
18	1897	H.W. Moore	Money	Edward Giles	Draper
20	1899	H.W. Moore	Money	Mary Bennett	Widow
22	1899	H.W. Moore	Money	Mary Bennett	Widow
24	1900	H.W. Moore	Money	Frances Bull	Spinster
26	1899	H.W. Moore	Money	Thomas Hodges	Clerk
28	1899	H.W. Moore	Money	Thomas Hewitt	Compositor
30	1899	H.W. Moore	Money	Thomas Hewitt	Compositor
32	1906	H.W. Moore	Money	Walter Gray	Auctioneer
34	1906	H.W. Moore	Money	Walter Gray	Auctioneer
36	1906	H.W. Moore	Money	Walter Gray	Auctioneer
38	1906	H.W. Moore	Money	Walter Gray	Auctioneer
40	1906	H.W. Moore	Money	Herbert Marston	Clerk
42	1906	H.W. Moore	Money	Herbert Marston	Clerk

Address	Date of Lease	Architect	Builder	Leaseholder	Occupation
Fyfield Rd					
1	1878	Codd		Rev Sir W. Clarke	Clergyman
2	1881	Wilkinson	Dorn	William Baker	Upholsterer
3	1881	Wilkinson	Dorn	William Baker	Upholsterer
4	1881	Wilkinson	Dorn	William Baker	Upholsterer
5	1888	Pike & Mess.	T. Jones	Eliza Hales	Spinster
6	1888	Pike & Mess.	T. Jones	Eliza Hales	Spinster
7	1888	Pike & Mess.	T. Jones	Eliza Hales	Spinster
8	1882	Pike & Mess.	Ward & Curtis	Emily Messenger	Wife/Auctioneer
9	1882	Pike & Mess.	Ward & Curits	Emily Messenger	Wife/Auctioneer
10	1881	Pike & Mess.	Ward & Curtis	Erastus Rogers	Gentleman
11	1884	Pike & Mess.	Ward & Curtis	Mary Bloxham	Spinster
12	1882	Pike & Mess.	T. Jones	Richard Shute	Senior Student, ChCh
13	1878	Codd		Rev Arthur Acland	Tutor, ChCh
14	1887	Codd		Thomas Wheatley	Esquire
Garford Rd					
Garford House	1930			Frederick Penny	Esquire
1A	1959			Brebis Bleaney	Prof Exp Philosophy
1	1928	C. Wright	Organ	Georgina Galbraith	Wife/Reader
2	1929	C. Wright	Organ	Frances Gray	Widow
3	1929	C. Wright	Organ	Emily Graham	Widow
4	1928	C. Wright	Organ	Carleton Allen	Fellow Univ
5	1928	C. Wright	Organ	Ernest Greswell	Esquire
Hayfield Rd					
3	1887	H.W. Moore		William Tombs	Carpenter
5	1887	H.W. Moore		Edwin Butler	Tailor
7	1887	H.W. Moore		Charlotte Blencowe	Spinster
9	1887	H.W. Moore		James Nix	PO Clerk
11	1887	H.W. Moore		Kezia Butler	Wife/Tailor
13	1887	H.W. Moore		Alfred Goodall	Tailor
15	1887	H.W. Moore		Walter Collett	Carpenter
17	1887	H.W. Moore		William Haines	Grocer
19	1887	H.W. Moore		Joseph Richardson	Schoolmaster
21	1887	H.W. Moore		Clara Blencowe	Spinster
23	1887	H.W. Moore		Emmala Richardson	Wife/Schoolmaster
25	1887	H.W. Moore		James Stuart	College Servant
27	1887	H.W. Moore		John Hough	Carpenter
29	1887	H.W. Moore		Thomas Green	College Servant
31	1887	H.W. Moore		George Busby	Builder
33	1887	H.W. Moore		Charles Cox	Teacher
35	1887	H.W. Moore		Thomas Payne	College Servant
37	1887	H.W. Moore		Thomas Hull	Inspector of Nuisances
39	1887	H.W. Moore		Charlotte Bridgwater	Wife/Policeman
41	1887	H.W. Moore		Thomas Hull	Inspector of Nuisances
43	1887	H.W. Moore	Kingerlee	Jane Plummer	Wife/Tailor
45	1887	H.W. Moore	Kingerlee	Henry Wild	Carpenter

Address	Date of Lease	Architect	Builder	Leaseholder	Occupation
47	1887	H.W. Moore	Kingerlee	Eliza Blencowe	Spinster
49	1887	H.W. Moore	Kingerlee	Jonathan Strange	Corn Traveller
51	1887	H.W. Moore	Kingerlee	Walter Payne	Tailor
53	1887	H.W. Moore	Kingerlee	Edwin Goddard	Police Constable
55	1887	H.W. Moore	Kingerlee	Sidney French	Joiner
57	1887	H.W. Moore	Kingerlee	Alfred Webb	Carpenter
59	1887	H.W. Moore	Kingerlee	David Francombe	Commercial Clerk
61	1887	H.W. Moore	Kingerlee	Dan Symes	Coal Merchant
63	1887	H.W. Moore	Kingerlee	Richard Davis	Carpenter
65	1887	H.W. Moore	Kingerlee	Emmala Richardson	Wife/Schoolmaster
67	1887	H.W. Moore	Kingerlee	Emmala Richardson	Wife/Schoolmaster
69	1887	H.W. Moore	Kingerlee	Charles Cox	Teacher
71	1887	H.W. Moore	Kingerlee	Charles Blencowe	Baker
73	1887	H.W. Moore	Kingerlee	Charles Woolf	Hairdresser
4	1889	H.W. Moore		George Newman	Baker
6	1889	H.W. Moore		Harry Bishop	Waiter
8	1888	H.W. Moore		Alfred Quelch	Green Grocer
10	1888	H.W. Moore		Mary Ann Eaton	Widow
12	1888	H.W. Moore		John Wooldridge	Carpenter
14	1888	H.W. Moore		William Winfield	Carpenter
16	1888	H.W. Moore		Joseph Richardson	Schoolmaster
18	1888	H.W. Moore		Emmala Richardson	Wife/Schoolmaster
20	1888	H.W. Moore		William Phillips	Carpenter
22	1888	H.W. Moore		Ellen Martin	Wife/Not Known
24	1887	H.W. Moore		William Sheppard	Compositor
26	1887	H.W. Moore	Kingerlee	Emma Davis	Spinster
28	1887	H.W. Moore	Kingerlee	William Wyatt	College Servant
30	1887	H.W. Moore	Kingerlee	Robert Thomas	Schoolmaster
32	1887	H.W. Moore	Kingerlee	Moses Adkins	Joiner
34	1887	H.W. Moore	Kingerlee	Charles Cox	Teacher
36	1887	H.W. Moore	Kingerlee	Sarah Cummings	Widow
38	1887	H.W. Moore	Kingerlee	Charlotte Maltby	Spinster
40	1887	H.W. Moore	Kingerlee	Walter Gray	Auctioneer
42	1887	H.W. Moore	Kingerlee	Walter Gray	Auctioneer
44	1887	H.W. Moore	Kingerlee	Henry Foster	Innkeeper
46	1887	H.W. Moore	Kingerlee	John Harris	Wharfinger
48	1887	H.W. Moore	Kingerlee	Alfred Evetts	Carpenter
50	1887	H.W. Moore	Kingerlee	William Williamson	College Servant
52	1887	H.W. Moore	Kingerlee	William Judge	Joiner
54	1887	H.W. Moore	Kingerlee	Henry Foster	Innkeeper
56	1887	H.W. Moore	Kingerlee	Elizabeth Ariss	Widow
58	1887	H.W. Moore	Kingerlee	Benjamin Harse	Ball Maker
60	1887	H.W. Moore	Kingerlee	William Sheppard	Carpenter
62	1887	H.W. Moore	Kingerlee	Emmala Richardson	Wife/Schoolmaster
64	1887	H.W. Moore	Kingerlee	Charlotte Blencowe	Spinster
66	1887	H.W. Moore	Kingerlee	William Harris	Shoemaker
68	1887	H.W. Moore	Kingerlee	Henry Wild	Carpenter
70	1887	H.W. Moore	Kingerlee	Henry Wild	Carpenter
72	1887	H.W. Moore	Kingerlee	Edwin Butler	Tailor
74	1887	H.W. Moore	Kingerlee	Kate Annis	Widow
76	1887	H.W. Moore	Kingerlee	Jonathan Strange	Corn Traveller
78	1887	H.W. Moore	Kingerlee	Charles Kearsey	Tailor
80	1887	H.W. Moore	Kingerlee	Mary Restall	Wife/Tobacconist
82	1887	H.W. Moore	Kingerlee	William Walker	Shopkeeper
84	1887	H.W. Moore	Kingerlee	William Hancock	Labourer

Address	Date of Lease	Architect	Builder	Leaseholder	Occupation
86	1887	H.W. Moore	Kingerlee	Richard Davis	Carpenter
88	1887	H.W. Moore	Kingerlee	Emily Foster	Wife/Innkeeper
90	1887	H.W. Moore	Kingerlee	William Winfield	Carpenter

Keble Rd

Address	Date of Lease	Architect	Builder	Leaseholder	Occupation
1	1874	Wilkinson		Rev John Wordsworth	Tutor, BNC
2	1871	Wilkinson		Rev Francis Jayne	Tutor, Jesus
3	1871	Wilkinson	Honour & Castle	Mary E. Corbet	Spinster
4	1871	Wilkinson	Honour & Castle	John Rippington	Farmer
5	1869	Wilkinson	Dorn	Elizabeth Cox	Widow
6	1870	Wilkinson	Dorn	John Dorn	Builder
7	1870	Wilkinson	M. Gray	Rev Richard Greaves	Clergyman
8	1870	Wilkinson		James Turrill	Poulterer
9	1869	Wilkinson	M. Gray	William Bramwell	Architect
10	1870	Wilkinson		William Wilkinson	Architect
11	1870	Wilkinson		William Wilkinson	Architect

Kingston Rd

Address	Date of Lease	Architect	Builder	Leaseholder	Occupation
14	1883		Hutchins	William Young	Butcher
15	1883		Hutchins	William Young	Butcher
16	1883		Hutchins	John Peattie	Plumber
17	1883		Hutchins	Samuel Hutchins	Builder
18	1878		Brucker	John Kilburn	Commercial Traveller
19	1878		Brucker	John Kilburn	Commercial Traveller
20	1875		J. Horne	John Blencowe	Baker
21	1875		J. Horne	William Mallett	Clothier
22	1874		J. Horne	James Webb	Engine Driver
23	1872		J. Horne	Anne Scarsbrook	Spinster
24	1875		J. Horne	Rowland Hale	Printer
25	1875		J. Horne	Maria Hull	Spinster
26	1875		J. Horne	William Cleaver	Bootmaker
27	1875		J. Horne	John Horne	Builder
28	1872		Holt	Mary Ann Leach	Widow
29	1874		Holt	Jabez Sumner	Printer
30	1873		Holt	Charlotte Gadney	Spinster
31	1873		Holt	Charlotte Gadney	Spinster
32	1874		Holt	Richard Graham	PO Clerk
33	1874		Holt	Henry Aldred	Draper
34	1877		Holt	Charles Wood	Cook
35	1873		Holt	Elizabeth Rose	Widow
36	1874		Holt	Richard Tanner	Surveyor
37	1874		Holt	Richard Tanner	Surveyor
38	1874		Holt	Richard Tanner	Surveyor
39	1874		Holt	Richard Tanner	Surveyor
40	1874		Holt	Josiah Nix	Grocer
41	1875	Geo Shirley		Charles Rooke	Builder
42	1877	Geo Shirley		James Panter	Engine Driver
43	1876	Geo Shriley		George Barker	Cabinetmaker
44	1876	Geo Shirley		Robert Parish	Engineer
45	1875	Geo Shirley		Emanuel Carpenter	Shoemaker
46	1875	Geo Shirley		Emanuel Carpenter	Shoemaker

Address	Date of Lease	Architect	Builder	Leaseholder	Occupation
47	1873		Money	John Money	Builder
48	1873		Money	John Money	Builder
49	1873		Money	John Money	Builder
50	1873		Money	John Money	Builder
51	1875		Money	John Money	Builder
52	1875		Money	John Money	Builder
53	1883		Crapper	Charles Hartwell	Grocer
54	1883		Crapper	Charles Hartwell	Grocer
55	1881		Crapper	Harriet Tombs	Spinster
56	1881		Crapper	Harriet Tombs	Spinster
57	1880		Crapper	Robert Peel	Shoemaker
58	1882		Crapper	Alfred Wiblin	Butcher
59	1883		Crapper	John Thorogood	Schoolmaster
60	1883		Crapper	Thomas Newton	China Dealer
61	1877		Parnell	James Turrill	Poulterer
62	1877		Parnell	James Turrill	Poulterer
63	1888		Parks	George Hebbes	Cook
64	1888		Parks	George Hebbes	Cook
65	1878		Parks	George Hebbes	Cook
66	1878		Parks	William Purnell	Mercer
67	1877		Gray	Walter Turrill	Poulterer
68	1877		Gray	Walter Turrill	Poulterer
69	1877		Brucker	Elizabeth West	Widow
70	1877		Brucker	Elizabeth West	Widow
71	1878		Brucker	Ann Elizabeth Lane	Widow
72	1878		Brucker	Ann Elizabeth Lane	Widow
73	1877		J. Horne	Charles Swearse	Solicitor
74	1879		J. Horne	William Godfrey	Gentleman
75	1879		J. Horne	Elizabeth Rose	Widow
76	1879		J. Horne	Elizabeth Rose	Widow
77	1880		J. Horne	William Thomas	Fishmonger
78	1880		J. Horne	William Thomas	Fishmonger
79	1884		J. Horne	Robert Nix	Provision Merchant
80	1888		G. Horne	Charlotte Horne	Widow
81	1886	Wilk. & Moore	Money	John Money	Builder
82	1886	Wilk. & Moore	Money	John Money	Builder
83	1886	Wilk. & Moore	Money	John Money	Builder
84	1886	Wilk. & Moore	Money	John Money	Builder
85	1884	Wilk. & Moore	Money	Frank Restall	Gentleman
86	1884	Wilk. & Moore	Money	Frank Restall	Gentleman
87	1887	H.W. Moore	G. Horne	William Barrett	Gentleman
88	1887	H.W. Moore	G. Horne	William Barrett	Gentleman
89	1889	H.W. Moore	G. Horne	Frederick Butler	Clerk
90	1889	H.W. Moore	G. Horne	George Horne	Builder
91	1890		Money	John Money	Builder
92	1890	H.W. Moore	Money	Emma Stevens	Widow
93	1890	H.W. Moore	Money	John Money	Builder
94	1890	H.W. Moore	Money	John Money	Builder
95	1889	H.W. Moore	Buckingham	James Boffin	Gentleman
96	1889	H.W. Moore	Buckingham	James Boffin	Gentleman
97	1889	H.W. Moore	Buckingham	James Boffin	Gentleman
98	1889	H.W. Moore	Buckingham	James Boffin	Gentleman
99	1879		Bossom	Thomas Wheeler	Builder
100	1884		Bossom	Francis Turning	Grocer
101	1881		Curtis	Robert Hills	Photographer

228

Address	Date of Lease	Architect	Builder	Leaseholder	Occupation
102	1880		Curtis	Henry Cowley	Builder
103	1880		Curtis	Frank Long	Cutler
104	1880		Curtis	Frank Long	Cutler
105	1887		Curtis	Arthur Edmonds	Dairyman
106	1875		Wheeler	Charles Holloway	Accountant
107	1875		Wheeler	Charles Holloway	Accountant
108	1873		Wheeler	Thomas Newton	China Merchant
109	1873		Wheeler	Thomas Newton	China Merchant
110	1875		Wheeler	Charles Holloway	Accountant
111	1875		Wheeler	Charles Holloway	Accountant
112	1873		Wheeler	Charles Wright	Compositor
113	1875		Wheeler	Charles Holloway	Accountant
114	1872	C.C. Rolfe	Bryer	Robert Hills	Photographer
115	1872	C.C. Rolfe	Bryer	Robert Hills	Photographer
116	1872	C.C. Rolfe	Bryer	Robert Hills	Photographer
117	1872	C.C. Rolfe	Bryer	Robert Hills	Photographer
118	1872	C.C. Rolfe	Bryer	Robert Hills	Photographer
119	1877	C.C. Rolfe	Long	Eliza Hailstone	Spinster
120	1877	C.C. Rolfe	Long	Eleanor Hailstone	Spinster
121	1872	C.C. Rolfe	Long	Mary Wotton	Stationer
122	1872	C.C. Rolfe	Long	Mary Wotton	Stationer
123	1972	C.C. Rolfe	Long	George Yeatman	Mason
124	1872	C.C. Rolfe	Long	George Yeatman	Mason
125	1872	C.C. Rolfe	Long	John Payne	College Servant
126	1872	C.C. Rolfe	Long	John Payne	College Servant
127	1874	C.C. Rolfe	Long	Margaretha Winkler	Spinster
128	1874	C.C. Rolfe	Long	Margaretha Winkler	Spinster
129	1874	C.C. Rolfe	Walter	Francis Tuck	Chemist
130	1874	C.C. Rolfe	Walter	Francis Tuck	Chemist
131	1874	C.C. Rolfe	Walter	Francis Tuck	Chemist
132	1874	C.C. Rolfe	Walter	Francis Tuck	Chemist
133	1874	C.C. Rolfe	Walter	Francis Tuck	Chemist
134	1874	C.C. Rolfe	Walter	Francis Tuck	Chemist
135	1874	C.C. Rolfe	Walter	Francis Tuck	Chemist
136	1874	C.C. Rolfe	Walter	Francis Tuck	Chemist
137	1874	C.C. Rolfe	Walter	Francis Tuck	Chemist
138	1874	C.C. Rolfe	Walter	Francis Tuck	Chemist
139	1872		Wheeler	Charles Holloway	Accountant
140	1872		Wheeler	Charles Holloway	Accountant
141	1871			William Kay	Lay Clerk
142	1871			William Kay	Lay Clerk
143	1872		Wheeler	Henry Clarke	Draper
144	1876		Wheeler	Charles Holloway	Accountant
145	1871		Wheeler	Stephen Hazell	Chairmaker
146	1871		Wheeler	Stephen Hazell	Chairmaker
147	1871		Wheeler	Stephen Hazell	Chairmaker
148	1871		Wheeler	Stephen Hazell	Chairmaker
149	1870	C.C. Rolfe		Thomas Walter	Gent's Servant
150	1870	C.C. Rolfe		Thomas Walter	Gent's Servant
151	1870	C.C. Rolfe		Thomas Walter	Gent's Servant
152	1870	C.C. Rolfe		Thomas Walter	Gent's Servant
153	1871	C.C. Rolfe		Thomas Walter	Gent's Servant
154	1871	C.C. Rolfe		Thomas Walter	Gent's Servant
155	1871	C.C. Rolfe		Thomas Walter	Gent's Servant
156	1871	C.C. Rolfe		Thomas Walter	Gent's Servant

Address	Date of Lease	Architect	Builder	Leaseholder	Occupation
157	1868			Thos Harris	Publican
158	1868			Thos Harris	Publican
159	1870	C.C. Rolfe	Walter	Edwin Butler	Tailor
160	1870	C.C. Rolfe	Walter	Stephen Roberts	Compositor
161	1871	C.C. Rolfe	Walter	Thomas Markham	Tailor
162	1875	C.C. Rolfe	Walter	Richard Beckley	Gentleman
163	1875	C.C. Rolfe	Walter	Richard Beckley	Gentleman
164	1870	C.C. Rolfe	Walter	James Walters	Builder
165	1870		Walter	James Slatter	Carpenter
166	1870		Walter	Hannah Shelton	Widow
167	1870		Walter	James Prickett	Carpenter
168	1870		Walter	Stephen Large	Boat Builder
169	1870		Walter	Stephen Large	Boat Builder
170	1870		Walter	Richard Smith	Cabinetmaker
171	1870		Walter	Susanna Barnes	Widow
172	1870		Walter	Susanna Barnes	Widow
173	1870		Walter	Richard Beckley	Gentleman
174	1870		Walter	Josiah Cantwell	Dairyman

Leckford Rd

Address	Date of Lease	Architect	Builder	Leaseholder	Occupation
1	1875		Walter	William Perry	Engine Driver
2	1875		Walter	Charles Palmer	Coachman
3	1875		Walter	Henry Cowley	Clerk
4	1875		Walter	Thomas Newton	China Merchant
5	1874		Walter	Charles Curtis	Builder's Foreman
6	1874		Walter	William Wynch	Coachman
7	1874		Walter	Ann Lane	Widow
8	1874		Walter	Ann Lane	Widow
9	1874		Walter	Benjamin Bennett	Dyer
10	1874		Walter	Benjamin Bennett	Dyer
11	1873		Williams	Benjamin Roberts	Tailor
12	1873		Williams	Job Bryan	Tea Dealer
13	1873		Williams	Edmund Peacy	College Servant
14	1873		Williams	Thomas Hull	Inspector Nuisances
15	1873		Williams	James Minn	Jeweller
16	1873		Williams	Aaron Soanes	Not Known
17	1873		Williams	Richard Gillman	Bootmaker
18	1873		Williams	Richard Gillman	Bootmaker
19	1873		Williams	Richard Gillman	Bootmaker
20	1873		Williams	Richard Gillman	Bootmaker
21	1875			William Orpwood	Saddler
22	1875			James Hall	Printer
23	1877	Connell		John W. Hallam	Architect
24	1877	Connell		Rev Henry Pickard	School Inspector
25	1876	Connell		Thomas Green	Ironmonger
26	1875	Connell		Louisa Johnson	Spinster
27	1873			John Barnett	Gent's Servant
28	1873			John Barnett	Gent's Servant
29	1876		Reynolds	Sarah Monsell	Widow
30	1876		Reynolds	Frank Webb	Cutler
31	1878		Reynolds	Charles Williams	Builder
32	1878		Reynolds	Charles Williams	Builder
33	1883		Holt	Oxford Building Co.	Building Society
34	1885		Holt	George Gillman	Bootmaker
35	1875		Reynolds	Edward Turner	Gentleman

Address	Date of Lease	Architect	Builder	Leaseholder	Occupation
36	1875		Reynolds	Edward Turner	Gentleman
37	1875		Reynolds	Sarah Painton	Widow
38	1878		Reynolds	Alfred Nicholson	Clerk
39	1881		Williams	Oxford Building Co.	Building Society
40	1881		Williams	Oxford Building Co.	Building Society
41	1881		Williams	Oxford Building Co.	Building Society
42	1881		Williams	Oxford Building Co.	Building Society
43	1881		Williams	Oxford Building Co.	Building Society
44	1881		Williams	Oxford Building Co.	Building Society
45	1881		Williams	Oxford Building Co.	Building Society
46	1881		Williams	Oxford Building Co.	Building Society
47	1876		Walter	Robert Horton	Pattern Maker
48	1876		Walter	Ann Lane	Widow
49	1876		Walter	Ann Lane	Widow
50	1876		Walter	Ann Lane	Widow
51	1876		Walter	Ann Lane	Widow
52	1876		Walter	Richard Beckley	Gentleman
53	1876		Walter	Richard Beckley	Gentleman

Linton Rd

Address	Date of Lease	Architect	Builder	Leaseholder	Occupation
1	1896	J.C. Gray		Benjamin Blackwell	Bookseller
3	1904	H.W. Moore	Hutchins	Samuel Hutchins	Builder
5	1903	H.W. Moore	Hutchins	John Moberly	Gentleman
7	1903	A.H. Moberly	Hutchins	John Moberly	Gentleman
9	1905	G. Gardiner		Rev Walter Merry	Clergyman
11	1906	G. Gardiner		George Gardiner	Architect
13	1905	S. Stallard		Charles Edmunds	Gentleman
15	1912		Hutchins	John Behan	Esquire
19	1908	G. Gardiner		Paul Vinogradoff	Prof Jurisprudence
21	1908	G. Gardiner		George Gardiner	Architect
23	1909	G. Gardiner	Pipkin	George Gardiner	Architect
25	1909	G. Gardiner	Pipkin	George Gardiner	Architect
27	1912	G. Gardiner	Inness	John Stenning	Fellow, Wadham
31	1925	A.C. Martin	Hinkins	Isabella Mullaly	Widow
'Cherwell' Linton Rd	1921	G. Gardiner		John S. Haldane	Fellow, New Coll
2	1895	H.W. Moore	Hutchins	Henry Adair	Major Army
4	1902	H.W. Moore	Capel	Noah Capel	Builder
6	1904	H.W. Moore	Capel	R. Dunn-Pattison	Fellow, Magdalen
8	1901	E.J. Marriott	Higgs	Katharine Hopkins	Widow
12	1910	N.W. Harrison	Grimsley	Fred Blencowe	Builder
14	1905	N.W. Harrison	Money	Henry Cooper	MA
16	1909	G. Gardiner		William Bloxham	Builder
18	1908	G. Gardiner		George Gardiner	Architect
20	1911	G. Gardiner		George Gardiner	Architect

Longworth Rd

Address	Date of Lease	Architect	Builder	Leaseholder	Occupation
Belmont	1888		Buckingham	Susan Claridge	Wife/Engine Driver
1	1887		Buckingham	Rosetta Turrill	Widow
2	1888		Buckingham	Ellen Bayzand	Spinster
3	1887		Buckingham	William Wood	Carpenter
4	1887		Buckingham	Mary Clarke	Spinster

Address	Date of Lease	Architect	Builder	Leaseholder	Occupation
5	1890		Dines	Elizabeth Workman	Widow
6	1890		Dines	Elizabeth Workman	Widow
7	1890		Dines	Elizabeth Workman	Widow
8	1889		Dines	Thomas Newman	College Cook

Marston Ferry Rd

Address	Date of Lease	Architect	Builder	Leaseholder	Occupation
1	1905	Gardiner	Pipkin	Rev J. Betteridge	Clergyman
3	1905	Gardiner	Pipkin	John Allen	Esquire
5	1905	Gardiner	Pipkin	John Allen	Esquire
7	1907	Gardiner	Pipkin	John Allen	Esquire
9	1909	Gardiner	Pipkin	John Allen	Esquire
11	1909	Gardiner	Pipkin	John Allen	Esquire
15	1937			Claude Douglas	Fellow, SJC
2	1905	Gardiner		Ernest Trevelyan	Reader, All Souls
4	1907	Gardiner	Pipkin	John Allen	Esquire
6	1907	Gardiner	Pipkin	John Allen	Esquire
8	1907	Gardiner	Pipkin	John Allen	Esquire
10	1907	Gardiner	Pipkin	John Allen	Esquire
12	1907	Gardiner	Pipkin	John Allen	Esquire

Museum Road

Address	Date of Lease	Architect	Builder	Leaseholder	Occupation
33[7]	1899		Kingerlee	Edgar Mills	Gentleman
35	1899		Kingerlee	Jessie Rowden	Spinster
37	1899		Kingerlee	Thomas Potts	DCL Lincoln
39	1899		Kingerlee	Annie Rogers	Spinster
41	1898		Kingerlee	St John's College	Tutor's House
2	1864			Frederick Irwin	Hairdresser
4	1864			Frederick Irwin	Hairdresser
6	1865			James Slatter	Builder
8	1865			James Slatter	Builder
10	1866			Josiah Watson	Contractor
12	1866			Josiah Watson	Contractor
14	1873		Dorn	John Dorn	Builder
16	1873		Dorn	John Dorn	Builder
18	1873		Dorn	John Dorn	Builder
20	1873		Dorn	John Dorn	Builder
22	1873		Dorn	John Dorn	Builder
24	1873		Dorn	John Dorn	Builder
26	1938	Edward Maufe		SJC	Tutor's House
28	1938	Edward Maufe		SJC	Tutor's House

Norham Gardens

Address	Date of Lease	Architect	Builder	Leaseholder	Occupation
1	1865	Wilkinson		Elizabeth Huckvale	Spinster
3	1868	Buckeridge	G & T Jones	Henry Hammons	Bookseller
5	1865	Wilkinson		Robert Pike	Auctioneer
7	1862	Wilkinson		Goldwin Smith	Prof Modern History
9	1868	Buckeridge	Jos Castle	Montagu Burrows	Prof Modern History
11	1866	Wilkinson		George Mallam	Solicitor
13	1869	Wilkinson	G. Jones	Thos Dallin	Tutor, Queens

Address	Date of Lease	Architect	Builder	Leaseholder	Occupation
15	1873	Codd		William Odling	Prof Chemistry
17	1874	Codd		William Aldridge	Gentleman
19	1877	Codd		Mary Jephson	Spinster
21	1879	Willson Beasley	H. Castle	Lady Margaret Hall	Women's Hall
2	1870	Codd	M. Gray	Bonamy Price	Prof Politics and Economics
4	1873	Codd		Richard Gillett	Gentleman
6	1870	Codd	M. Gray	Patrick Henderson	Fellow, Wadham
8	1871	Codd		Charles F.C. West	Fellow, SJC
10	1868		Jones	John Mawer	Hatter
12	1868		Jones	Robert Modlen	Commercial Traveller
14	1873	Codd		Hon W. Sackville-West	Bursar Keble
16	1872	Codd		Caroline Johnson	Widow
18	1872	Codd		Rev Edwin Palmer	Prof Latin Literature
20	1873	Galp. & Shir.	Dover	John Dover	Builder
22	1873	Galp. & Shir.	Dover	Arthur Johnson	Fellow, All Souls
24	1873	Galp. & Shir.	Dover	Thomas Case	Fellow, BNC
26	1877	Galp. & Shir.	Dover	John Dover	Builder
28	1876	Galp. & Shir.	Dover	John Dover	Builder
30	1876	Galp. & Shir.	Dover	John Dover	Builder

Norham Rd

Address	Date of Lease	Architect	Builder	Leaseholder	Occupation
Westbury	1874		Jones	George Jones	Builder
1	1863		Jones	Deborah Brain	Spinster
2	1875		Jones	Charles Laker	Grocer
3	1875		Jones	Charles Laker	Grocer
4	1875		Jones	Charles Laker	Grocer
5	1864		J. Gardiner	James Gardiner	Builder
6	1864		J. Gardiner	James Gardiner	Builder
7	1863		J. Gardiner	John Penson	Banker's Clerk
8	1863		J. Gardiner	William Cheney	Gentleman
9	1864		Dorn	John Dorn	Builder
10	1864		Dorn	John Dorn	Builder
11	1875	Galp. & Shir.	Dover	John Dover	Builder
12	1875	Galp. & Shir.	Dover	John Dover	Builder
13	1878	Codd		Chas Shillingford	Brewer
14	1878	Wilkinson	Dorn	Chas Mount	Clergyman
15	1878	Wilkinson	Dorn	Elizabeth Perry	Spinster
16	1878	Wilkinson	Dorn & Brown	James Griffin	Gentleman
17	1878	Wilkinson	Dorn & Brown	Hugh Eldrid	China Merchant
18	1879	Wilkinson	Dorn & Brown	Charles Wyndham	Captain/Army
19	1882	Wilkinson	Dorn & Brown	Elizabeth Cox	Widow
20	1880	Wilkinson	Dorn & Brown	Eliza Draper	Spinster
21	1880	Wilkinson	Dorn & Brown	Wm Henry Ward	Gentleman
22	1884	Wilkinson	Dorn & Brown	William Belson	MA Oriel
23	1884	Wilkinson	Dorn & Brown	Edward Hall	Esquire
24	1881	Wilkinson	Brucker	William Baker	Upholsterer
25	1881	Wilkinson	Brucker	John Thornton	Bookseller
26	1881	Wilkinson	Brucker	Edwin Wallace	Fellow, Worcs
27	1886	Pike & Mess.		Archibald Prankerd	Fellow, Trinity
28	1883	Pike & Mess.	Curtis	Charles Bigg	Chaplain, Corpus

Address	Date of Lease	Architect	Builder	Leaseholder	Occupation
29	1885	Pike & Mess.	Curtis	Mary Hall Souttar	Wife/Gentleman
30	1881	Wilkinson	Brown	Frederick Tasker	Esquire
31	1881	Wilkinson	Brown	Sarah Ansell	Widow
32	1884	Wilkinson	Brown	Alfred Brown	Builder
33	1883	Wilkinson	Brown	Charles Firth	Fellow, Balliol
34	1885	Wilkinson	Brown	Jane Dorn	Wife/Builder
35	1883	Wilkinson	Brown	John Goundrey	Ironmonger
36	1880	F. Connell	Wells	Augustus Westmacott	Fellow, Merton
37	1880	F. Connell	Wells	Frederick Spurling	Fellow, Keble
38	1874	Galp. & Shir.		Robert Hills	Photographer
Norham End	1911	G. Gardiner		C.R.L. Fletcher	Delegate/Press
Lane House	1905	G. Gardiner			

Northmoor Rd

Address	Date of Lease	Architect	Builder	Leaseholder	Occupation
1	1899	G. Gardiner	Wooldridge	Adam Kirkaldy	BA Wadham
3	1897		Wooldridge	Thomas Blockley	Chaplain, New Coll
5	1902	H.W. Moore	Wild	George Wakeling	Fellow, BNC
7	1902	H.W. Moore	Wild	Charles Haselfoot	Fellow, Hertf
9	1905	H.W. Moore	Wild	Bertha Harvey	Spinster
11	1906	H.W. Moore & Warwick	Wild	Mary West	Widow
13	1904	H.W. Moore	Wild	Blanche Wroughton	Spinster
17	1903	H.W. Moore	Wild	George Wells	Gentleman
19	1903	H.W. Moore	Wild	George Wells	Gentleman
21	1915	N.W. Harrison	Grimsley	Matthew Peacock	MA
23	1930	A.C. Martin	Capel	Alice Seaton Tribe	Wife/Not Known
25	1928	A.C. Martin	Capel	Alfred Brown	Principal, Ruskin
27	1926	F.E. Openshaw	Hutchins	Charles Seddon	Univ Lecturer
29	1926	T. Rayson	Organ	Margaret Lilly	Wife/Clergyman
31	1925	C. Wright	Organ	Laura Bickmore	Widow
33	1926	C. Wright	Organ	Horace Joseph	Fellow, New Coll
2	1908	E.W. Allfrey	Hutchins	Charles Firth	Prof Modern History
4	1906	H.W. Moore	Wild	Walter Gray	Auctioneer
6	1902	H.W. Moore	Wild	William Baker	Gentleman
8	1913	H.W. Moore	Kingerlee	Augustus Hoernle	MA, Worcs
10	1904	H.W. Moore	Wild	George Underhill	Fellow, Magdalen
12	1905	H.W. Moore	Wild	Walter Raleigh	Prof English Literature
14	1912	F. Mountain	Inness	George Inness	Builder
16	1912	F. Mountain	Inness	George Inness	Builder
18	1957	T. Rayson		Irma Simonis	
20	1926	F.E. Openshaw	Hinkins & Frewin	Basil Blackwell	Bookseller
22	1925	C. Wright	Wooldridge	J.R.R. Tolkien	Prof Anglo-Sax
24	1925	C. Wright	Wooldridge	Norman Swan	Lieut-Col/Army
26	1925	C. Wright	Wooldridge	Thomas Higham	Fellow, Trinity

Parks Road

Address	Date of Lease	Architect	Builder	Leaseholder	Occupation
12	1868		M. Gray	Thomas Sammons	College Servant

Address	Date of Lease	Architect	Builder	Leaseholder	Occupation
13	1868		M. Gray	Thomas Sammons	College Servant
14	1869		Dorn	Frederick Irwin	Hairdresser
15	1869		Dorn	John Dorn	Builder
16	1895		Money	Walter Gray	Auctioneer
17	1872		G. Jones	William Merry	Fellow, Lincoln
18	1872		T. Jones	Elizabeth Fussell	Spinster

Polstead Road

Address	Date of Lease	Architect	Builder	Leaseholder	Occupation
1	1890	H.W.Moore	Kingerlee	Thos Kingerlee	Builder
3	1890	H.W.Moore	Kingerlee	Thos Kingerlee	Builder
5	1889	H.W.Moore	Arnett	John W.Hallam	Architect
7	1889	H.W.Moore	Arnett	Richard Cross	JP
9	1892	H.W.Moore	Hutchins	Laura Green	Spinster
11	1892	H.W.Moore	Hutchins	Mary Ellen Beard	Widow
13	1894	H.W.Moore	Hutchins	Samuel Hutchins	Builder
15	1894	H.W.Moore	Hutchins	Samuel Hutchins	Builder
17	1892	H.W.Moore	Hutchins	Walter Richmond	Clothier
19	1892	H.W.Moore	Hutchins	Samuel Mowbray	Publisher
21	1888	H.W.Moore	Castle & Martin	Isaac Castle	Builder
23	1888	H.W.Moore	Castle & Martin	Isaac Castle	Builder
25	1890	H.W.Moore	G. Horne	Ellen Parsons	Spinster
27	1890	H.W.Moore	G. Horne	Ellen Parsons	Spinster
29	1890	H.W.Moore	Money	John Money	Builder
31	1890	H.W.Moore	Money	John Money	Builder
33	1890	H.W.Moore	Money	John Money	Builder
2	1889	H.W.Moore	Hutchins	William Glasson	Bursar, SJC
4	1889	H.W.Moore	Hutchins	Ellen Pullen	Widow
6	1890	H.W.Moore	Hutchins	Jane Abbott	Widow
8	1891	H.W.Moore	Hutchins	W. Hallam	Gentleman
10	1889	H.W.Moore	Castle & Martin	Elizabeth Macdonald	Wife/Clergyman
12	1889	H.W.Moore	Castle & Martin	Jesse Hughes	Farmer
14	1896	H.W.Moore	Hastings	James Hastings	Surveyor
16	1892	H.W.Moore	Hastings	Jessie Holloway	Spinster
18	1892	H.W.Moore	Hastings	Herbert Quinton	Architect
20	1896	H.W.Moore	Hastings	James Hastings	Surveyor
22	1891	H.W.Moore	Hastings	Dan Symes	Coal Merchant
24	1894	H.W.Moore	Hastings	Charlotte Staniland	Widow
26	1890	H.W.Moore	Hastings	Arthur Martin	Wes Minister
28	1890	H.W.Moore	Hastings	Arthur Martin	Wes Minister
Parish Institute	1891			H.G.W. Drinkwater	Architect

Rawlinson Rd

Address	Date of Lease	Architect	Builder	Leaseholder	Occupation
1	1888	H.W.Moore	Castle & Martin	James Rose	MA, Exeter
3	1888	H.W.Moore	Castle & Martin	Edward Burstal	Gentleman
5	1890	H.W.Moore	Castle & Martin	Edward Hayes	Fellow, New Coll
7	1890	H.W.Moore	Money	Alexander Bell	Private Tutor
9	1890	H.W.Moore	Money	Emily Baird	Not Known
11	1890	H. Quinton		Francis Gotch	MA
13	1892	H. Quinton		Elizabeth Johnson	Spinster
15	1893	H. Quinton	Jarvis	Peyton Mackeson	MA, Univ

Address	Date of Lease	Architect	Builder	Leaseholder	Occupation
2	1889	H.W.Moore	Money	Henry Stilwell	Esquire
4	1889	H.W.Moore	Money	Francis Jeune	Lawyer
6	1889	H. Quinton		Charles Laing	MA, Madgalen
8	1889	H. Quinton		Helen Egerton	Widow
10	1889	H. Quinton		J.W. Messenger	Auctioneer
12	1889	H.W.Moore		Robert McDonald	Gentleman
14	1889	H.W.Moore		Emily Butler	Spinster
16	1890	H.W.Moore		William Baker	Upholsterer
18	1889	H.W.Moore		James Drummond	Principal, Man Coll

St Margaret's Rd

Address	Date of Lease	Architect	Builder	Leaseholder	Occupation
1	1884	Wilk. & Moore	Brucker	Henry Wakeman	Fellow, All Souls
2	1884	Wilk. & Moore		Georgina Whigham	Spinster
3	1884	Wilk. & Moore		Caleb Bolton	Draper
4	1884	Wilk. & Moore		Rev Thomas Gorman	Clergyman
5	1884		Curtis	Walter Fisher	MA/Analyst
6	1882	Connell		Edwin Brooks	Tailor
7	1880	Connell		George Dudley	Gentleman
8	1884	Wilk. & Moore	Money	William White	Engineer
9	1884	Wilk. & Moore	Money	Albert Payne	Commercial Traveller
10	1885	Wilk. & Moore	Money	Henry F.Galpin	Solicitor
11	1885	Wilk. & Moore	Money	Henry F.Galpin	Solicitor
12	1885	Wilk. & Moore		John Parker	Upholsterer
13	1885	Wilk. & Moore		John Parker	Upholsterer
14	1886	Wilk. & Moore	Hutchins	John Henderson	Commercial Traveller
15	1886	Wilk. & Moore	Hutchins	Edward Beaumont	Draper
16	1886	Wilk. & Moore	Hutchins	Edwin Slaughter	Grocer
17	1879	Galp. & Shir.	Bossom	James Gardiner	Gentleman
18	1879	Galp. & Shir.	Bossom	James Soame	Photographer
19	1886	Wilk. & Moore	E. Webb	George Bliss	Clergyman
20	1886	Wilk. & Moore	E. Webb	George Bliss	Clergyman
21	1886	Wilk. & Moore	E. Webb	William Barrett	Gentleman
22	1886	Wilk. & Moore	E. Webb	William Barrett	Gentleman
23	1886	Wilk. & Moore	E. Webb	Frederick Lovegrove	Tutor
24	1886	Wilk. & Moore	E. Webb	John Hughes	Keeper
25	1887	Wilk. & Moore	E. Webb	John Thomas Green	College Servant
26	1887	Wilk. & Moore	E. Webb	Julia B-Webster	Widow
27	1886	Wilk. & Moore	Money	John Money	Builder
28	1886	Wilk. & Moore	Money	John Money	Builder
29	1885	Wilk. & Moore	Money	William Hallam	Architect
30	1885	Wilk. & Moore	Money	John W. Hallam	Architect
31	1886	Wilk. & Moore	Newcombe	Mary Ann Sadler	Wife/Fellow, ChCh
32	1885	Wilk. & Moore Wilk. & Moore	Newcombe	William Newcomb	Commercial Traveller
33	1885	Wilk. & Moore	Gray	Lewis Bigge	MA
34	1885	Wilk. & Moore	Gray	Emma Davenport	Widow
35	1886	J. Messenger		George Jones	Hotel Prop
36	1886	Wilk. & Moore		Reginald Macan	Fellow, Univ
37	1887	Wilk. & Moore		Richard Lodge	Fellow, BNC

Address	Date of Lease	Architect	Builder	Leaseholder	Occupation
38	1887	Wilk. & Moore		Ebenezer Jenkins	Gentleman
39	1887	Wilk. & Moore		John B. Thompson	MA, ChCh
40	1887	Pike & Mess.		Frederick Pike	Auctioneer
41	1887	Pike & Mess.		Thomas Rose	Draper

Southmoor Rd

Address	Date of Lease	Architect	Builder	Leaseholder	Occupation
1	1885	H.W. Moore	Hutchins	George Cooper	Hardware Dealer
3	1885	H.W. Moore	Hutchins	George Cooper	Hardware Dealer
5	1886	Wilk. & Moore	Hutchins	Samuel Hutchins	Builder
7	1886	Wilk. & Moore	Hutchins	Emily Pannell	Spinster
9	1882	Wilk. & Moore	Chaundy	Henry Chaundy	Cabinetmaker
11	1882		Chaundy	Charles Maxey	Tailor
13	1887	Wilk. & Moore	Prickett	Mary Ann Mollison	Wife/Hairdrssr
15	1885	Wilk. & Moore	Prickett	Ellen Hull	Spinster
17	1889	Wilk. & Moore	Prickett	John Wooldridge	Builder
19	1889	Wilk. & Moore	Prickett	John Wooldridge	Builder
21	1884	Wilk. & Moore	Bayliss	Mark Bayliss	Builder
23	1884	Wilk. & Moore	Bayliss	Mark Bayliss	Builder
25	1885		Collier	William Scroggs	Gentleman
27	1885		Collier	William Scroggs	Gentleman
29	1884		Collier	Charles Davis	College Servant
31	1884		Collier	Charles Davis	College Servant
33	1883	Wilk. & Moore	Money	Ellen Pullen	Widow
35	1883	Wilk. & Moore	Money	Ellen Pullen	Widow
37	1887		E. Webb	Sarah Ann Spencer	Spinster
39	1887		E. Webb	Helen Forrest	Spinster
41	1892		Collier	Sarah Ann Collier	Widow
43	1892		Collier	Sarah Ann Collier	Widow
45	1892		Collier	Sarah Ann Collier	Widow
47	1892		Collier	Sarah Ann Collier	Widow
49	1883	J.C. Gray	Matthew Gray	Edward Bond	Draper
51	1883	J.C. Gray	Matthew Gray	Edward Bond	Draper
53	1883	Wilk. & Moore	Lambourne	William Lambourne	Cabinetmaker
55	1883	Wilk. & Moore	Lambourne	William Lambourne	Cabinetmaker
57	1885	H.W. Moore	Bossom	Martha Webb	Spinster
59	1886	H.W. Moore	Bossom	John Money	Builder
61	1886	H.W. Moore	Bossom	John Money	Builder
63	1886	H.W. Moore	Bossom	John Money	Builder
65	1883		Arnett	Harry J. Arnett	Builder
67	1883		Arnett	Harry J. Arnett	Builder
69	1886	Wilk. & Moore	Dines	Walter Turrill	Poulterer
71	1886	Wilk. & Moore	Dines	Walter Turrill	Poulterer
73	1888	Wilk. & Moore	Dines	Mary Ann Proctor	Spinster
75	1888	Wilk. & Moore	Dines	Mary Ann Proctor	Spinster
77	1885	Wilk. & Moore	E. Webb	Jabez Marston	Goods Agent
79	1884	Wilk. & Moore	E. Webb	John Skuce	Commission Agent
81	1883	Wilk. & Moore		Anne Lucas	Spinster
83	1883	Wilk. & Moore		Harry Smith	Ironmonger
85	1885	Wilk. & Moore		Anne Lucas	Spinster
87	1885	Wilk. & Moore		Anne Lucas	Spinster
89	1885	Wilk. & Moore		Anne Lucas	Spinster
91	1885	Wilk. & Moore		Anne Lucas	Spinster
93	1886	Wilk. & Moore	Alfred Webb	Edward Webb	Builder
95	1886	Wilk. & Moore	Alfred Webb	Edward Webb	Builder

Address	Date of Lease	Architect	Builder	Leaseholder	Occupation
97	1885	Wilk. & Moore	E. Webb	William Hallam	Architect
99	1885	Wilk. & Moore	E. Webb	William Hallam	Architect
101	1885	Wilk. & Moore	E. Webb	Josiah Stevenson	Upholsterer
103	1885	Wilk. & Moore	E. Webb	Thomas Collier	Gentleman
105	1885	Wilk. & Moore	Prickett	Thomas Lucas	Gentleman
107	1885	Wilk. & Moore	Prickett	Thomas Soanes	Tailor
109	1886	Wilk. & Moore		Thomas Webb	Clerk
111	1886	Wilk. & Moore		Thomas Webb	Clerk
2	1885	Wilk. & Moore		John W. Scott	Fishmonger
4	1885	Wilk. & Moore		John W. Scott	Fishmonger
6	1885	Wilk. & Moore		John W. Scott	Fishmonger
8	1886	Wilk. & Moore		John W. Scott	Fishmonger
10	1886	Wilk. & Moore		John W. Scott	Fishmonger
12	1886	Wilk. & Moore		John W. Scott	Fishmonger
14	1889	Wilk. & Moore		James Scott	Pilot
16	1889	Wilk. & Moore		James Scott	Pilot
18	1889	Wilk. & Moore		Edward Money	Printer
20	1889	Wilk. & Moore		William Sheppard	Compositor
22	1895	Wilk. & Moore		Walter Butler	Accountant
24	1895	Wilk. & Moore		Edwin Butler	Victualler
26	1889	Wilk. & Moore		George Shelton	Clerk
28	1889	Wilk. & Moore		George Shelton	Clerk
30	1895	Wilk. & Moore		Thomas Griffiths	Compositor
32	1896	Wilk. & Moore		James Wakelin	Clerk
34	1883	Wilk. & Moore	Money	Rev E.S. Talbot	Warden, Keble
36	1883	Wilk. & Moore	Money	Rev E.S. Talbot	Warden, Keble
38	1883	Wilk. & Moore	Money	Rev E.S. Talbot	Warden, Keble
40	1883	Wilk. & Moore	Money	Rev E.S. Talbot	Warden, Keble
42	1884	Wilk. & Moore		John W. Scott	Fishmonger
44	1884	Wilk. & Moore		John W. Scott	Fishmonger
46	1884	Wilk. & Moore		John W. Scott	Fishmonger
48	1884	Wilk. & Moore		John W. Scott	Fishmonger
50	1884	Wilk. & Moore		John W. Scott	Fishmonger
52	1884	Wilk. & Moore		John W. Scott	Fishmonger
54	1883		Bedding	Harry Bedding	Builder
56	1883		Bedding	Harry Bedding	Builder
58	1883		Bedding	Harry Bedding	Builder
60	1883		Bedding	Harry Bedding	Builder
62	1883		Bedding	Harry Bedding	Builder
64	1883		Bedding	Harry Bedding	Builder
66	1884	Wilk. & Moore	Buckingham	George Reid	Printer
68	1884	Wilk. & Moore	Buckingham	George Reid	Printer
70	1885	Wilk. & Moore	Buckingham	George Reid	Printer
72	1885	Wilk. & Moore	Buckingham	George Reid	Printer
74	1885	Wilk. & Moore	Buckingham	George Reid	Printer
76	1885	Wilk. & Moore	Buckingham	George Reid	Printer
78	1885		Dover	Thomas Lucas	Gentleman
80	1885		Dover	Thomas Lucas	Gentleman
82	1885		Dover	Thomas Lucas	Gentleman
84	1885		Dover	Thomas Lucas	Gentleman
86	1888		E. Webb	Edward Webb	Brickmaker
88	1888		E. Webb	Edward Webb	Brickmaker
90	1887		Horseman	Rupert Hall	Not Known
92	1887		Horseman	Rupert Hall	Not Known

238

Address	Date of Lease	Architect	Builder	Leaseholder	Occupation
94	1885	Wilk. & Moore	E. Webb	Daniel Deverell	College Servant
96	1885	Wilk. & Moore	E. Webb	Edward Webb	Brickmaker
98	1885	Wilk. & Moore	E. Webb	Edward Webb	Brickmaker
100	1885	Wilk. & Moore	E. Webb	Edward Webb	Brickmaker
102	1885	Wilk. & Moore	E. Webb	Edward Webb	Brickmaker
104	1885	Wilk. & Moore	E. Webb	Matilda Gibson	Spinster
106	1887		Horseman	Walter Burgess	Compositor
108	1886		Horseman	Henry Bowen	Compositor
110	1887	Wilk. & Moore	Hutchins	Ernest Alden	Butcher
112	1887	Wilk. & Moore	Hutchins	Emily Bennetts	Widow
114	1888	Wilk. & Moore	Hutchins	James Jackson	Draper
116	1888	Wilk. & Moore	Hutchins	Elizabeth Pannell	Spinster
118	1890	Wilk. & Moore	Hutchins	George Symonds	Gentleman

Tackley Place

Address	Date of Lease	Architect	Builder	Leaseholder	Occupation
1	1882		Williams	Oxford Building Co.	Building Society
2	1882		Williams	Oxford Building Co.	Building Society
3	1882		Williams	Oxford Building Co.	Building Society
4	1882		Williams	Oxford Building Co.	Building Society
5	1882		Williams	Oxford Building Co.	Building Society
6	1882		Williams	Oxford Building Co.	Building Society
7	1882		Williams	Oxford Building Co.	Building Society
8	1887		Gray	Alfred Clark	Hatter
9	1877		Gray	Alfred Clark	Hatter
10	1877		Gray	Richard Bishop	Gentleman
11	1877		Gray	Richard Bishop	Gentleman
12	1877		Gray	Chas Cracknell	Draper
13	1877		Gray	Chas Cracknell	Draper

Walton Well Rd

Address	Date of Lease	Architect	Builder	Leaseholder	Occupation
1	1897			Thomas Johnson	Wheelwright
3	1897			Thomas Johnson	Wheelwright
5	1897			Thomas Johnson	Wheelwright
7	1873			Stephen Large	Boat Builder
9					
11	1884		Curtis	Joseph Curtis	Builder
13	1886		Curtis	Joseph Curtis	Builder
15	1886		Curtis	Joseph Curtis	Builder
17	1889		Curtis	Joseph Curtis	Builder
19	1889		Curtis	Joseph Curtis	Builder
21	1889		Curtis	Joseph Curtis	Builder
23	1889		Curtis	Joseph Curtis	Builder
25	1889		Curtis	Joseph Curtis	Builder
27	1884	Wilk. & Moore	Horseman	James Horseman	Builder
29	1884	Wilk. & Moore	Horseman	James Andrews	Bookseller
31	1887	Wilk. & Moore	Arnett	James Turrill	Poulterer
33	1887	Wilk. & Moore	Arnett	James Turrill	Poulterer
35	1887	Wilk. & Moore	Arnett	James Turrill	Poulterer
37	1887	Wilk. & Moore	Arnett	James Turrill	Poulterer
39	1887	Wilk. & Moore	Arnett	William Chennell	Saddler
41	1888	Wilk. & Moore	Arnett	James Turrill	Poulterer
10[8]	1886	H.W. Moore	Buckingham	Asaph Pauling	Tailor
12	1886	H.W. Moore	Buckingham	John Mansell	Clerk

Address	Date of Lease	Architect	Builder	Leaseholder	Occupation
14	1886	H.W. Moore	Buckingham	Clara Blencowe	Spinster
16	1886	H.W. Moore	Buckingham	Clara Blencowe	Spinster
18	1888		Buckingham	Mary Ann Thomas	Widow
20	1889	H.W. Moore	Arnett	Francis Andrews	Secretary
22	1889	H.W. Moore	Arnett	Caroline Goundrey	Widow
24	1889	H.W. Moore	Arnett	Francis Andrews	Secretary
26	1888	H.W. Moore	Arnett	Charlotte Spiers	Widow
28	1888	H.W. Moore	Arnett	George Gardiner	Architect
30	1888	H.W. Moore	Arnett	William Timberlake	Librarian

Warnborough Rd

Address	Date of Lease	Architect	Builder	Leaseholder	Occupation
1	1877		Reynolds	Oxford Building Co.	Building Society
2	1877		Reynolds	Oxford Building Co.	Building Society
3	1882		Williams	Oxford Building Co.	Building Society
4	1882		Williams	Oxford Building Co.	Building Society
5	1882		Williams	Oxford Building Co.	Building Society
6	1882		Williams	Oxford Building Co.	Building Society
7	1880	Wilkinson	Brucker	Hon W. Sackville-West	Gentleman
8	1880	Wilkinson	Brucker	Hon W. Sackville-West	Gentleman
9	1879		Brucker	Hon W. Sackville-West	Gentleman
10	1879		Brucker	Hon W. Sackville-West	Gentleman
11	1879		Brucker	Hon W. Sackville-West	Gentleman
12	1879		Brucker	Hon W. Sackville-West	Gentleman
13	1883		Curtis	Frederick Hiffe	Schoolmaster
14	1883		Curtis	Thomas Wyatt	Builder
15	1886		Curtis	William Hurst	Gentleman
16	1886		Curtis	William Hurst	Gentleman
17	1888		Curtis	Sidney Venables	Gunmaker
18	1888		Curtis	Sidney Venables	Gunmaker
19	1887	Galp. & Shir.	Dover	John Thos Green	College Servant
20	1886	Galp. & Shir.	Dover	John Dorn	Builder
21	1885	Galp. & Shir.	Dover	James Nix	PO Clerk
22	1884	Galp. & Shir.	Dover	Thomas Eldrid	Commercial Traveller
23	1884	Galp. & Shir.	Dover	Thomas Andrews	Commercial Traveller
24	1886	Galp. & Shir.	Dover	John Dorn	Builder
25	1886	Galp. & Shir.	Dover	John Dorn	Builder
26	1885	Galp. & Shir.	Holt	Ann Thornton	Wife/Bookseller
27	1885	Galp. & Shir.	Holt	William Cannon	Butcher
28	1896	Galp. & Shir.		Graham Squire	Cleric
29	1895	Galp. & Shir.		Graham Squire	Cleric
30	1891	Galp. & Shir.		Henry Marsh	Paymaster RN
31	1881	Galp. & Shir.		William Duck	BA Hertf
32	1885	Galp. & Shir.	Hall	William Hurcomb	Bookseller
33	1882	Galp. & Shir.	Hall	Oxford Building Co.	Building Society
34	1885		Holt	Ann Sillman	Widow
35	1885		Holt	Ann Sillman	Widow

Address	Date of Lease	Architect	Builder	Leaseholder	Occupation
Winchester Rd					
1	1877	Cross	Dover	William Cross	Builder
2	1877	Cross	Dover	Richard Sexton	Tea Dealer
3	1875	Cross	Dover	Lucy Ham	Spinster
4	1876	Cross	Dover	Lucy Ham	Spinster
5	1875	Wilkinson	Dorn	Alfred Boffin	Confectioner
6	1875	Wilkinson	Dorn	Elizabeth Dudley	Spinster
7	1875	Wilkinson	Dorn	Edward Beaumont	Draper
8	1876	Wilkinson	Dorn	John Smith	Bootmaker
9	1876	Wilkinson	Dorn	Emily Williams	Widow
10	1880	Wilkinson	Dorn	Edwin Elliott	Bootmaker
21[9]	1876	Codd		Frederick Codd	Architect
22	1882	Wilkinson	Dorn	John Dorn	Builder
23	1882	Wilkinson	Dorn	John Dorn	Builder
24	1882	Wilkinson	Dorn	John Dorn	Builder
25	1882	Wilkinson	Dorn	John Dorn	Builder
26	1882	Wilkinson	Dorn	John Dorn	Builder
Woodstock Rd					
99	1865		Watson	Josiah Watson	Contractor
101	1865		Watson	Josiah Watson	Contractor
103	1865			John Lovis	Commercial Traveller
105	1865			John Lovis	Commercial Traveller
107	1866			William Lucy	Iron Founder
109	1866			Catherine Lucy	Widow
111	1866	Wilkinson		Robert Hills	Photographer
113	1863	Wilkinson		Edwin Butler	Wine Merchant
115	1869			Titus Wray	Grocer
117	1865			Henry Yule	Esquire
119	1863			Robert Hawkins	Solicitor
121	1856	Seckham	Dyne	John Dyne	Builder
123	1856	Seckham	Dyne	John Dyne	Builder
125	1868	Bruton		Edward G. Bruton	Architect
127	1868	Bruton		Alexander Hurford	Gentleman
129	1876	Galpin		John Dover	Builder
131	1876	Galpin		Philip Tyrwhitt	Commander RN
133	1870		Symm	Titus Wray	Grocer
135	1871		Symm	Thomas Hyde	Gentleman
137	1884		Symm	Edmund Bevers	Surgeon
139	1884		Symm	William Leary	Gentleman
141	1865			John O. Westwood	Prof Zoology
143	1887	Wilk. & Moore	Kingerlee	Montague Wootten	Banker
145	1888	Wilk. & Moore	Kingerlee	Robert Hartley	BA, Exeter
147	1889	H.W. Moore	Kingerlee	Thomas Withington	Esquire
149	1890	H.W. Moore	Hutchins	George Carter	Inland Revenue
151	1890	H.W. Moore	Hutchins	Sally Stevens	Spinster
153	1914	H.W. Moore	Hutchins	Samuel Hutchins	Builder
155	1914	H.W. Moore	Hutchins	Samuel Hutchins	Builder
157	1905	H.W. Moore	Hutchins	Samuel Hutchins	Builder
159	1905	H.W. Moore	Hutchins	John Chillingworth	Farmer

241

Address	Date of Lease	Architect	Builder	Leaseholder	Occupation
161	1891	H.W. Moore	Castle & Martin	James Millard	Fellow, Magdalen
163	1892	H.W. Moore	Castle & Martin	Arthur Thomson	Lecturer, Exeter
165	1891	H.W. Moore	Castle & Martin	Robert Buckell	Auctioneer
167	1900	H.W. Moore	Inness	Arthur Castle	Gentleman
169	1900	H.W. Moore	Inness	Arthur Castle	Gentleman
171	1898		Jarvis	Edwin Parry	Contractor
173	1898		Jarvis	Edwin Parry	Contractor
175	1900		Jarvis	Thomas Cross	Gentleman
177	1898		Jarvis	Thomas Cross	Gentleman
179	1900	H.W. Moore	Buckingham	George Blake	Furnisher
181	1900	H.W. Moore	Buckingham	George Blake	Furnisher
183	1902	H.W. Moore	Buckingham	Herbert Blunt	Tutor, ChCh
185	1904	H.W. Moore	Buckingham	Thomas Grimsley	Builder
187	1904	H.W. Moore	Buckingham	Thomas Grimsley	Builder
189	1904	H.W. Moore	Buckingham	Thomas Grimsley	Builder
191	1903	H.W. Moore	Wooldridge	Alfred Boffin	Confectioner
193	1906	H.W. Moore	Wooldridge	Mary Ann Ray	Wife/Gentleman
195	1901	H.W. Moore	Wooldridge	Ellen Dore	Widow
197	1901	H.W. Moore	Wooldridge	Arthur Kerry	Fellow, Exeter
199	1909	N.W. Harrison	Wooldridge	Frank Gadney	Esquire
201					
203	1903	H.W. Moore	Blencowe	Sydney Underhill	Grocer
205	1903	H.W. Moore	Blencowe	Frederick Blencowe	Builder
207	1903	H.W. Moore	Blencowe	Flora Sidebottam	Widow
209	1903	H.W. Moore	Blencowe	Frederick Blencowe	Builder
213	1914	H.W. Moore		Ethel Pogson-Smith	Widow
215	1914	H.W. Moore		Ethel Pogson-Smith	Widow
217	1900			Frances Richardson	Wife/Clergyman
219	1900			Sarah Gillett	Spinster
221	1902	H.W. Moore	Wild	Alfred Boffin	Confectioner
223	1902	H.W. Moore	Wild	Josiah Nix	Gentleman
225	1901	H.W. Moore	Wild	Samuel Watson	Builder
227	1903	H.W. Moore	Wild	Arthur Jolliffe	Fellow, Corpus
229	1906		Wild	Hortense Dulake	Wife/Auctioneer
231	1906		Wild	George Underhill	Esquire
233	1907		Brucker	Fanny Potter	Wife/Draper
235	1907		Brucker	Alice Maltby	Wife/Bookbinder
237	1915		Cowley	Henry Cowley	Builder
239	1915		Cowley	Henry Cowley	Builder
241	1913		Blencowe	Frederick Blencowe	Builder
243	1913		Blencowe	Thomas Grimsley	Builder
245	1914		Blencowe	Ellen Barker	Widow
247	1914		Blencowe	Frederick Blencowe	Builder
251	1896		E. Webb	Edward Webb	Brickmaker
253	1924		Capel	Brenda DeButts	Spinster
255	1931		Hutchins	Gerald McMichael	MD
257	1926		Hinkins & Frewin	Dorothy Bigg	Spinster
259	1927		Capel	L. Dudley-Buxton	MA, Exeter
261	1913		E. Webb	Edward Webb	Brickmaker
263	1911		E. Webb	F. John Hanks	Bookseller
265	1910		E. Webb	Edward Webb	Brickmaker
38	1884	Wilk. & Moore		Moses Allnutt	College Servant
40	1884	Wilk. & Moore		Moses Allnutt	College Servant

Address	Date of Lease	Architect	Builder	Leaseholder	Occupation
8[10]	1882	H.G.W. Drinkwater	Williams	Frederick Smith	Maltster
0	1882	Wilk. & Moore	Franklin	Alexander Macdonald	Art Teacher
6[11]	1868			Robert Charsley	Lecturer Maths
8	1872	Codd		Charles Hoole	Senior Student, ChCh
0	1872	Codd		Daniel Parsons	MA, Oriel
2	1868	Buckeridge	Wyatt	Marion Hughes	Spinster
4	1875	Galp. & Shir.		John Nutt	Fellow, All Souls
6	1875	Galp. & Shir.		John Hanbury	Fellow, Wadham
8	1887	Drinkwater	Wilkins	SS Philip & James	Vicarage
0	1872	Codd		Samuel Merriman	Esquire
4	1882	Wilk. & Moore	Brucker	Thomas Holland	Prof Int Law
6	1882	Wilk. & Moore	Brucker	Thomas Gorman	Cleric
8	1882	Wilk. & Moore	Brucker	Thomas Gorman	Cleric
0	1884	Wilk. & Moore	Brucker	Richard Rowell	Silversmith
2	1887	Wilk. & Moore	Hutchins	Thomas Gorman	Cleric
4	1886	Wilk. & Moore	Brucker	Frances Bull	Spinster
6	1889	Wilk. & Moore	Colston	Sarah Crow	Wife/Draper
8	1892	H. Quinton	Jarvis	David Margoliouth	Prof Arabic
0	1892	H. Quinton	Jarvis	Edward Rice	MD
2	1891	H. Quinton	Jarvis	Daniel Jarvis	Builder
4	1888	H.G.W. Drinkwater		Thomas Lucas	Gentleman

SJC   St John's College
New Coll New College
ChCh   Christ Church
BNC   Brasenose College

Galp. & Shir   Galpin & Shirley
Pike & Mess.   Pike & Messenger
Radcl. & Wat.   Radclyffe & Watson
Wilk. & Moore   Wilkinson & Moore.

NOTES

CHAPTER ONE

1 For the concept of the 'walking suburb' see Sam B. Warner, *Streetcar Suburbs*, 1976, Chapter 2; and for eighteenth- and nineteenth-century suburban growth in English towns see C.W. Chalklin, *The Provincial Towns of Georgian England*, 1974.
2 Quoted in Georgiana Goddard King ed., *George Edmund Street Unpublished Notes and Reprinted Papers*, 1916, p. 14.
3 *Jackson's Oxford Journal*, 7 January 1860; *Oxford Chronicle*, 4 February 1882.
4 A variety of nineteenth-century suburbs are discussed in F.M.L. Thompson ed., *The Rise of Suburbia*, 1982.
5 D.J. Olsen, *Town Planning in London*, 1964, Chapter 4; D.J. Olsen, *The Growth of Victorian London*, 1976, pp. 247–64.
6 W.H. Stevenson and H.E. Salter, *The Early History of St John's College Oxford*, 1939, pp. 116–22.
7 C.M. Clode, *The Early History of the Guild of Merchant Taylors of the Fraternity of St John the Baptist*, 1888, II.
8 W.K. Jacob, *The Charities of London 1480–1660*, 1960, p. 174.
9 Stevenson and Salter, *Early History of St John's*, p. 114.
10 *Ibid.*, p. 197.
11 J.R.L. Highfield, 'The Early Colleges', in J.I. Catto ed., *The Early Oxford Schools*, 1984.
12 Stevenson and Salter, *Early History of St John's*, pp. 151–6.
13 Victoria County History (hereafter VCH), *Oxon*, 1954, III, p. 245.
14 Christopher Hill, *Economic Problems of the Church*, 1956, p. 30.
15 13 Elizabeth c 10; 18 Elizabeth c 11.
16 *Report of the Commissioners appointed to inquire into the property and income of the Universities of Oxford and Cambridge . . .* , 1874, I, p. 26.
17 Saint John's College (hereafter SJC), *Register*, 8 October 1828.
18 SJC, *Computus Annuus*, Muniments, ACC I A, 1800–65.
19 *Universities and College Estates Act Extension*, 23 and 24 Vict c 59.
20 For nineteenth-century University Reform see A.I. Tillyard, *A History of University Reform*, 1913;

W.R. Ward, *Victorian Oxford*, 1965; and A.J. Engel, *From Clergyman to Don*, 1983.
21 SJC, *Register*, 7 April 1837.
22 *Oxford University Act*, 17 and 18 Vict c 81.
23 Stevenson and Salter, *Early History of St John's*, p. 122.
24 E.P. Hart ed., *Merchant Taylors' School Register, 1851–1920*, 1923.
25 W.C. Costin, *The History of St John's College Oxford 1598–1860*, 1958, p. 277.
26 *Letter from the President of St John's College, Oxford to the Master of Merchant Taylors' Company*, 8 June 1888.
27 *University of Oxford and Cambridge Act*, 40 and 41 Vict c 48.
28 *Report of the Commissioners . . .* 3 vols., 1874.
29 *Ibid.*, II, p. 769.
30 *Ibid.*, I, p. 109.
31 *Ibid.*, II, p. 767.
32 *Ibid.*, II, p. 748.
33 *Ibid.*, II, p. 781.
34 *Ibid.*, II, pp. 327–32.
35 Alan Crossley, Chris Day and Janet Cooper, *Shopping in Oxford*, 1983, pp. 23–5.

CHAPTER TWO

1 *Jackson's Oxford Journal*, 30 July 1853.
2 *Select Committee on Oxford and Great Western Union Railway Bill*, PRO HL 227, XX, 1837–8, p. 648, quoted in VCH, *Oxon*, 1979, IV, p. 186.
3 William Morris, 'Art Under Plutocracy', in A.L. Morton ed., *Political Writings of William Morris*, 1979, p. 62.
4 Richard Rodger, 'Rents and ground rents', in James H. Johnson and Colin G. Pooley, *The Structure of Nineteenth Century Cities*, 1982, pp. 39–74.
5 E.T. MacDermott, *History of the Great Western Railway*, 1964, I, pp. 86–7.
6 VCH, *Oxon*, 1979, IV, p. 209.
7 *Report of the Commission appointed to inquire into the property and income of the Universities of Oxford and Cambridge . . .* , C-856, 1874, II.
8 R.J. Morris, 'The Friars and Paradise: An Essay in the Building History of Oxford 1801–1861', *Oxoniensia*, 1971, XXXVI, p. 76.
9 A.J. Engel, *From Clergyman to Don*, 1983, p. 61.
10 For general discussions of the suburb see

F.M.L. Thompson ed., 'Introduction', *The Rise of Suburbia*, 1982; C.W. Chalklin, *The Provincial Towns of Georgian England. A Study of the Building Process 1740–1820*, 1974.

11 See Leonore Davidoff and Catherine Hall, *Family Fortunes Men and Women of the English Middle Class 1780–1850*, 1987.

12 An example of these two types in close proximity to each other are Clissold House, *c.* 1820, and Highbury Terrace, 1789, in north London.

13 Ann Bermingham, *Landscape and Ideology the English Rustic Tradition, 1740–1860*, 1987.

14 VCH, *Oxon*, 1979, IV, p. 209.

15 H.E. Salter ed., *A Cartulary of the Hospital of St John the Baptist*, 1917, III, p. 336.

16 SJC, Muniments, VB 74.

17 See Anson Osmond, 'Building on the Beaumonts: An Example of Early 19th-Century Housing Development', *Oxoniensia*, 1984, XLIX, pp. 301–25.

18 J.P.D. Dunbabin, 'College Estates and Wealth 1660–1815', in L.S. Sutherland and L.G. Mitchell, eds., *The Eighteenth Century*, vol. v of *The History of the University of Oxford* ed. T.H. Aston, 1986, p. 288.

19 SJC, *Register*, 24 October 1804.

20 *Ibid.*, 19 May and 9 October 1822.

21 SJC, *Computus Annuus*, Muniments, ACC I, A, 1822. My thanks to H.M. Colvin for drawing my attention to this reference.

22 SJC, *Register*, 8 October 1823.

23 *Ibid.*, 7 April and 26 June 1824.

24 SJC, *Lease Book and General Ledger*, 1821–41.

25 SJC, Muniments, EST III, MP 185.

26 SJC, *Lease Book and General Ledger*, 1821–41.

27 *Notes on Oxford Market*, Bodleian, MS Top Oxon, e. 620.

28 *Oxford Canal Navigation*, Bodleian, MS Top Oxon c. 752–3.

29 *Census Enumerators' Returns*, 1841, HO 107 891.

30 See Harold Perkin, *Origins of Modern English Society*, 1969.

31 Pamela Horn, *The Rise and Fall of the Victorian Servant*, 1975, pp. 9–10.

32 F. Musgrove, 'Middle-class Education and Employment in the Nineteenth Century', *Economic History Review*, 2nd Series, XII (1959–60) p. 102.

33 *Census Returns*, 1841–1901.

34 *Census Enumerators' Returns*, 1841, HO 107 891.

35 *Jackson's Oxford Journal*, 19 March 1853.

36 SJC, *Register*, 6 April 1825.

37 *Jackson's Oxford Journal*, 20 October 1827; SJC, *Muniments*, MP 42.

38 SJC, *Lease Book and General Ledger*, 1821–9, p. 344.

39 SJC, *St Giles's Allottment Award*, Muniments, VB 101.

40 SJC, *Lease Book and General Ledger*, 1821–9, p. 344.

41 *Journals of the House of Commons*, LXXXIII, p. 173.

42 10 Geo IV, c 15.

43 *Jackson's Oxford Journal*, 19 September 1829.

44 SJC, *Mr Dixon's Valuation of Houses in St Giles's*, 1829, Muniments, VB 91.

45 *Ibid.*

46 SJC, *St Giles's Allottment Award*, Muniments VB 101.

47 SJC, Muniments VB 107; *Register*, 10 October 1842.

48 SJC, Muniments MP 52; Muniments VB 79.

49 SJC, *Register*, 7 October 1840.

50 *Ibid.*, 5 October 1842.

51 *Ibid.*, 11 October 1843.

52 *Ibid.*, 10 April 1844.

53 *Ibid.*, 30 January 1846.

54 *Ibid.*, 26 February 1847.

55 *Jackson's Oxford Journal*, 10 February 1849.

56 *Ibid.*

57 *Ibid.*, 10 March 1849.

58 SJC, Muniments VB 114.

59 *Ibid.*

60 *Ibid.*

61 *Jackson's Oxford Journal*, 27 July 1850.

62 *Ibid.*, 26 October and 21 December 1850.

63 *Ibid.*, 27 July 1850.

64 SJC, Muniments VB 114.

65 *Jackson's Oxford Journal*, 9 and 16 August; 15 November 1851.

66 *Ibid.*, 19 March 1853.

67 See J.R. Kellett, *The Impact of Railways on Victorian Cities*, 1969.

68 MacDermott, *Great Western Railway*, I, p. 86.

69 Margaret Jeune Gifford ed., *Pages from the Diary of an Oxford Lady, 1843–1862*, 1932.

70 MacDermott, *Great Western Railway*, I, p. 86.

71 *Ibid.*, p. 87.

72 *Ibid.*, pp. 100–51.

73 Oxford County Record Office, *London and Midwestern Railway*, PD 2 57.

74 SJC, *Register*, 22 December 1851 and 17 February 1852.

75 *Jackson's Oxford Journal*, 13 March 1852.

76 *Ibid.*, 20 March 1852.

77 *Ibid.*, 19 March 1853.

78 MacDermott, *Great Western Railway*, I, p. 261.

79 SJC, Muniments, VB 117.

80 SJC, *Leases and General Ledger*, 1841–60.

81 *Ibid.*

82 SJC, Muniments EST II.

83 SJC, Muniments MP 75.

84 *Jackson's Oxford Journal*, 19 March 1853; Bodleian MS Dep C. 541, d.

85 *Jackson's Oxford Journal*, 19 March 1853.

86 *Ibid.*, 2 April 1853.

87 See Peter Howell, 'Samuel Lipscomb Seckham', *Oxoniensia*, 1976, XLI, pp 337–47.

88 Bodleian MS Dep b. 217.

89 *Ibid.*

90 *Ibid.*

91 SJC, *Register*, 13 October 1854; Bodleian MS Top Oxon a. 28.

92 *Jackson's Oxford Journal*, 20 January 1883.

93 SJC, *Register*, 5 April 1854.

94 Bodleian MS Top Oxon a. 28.

95 SJC, *Register*, 5 April 1854.

96 SJC, *Bird's Eye View of the Walton Manor Estate*, Muniments MP 183.

97 SJC, *Register*, 13 October 1854; 18 and 19 Vict

c 10.

98 SJC, *Leases and General Ledger*, 1841–60, p. 358.

99 SJC, Muniments EST II.

100 *Census Returns*, 1861.

CHAPTER THREE

1 *Oxford Chronicle and Berks and Bucks Gazette*, 17 March 1883.

2 *Census Returns*, 1861 and 1871.

3 *Ibid.*

4 *Jackson's Oxford Journal*, 19 May 1860.

5 *Census Returns*, 1861 and 1871.

6 SJC, *Register*, 15 October 1859.

7 *Jackson Oxford Journal*, 14 April 1860; 2 February and 9 November 1861.

8 *Ibid.*, 8 September 1860.

9 *Ibid.*, 15 September 1860.

10 SJC, Muniments VC 7.

11 *Jackson's Oxford Journal*, 16 June 1860; SJC, *Estates Committee Minutes*, 28 April 1863; *Bursar's Incoming Letters*, 7 May 1879.

12 SJC, Muniments VC 8.

13 SJC, Muniments VC 11.

14 SJC, *Estates Committee Minutes*, 23 November 1871.

15 SJC, *Bursar's Incoming Letters*, 7 May 1879.

16 SJC, *College Leases*, Muniments V.

17 T.F.M. Hinchcliffe, 'Highbury New Park', *The London Journal*, 1981, no. 1, vii, pp. 29–44.

18 See SJC, *Register*, for the relevant years.

19 *Ibid.*, 3 February and 11 April 1860.

20 *Ibid.*, 17 October 1862.

21 SJC, *Bursar's Letters*, 23 January 1863.

22 E.T. MacDermott, *History of the Great Western Railway*, 1964, ii, pp. 16 and 19.

23 SJC, *Register*, 14 October 1864; *Estates Committee Minutes*, 20 February 1885.

24 SJC, *Bursar's Letters*, 13 March 1868.

25 Derived from SJC *Building Proposals*, *Building Agreements*, and *Leases*.

26 A data base has been made from SJC documents (hereafter SJC, *Data Base*).

27 *Oxford Building and Investment Company*, Bodleian, G.A. Oxon. c. 152.

28 *Oxford Chronicle*, 21 April 1883.

29 SJC, *Data Base*.

30 SJC, *Long Leases Ledgers*, 1863–84.

31 *London Directory*, 1860.

32 *Oxford Chronicle*, 14 October 1871.

33 *Ibid.*

34 SJC, *College Leases*, Muniments V.

35 *Ibid.*

36 *Jackson's Oxford Journal*, 8 January 1876.

37 *Ibid.*, 18 March and 12 August 1876.

38 University College, Muniments. I am indebted to David Sturdy for directing me to this correspondence held in the archives of University College.

39 C.J. Faulkner was a friend of William Morris and had been one of the original partners in 'The Firm' of Messrs Morris, Marshall, Faulkner and Co.

40 *Ibid.*, Letter from C.J. Faulkner to F.R. Pike, 25 January 1877.

41 *Ibid.*, Note on Letter from F.R. Pike to C.J. Faulkner, 27 June 1878.

42 *Ibid.*, Letter from T.S. Omond to C.J. Faulkner, 7 July 1878.

43 *Ibid.*

44 SJC, *Bursar's Incoming Letters*, 7 May 1879.

45 SJC, *Register*, 25 April 1878; *The City Press*, 28 February, 2 and 9 March 1878.

46 See J.P.D. Dunbabin, *Economic History Review* 2nd Series, 1975, xxviii, pp. 631–47; *Ibid.*, 1978 xxxi, pp. 446–9; A.J. Engel, *Ibid.*, pp. 437–45; Peter Mathias, *The First Industrial Nation*, 1983, pp 361–9.

47 *Jackson's Oxford Journal*, 11 May 1861.

48 *Oxford Building Investment Company*, Bodleian G.A. Oxon. c. 152. For Overend and Gurney see Mathias, *First Industrial Nation*, p. 176.

49 Mathias, *First Industrial Nation*, p. 328.

50 *The Oxford Chronicle*, 21 January 1871.

51 Sydney Galpin, *The Oxford Branch of Galpins* Bodleian, Top. Oxon. d. 473.

52 Malcolm Graham, *The Suburbs of Victorian Oxford*, unpublished Phd. thesis, University of Leicester, 1985, p. 93.

53 *The Oxford Chronicle*, 21 April 1883.

54 *Oxford Building and Investment Company*, Bodleian, G.A. Oxon. c. 152.

55 *The Oxford Chronicle*, 14 April 1883.

56 *Ibid.*, 30 June 1883.

57 Graham, *Suburbs of Victorian Oxford*, p. 99; *Oxford Building and Investment Company*, Bodleian, G.A. Oxon. c. 152.

58 *The Oxford Chronicle*, 30 June 1883.

59 *Ibid.*, 26 April 1883.

60 VCH, *Oxon*, iv, p. 231.

61 C. Fenby, *The Other Oxford*, 1970, p. 13.

62 SJC, *College Leases*, Muniments V.

63 *Oxford Building and Investment Company*, Bodleian, G.A. Oxon. c. 152.

64 *The Oxford Chronicle*, 17 March 1883.

65 *Ibid.*, 21 April 1883.

66 *Ibid.*

67 *Ibid.*, 5 May 1883.

68 *The Oxford Chronicle*, 5 and 12 February 1887.

69 *Ibid.*, 30 June 1883.

70 *Ibid.*, 20 January 1883.

71 *Census Enumerators' Returns*, 1881, RG11 1499.

72 *The Oxford Chronicle*, 14 July 1883.

CHAPTER FOUR

1 Richard Dennis, *English Industrial Cities of the Nineteenth Century*, 1984, p. 18.

2 Stefan Muthesius, *The English Terraced House*, 1982, pp. 12ff.

3 Donald J. Olsen, *Town Planning in London*, 2nd ed., 1982, p. 29.

4 F.M.L. Thompson, *Hampstead Building a Borough, 1650–1964*, 1974, p. 92.

5 R.J. Morris, 'The Middle Class and the Property Cycle during the Industrial Revolution', in T.C. Smout, ed., *The Search for Wealth and Stability*, 1979.

6 Mary Russell Mitford, *Our Village, Sketches of Rural Character and Scenery*, 1830, I, pp. 14–15.
7 J.M. Rawcliffe, 'Bromley: Kentish market town', in F.M.L. Thompson, ed., *The Rise of the Suburb*, 1982, pp. 48–53.
8 Sir John Summerson, *Georgian London*, revised ed., 1969, p. 175.
9 Sir John Summerson, 'The Beginnings of Regents Park', *Architectural History*, 1977, XX, pp. 56–62.
10 David Cannadine, *Lords and Landlords: the Aristocracy and the Towns, 1774–1967*, 1980, pp. 98ff.
11 Bodleian MS Dep. c. 541. item d.
12 SJC, *Bird's Eye View of Walton Manor Estate*, Muniments MP 183.
13 See George Chadwick, *The Park and the Town*, 1966.
14 *The Builder*, 1867, XXV, pp. 625–7.
15 VCH, *Oxon*, IV, p. 274.
16 *Jackson's Oxford Journal*, 13 October 1866; see also Peter Hayden, 'James Bateman', *Staffordshire History*, I, 1984, p. 11 and R.T. Gunther, *Oxford Gardens*, 1912, p. 238.
17 Bodleian MS Top. gen. a. 22, f. 27.
18 Andrew Saint, 'Three Oxford Architects', *Oxoniensia*, 1970, XXXV, p. 84 n. 82.
19 SJC, Muniments VC 8.
20 SJC, *Bursar's Incoming letters*, 7 November 1877.
21 SJC, Muniments VC 12.
22 SJC, Muniments VC 18–19, 21–42.
23 SJC, *Register*, 9 October 1822, 11 April 1855.
24 *Ibid.*, 25 February 1834, 29 January 1851, 6 April 1853, 3 February 1860, 11 April 1860.
25 SJC, *Bursar's Letters*, 11 February 1868.
26 SJC, *Register*, 16 October 1868, 9 April 1869.
27 SJC, *Observations on Statutes and Financial Statement*, [1880], Muniments.
28 J.P.D. Dunbabin, *Economic History Review*, 1975, 2nd Series, XXVIII, pp. 631–47; *Ibid.*, 1978, XXXI, pp. 446–9; A.J. Engel, *Ibid.*, pp. 437–45.
29 SJC, *Bursar's Incoming Letters*, 5 January 1877.
30 *Ibid.*, 10 May 1879.
31 *Ibid.*, 9 January 1880.
32 *Ibid.*, 24 March 1877.
33 SJC *Correspondence between T.S. Omond and President Bellamy*, 1885, Muniments File Box F No 217.
34 SJC, *Register*, 13 April 1882.
35 SJC, *Bursar's Reports*, 1886, 1887, Muniments File Box F No 217.
36 Howard Colvin, *The Canterbury Quadrangle*, 1988, p. 98.
37 *Letter of the President of St John's College, Oxford to the Master of Merchant Taylors' Company*, June 8, 1888, Guildhall Library London, Pam 12733.
38 SJC, *Appeal to the Visitor*, 1887, Muniments LII 173; *Register*, 20 December 1887. The College visitor was the external arbitrator to whom the fellows could appeal concerning internal disputes or their relations with the University.
39 *Ibid.*, 11 October 1888.
40 *The Oxford Chronicle*, 16, 23, 30 March 1889; *Jackson's Oxford Journal*, 16 March 1889.

41 SJC, *Appeal to Counsel*, 1889, Muniments File Box F No 217.
42 SJC, *Correspondence between Omond and President Bellamy*, Muniments File Box F No 217.
43 SJC, *Register*, 5 May 1889.
44 SJC, *Appeal to Counsel*, 1896, Muniments File Box B No 65.
45 *The Oxford Chronicle*, 17 March 1883.
46 SJC, *Bursar's Inward Letters*, 14 July 1877.
47 C. Fenby, *The Other Oxford*, 1970.
48 SJC, Data derived from College records (SJC Data Base).
49 SJC, *Long Lease Ledger*.
50 SJC, Muniments. VD.
51 University College, Muniments, *Letter from T.S. Omond to C.J. Faulkner*, 7 July 1878.
52 SJC, *Estates Committee Minutes*, 18 October 1880.
53 SJC, *Bursar's Letters*, 7 and 9 October 1882.
54 *Ibid.*, 1 December 1882.
55 *Ibid.*, 23 January 1883.
56 *Ibid.*, 17 November 1883.
57 Mitford, *Our Village*, pp. 1–16.
58 SJC, *Bursar's Letters*, 20 October 1882.
59 *Ibid.*, 30 October 1882.
60 *The Oxford Chronicle*, 14 July 1883.
61 SJC, *Estates Committee Minutes*, 26 October 1888.
62 Bodleian Per G.A. Oxon 4. 180.
63 SJC, *Estates Committee Minutes*, 6 February 1885.
64 SJC, *Bursar's Incoming Letters*, 16 February 1885.
65 SJC, *Estates Committee Minutes*, 29 January 1886.
66 Bodleian Per G.A. Oxon 4 161.
67 SJC, *Long Leases Ledgers*.
68 Bodleian Per G.A. Oxon 4 161.
69 SJC, *Bursar's Letters*, 7 April 1886.
70 SJC, *Data Base*.
71 VCH *Oxon*, IV, p. 359.
72 SJC, *Estates Committee Minutes*, 14 June 1895.
73 *Ibid.*, 27 July 1903.
74 *Ibid.*, 24 February 1875.
75 *Ibid.*, 24 April 1885.
76 SJC, *Bursar's Incoming Letters*, 23 May 1885.
77 *Ibid.*, 26 May 1885.
78 SJC, *Bursar's Letters*, 5 February 1886.
79 SJC, *Bursar's Incoming Letters*, 8 February 1886.

CHAPTER FIVE

1 Marcus Dick and A.F. Kersting, *Portrait of Oxford*, 1956, p. 12.
2 Sir John Summerson, 'The London Suburban Villa', *The Architectural Review*, 1948, CIV, pp. 63–74.
3 J.C. Loudon, *An Encyclopaedia of Cottage, Farm and Villa Architecture and Furniture*, 1836.
4 *Ibid.*, p. 774.
5 *The Ecclesiologist*, 1843, II, p. 145.
6 *Ibid.*, 1853, XII, p. 310. For writings by White see Paul Thompson, 'The Writings of William White', *Concerning Architecture*, ed. J. Summerson, 1968, pp. 226–37.

7 *Ibid.*

8 George Gilbert Scott, *Remarks on Secular and Domestic Architecture*, 1857, p. 7.

9 Robert Kerr, *The Gentleman's House or How to Plan English Residences, from the Parsonage to the Palace*, 1864, p. 76.

10 *The Builder*, 1866, xxiv, p. 209.

11 *Building News*, 1874, xxvi, p. 460.

12 *Ibid.*, 1875, xxvii, p. 640.

13 E. Viollet-le-Duc, *Habitations Modernes*, 1875, i, pp. 2–3.

14 Alan Savidge, *The Parsonage in England its History and Architecture*, 1969, p. 115.

15 *Ibid.*, p. 118.

16 SJC, *Bird's Eye View of the Walton Manor Estate*, Muniments MP 183; Bodleian, MS Top. Oxon. d. 501, fol 89.

17 Scott, *Remarks on Secular and Domestic Architecture*, pp. 114–15.

18 Details of Wilkinson's life are derived from Andrew Saint, 'Three Oxford Architects', *Oxoniensia*, 1970, xxxv, pp. 53–102.

19 *The Builder*, 1865, xxiii, pp. 145–6.

20 *Jackson's Oxford Journal*, 27 July 1861.

21 *The Builder*, 1861, xix, pp. 124–5.

22 SJC, *Estates Committee Minutes*, 19 February 1863.

23 *Ibid.*, 29 July 1865.

24 SJC, Printed Building Agreement Form.

25 William Wilkinson, *English Country Houses*, 1870.

26 H.S. Goodhart-Rendel, 'North Oxford', *Architecture and Building News*, 1936, cxlv, p. 284.

27 Wilkinson, *English Country Horses*, Nos 1–2.

28 *Ibid.*, Nos 7–8.

29 E. Viollet-le-Duc, *Habitations Modernes*, ii, plates 182–3.

30 *The Ecclesiologist*, 1863, xxiv, p. 68.

31 E.O. Dodgson, 'Notes on Nos 56, 58, 60, 62, and 64 Banbury Road', *Oxoniensia*, 1967, xxxii, pp. 53–9.

32 John Gibbs, *Designs for Gothic Ornaments and Furniture*, 1853; *English Gothic Architecture*, 1855.

33 Gibbs, *Designs*, pp. 5–6.

34 Goodhart-Rendel, 'North Oxford', p. 284.

35 *Jackson's Oxford Journal*, 13 October 1866.

36 *Census Enumerators' Returns*, 1871, RG 10 1439.

37 *Census*, 1871; *London Directory*, 1860.

38 A number of houses in North Oxford, especially those built during the first twenty years, were later enlarged. For example in 1874, Codd designed additions for Bonamy Price at 2 Norham Gardens and for Colonel the Hon. W.E. Sackville West at 14 Norham Gardens. See *The Oxford Chronicle*, 17 October 1874. Christina Colvin has attested to the fact that when the east side of 14 Norham Gardens was added, the entrance was moved from the side to the front of the house.

39 See Howard Colvin, *Unbuilt Oxford*, 1983, pp. 147–8, for Codd's dispute over Jackson's winning scheme for the Boys' High School in Oxford.

40 T.G. Jackson, *Modern Gothic Architecture*, 1873, p. 23.

41 Andrew Saint, *Richard Norman Shaw*, 1977, pp. 24–48.

42 Mark Girouard, *Sweetness and Light, the 'Queen Anne' Movement 1840–1900*, 1977, pp. 10–37.

43 J.J. Stevenson, *House Architecture*, 1880, i, p. 7.

44 SJC, *Bursar's Letters*, 7 July 1878.

45 Girouard, *Sweetness and Light*, pp. 114–16.

46 SJC, *Long Lease Ledger*, 1863–84.

47 *The Building News*, 1870, xvii, p. 93.

48 Wilkinson, *English Country Houses*, 2nd ed., 1875.

49 See *The Building News*, lii, p. 801; liii, p. 410; lv, p. 588, pp. 793–4; lvii, p. 493.

50 *The Oxford Chronicle*, 30 June 1883.

51 Sir John Summerson, *Architecture in Britain 1530 to 1830*, 1970, p. 155.

52 Alexander Robertson, *Atkinson Grimshaw*, 1988, pp. 97 and 99.

53 SJC, *College Leases*, Muniments V. For Edis see Shirley Neale, 'An Architect Presents Arms Col. Sir Robert Edis (1838–1927)', *Country Life*, 1985, pp. 1570–2.

54 R.W. Edis, *Decoration and Furniture of Town Houses*, 1881.

55 SJC, *College Leases*, Muniments V.

56 Peter Howell and Andrew Saint, *Notes on Victorian Architecture in Oxford*, MS in Local Studies Library, Oxford Central Library, 1970–6.

57 *Ibid.*

58 Library, Royal Institute of British Architects, *Biography File*.

59 Colvin, *Unbuilt Oxford*, p. 160.

60 Goodhart-Rendel, 'North Oxford', p. 284.

CHAPTER SIX

1 See Francis Thomas Mackreth, *Church Extension in Islington. A Letter*, 1856.

2 SJC, Muniments, VD. 4; MP 183.

3 Bodleian, MS Top. Oxon. a. 22.

4 SJC, *Register*, 12 October 1855.

5 Bodleian, MS Top. Oxon. d. 946.

6 SJC, *Register*, 2 April 1856.

7 *Ibid.*, 7 April 1858.

8 Bodleian, MS Top. Oxon. d. 946; MS Top. Oxon. a. 28.

9 *Ibid.*

10 *Ibid.*

11 A.E. Street, *Memoir of George Edmund Street, 1824–1881*, 1888 (Reissued 1972), p. 47.

12 Bodleian, MS Top. Oxon. d. 946.

13 *The Builder*, 1859, xvii, p. 749; *The Building News*, 1859, v, p. 1012.

14 *The Gentleman's Magazine*, January 1859, pp. 62–5; *The Building News*, 1858, iv, pp. 1291–2; 1859, v, p. 22; *The Builder*, 1859, xvii, pp. 5–6, 23–4, 45, 60–1.

15 *The Oxford Chronicle*, 26 November 1859.

16 Bodleian, MS Top. Oxon. a. 28.

17 *The Oxford Chronicle*, 5 November 1859.

18 Bodleian, MS Top. Oxon. a. 28.

19 *Ibid.*; *Jackson's Oxford Journal*, 12 May 1860.

20 Bodleian, MS Top. Oxon. a. 28.

21 Rev William Acworth, *The Acts of Uniformity*

Set at Nought in the Diocese of Oxford, 1866; see also Peter Maurice, *The Ritualism of Oxford Popery, a Letter to Dr Macbride*, 1869.

22 Margaret A. Crowther, *Church Embattled*, 1970, p. 21.

23 SJC, *Estates Committee*, 12 February 1874.

24 SJC, *Register*, 17 October 1879; *Estates Committee*, 27 June 1879.

25 SJC, *Bursar's Letters*, 23 November 1881.

26 SJC, *Estates Committee*, 12 May 1882.

27 SJC, *Bursar's Letters*, 21 July 1883.

28 SJC, *Muniments*, VD 11.

29 *Ibid.*

30 *Ibid.*

31 *Ibid.*

32 *Ibid.*

33 J.S. Reynolds, *The Evangelicals at Oxford 1735–1905*, 1975, p. 67.

34 SJC, *Register*, 26 April 1905.

35 A.I. Tillyard, *A History of University Reform*, 1913, pp. 170–5.

36 A. Crossley, C. Day, and J. Cooper, *Shopping in Oxford*, 1983, p. 22.

37 Maj O.C.C. Nicolls, *A Register of the Alumini of Keble College Oxford from 1870 to 1925*, 1927, p. 3.

38 SJC, *Estates Committee*, 24 November 1864.

39 *Ibid.*, 14 December 1865; for the foundation of Keble College see Geoffrey Rowell, '"Training in Simple and Religious Habits: Keble', in *History of the University of Oxford*, VII (forthcoming).

40 *Ibid.*, 19 April 1866.

41 *Ibid.*, 28 June 1866.

42 E.S. Talbot, *Memories of Early Life*, 1924, p. 53.

43 Nicolls, *Alumini of Keble College*, p. 5.

44 Paul Thompson, *William Butterfield*, 1971, p. 74.

45 Talbot, *Memories of Early Life*, p. 63.

46 *The Building News*, 1869, XVII, p. 284.

47 SJC, *Estates Committee*, 8 December 1864.

48 Grace Hargrave, *St Denys School Oxford, 1857–1957*, 1957, p. 3; *Census Enumerators' Returns*, 1841, HO 107 891.

49 SJC, *Estates Committee*, 8 December 1864.

50 *Ibid.*, 8 February 1866.

51 Andrew Saint and Michael Kaser, *St Anthony's College, Oxford*, 1973, p. 10. The convent was bought in 1954 by the University for St Anthony's College.

52 SJC, *Estates Committee*, 10 October 1872.

53 *Ibid.*

54 SJC, *Bursar's Letters*, 21 March 1873.

55 *Ibid.*, 28 April 1873, 3 February 1874.

56 *Ibid.*, 3 May 1873.

57 *Ibid.*, 11 December 1875.

58 *Ibid.*, 26 April 1876.

59 Thomas Jay Williams, *Priscilla Lydia Sellon*, 1965, p. 275.

60 SJC, *Estates Committee*, 8 December 1870.

61 SJC, *Bursar's Letters*, 9 December 1870.

62 James Bertram, *Letters of Thomas Arnold the Younger 1850–1900*, 1980, pp. 176–85.

63 Reynolds, *Evangelicals at Oxford*, p. 66.

64 SJC, *Bursar's Letters*, 9 November 1876.

65 *Ibid.*, 5 December 1876.

66 *Ibid.*, 14 December 1876.

67 SJC, *Register*, 14 October 1829.

68 SJC, *Estates Committee*, 20 April 1864.

69 SJC, *Bursar's Letters*, 23 October 1879.

70 *Ibid.*, 14 November 1879.

71 *Ibid.*, 18 May 1880.

72 SJC, *Leases and General Ledger*.

73 Girouard, *Sweetness and Light*, p. 70.

74 *The Building News*, 1883, XLIX, pp. 10, 20.

75 *Ibid.*, 1887, LIII, p. 410.

76 Elizabeth Wordsworth, *Glimpses of the Past*, 1913, p. 147.

77 *Ibid.*, pp. 147–8.

78 SJC, *Long Lease Ledger*.

79 SJC, *Bursar's Letters*, 31 July 1880.

80 *Ibid.*, 17 November 1880.

81 *Ibid.*, 12 November 1880.

82 SJC, *Estates Committee*, 18 March 1892.

83 *Ibid.*, 5 October 1932, 1 February 1933.

84 Annie M.A.H. Rogers, *Degrees by Degrees*, 1938, pp. 157–8.

CHAPTER SEVEN

1 A.J. Engel, *From Clergyman to Don*, 1983, p. 62.

2 Most of the streets in North Oxford were named for those parishes under the patronage of St John's.

3 Alan Ryan, 'Transformation 1850–1914', in John Buxton and Penry Williams eds., *New College Oxford, 1379–1979*, 1979, p. 79.

4 MacDermot, *Great Western Railway*, II, p. 16.

5 *Oxford Chronicle and Berks and Bucks Gazette*, 18 March 1865.

6 *Ibid.*, 20 May 1865.

7 *The Times*, 7 June 1865.

8 *Ibid.*, 8 June 1865.

9 MacDermot, *Great Western Railway*, II, p. 19.

10 Florence Mostyn Gamlen, *My Memoirs, 1856–1952*, N.D., p. 9.

11 E.M. Arnold, 'Social Life in Oxford', *Harper's Monthly Magazine*, July 1890, p. 248, quoted in VCH, *Oxon*, IV, p. 186.

12 *Jackson's Oxford Journal*, 16 February and 6 April 1861.

13 *Ibid.*, 24 May and 7 June 1862.

14 *The Builder*, 1853, XI, p. 500.

15 A.I. Tillyard, *A History of University Reform*, 1913, pp. 82ff.

16 SJC, *Appeal to the Visitor*, 1869, Muniments LII, 166.

17 34 Vict c 26.

18 40 and 41 Vict c 48.

19 SJC, *Correspondence between Omond and President Bellamy*, Muniments Files Box F No 217.

20 Louise Creighton, *Life and Letters of Mandel Creighton*, 1904, I, p. 84. In 1867 New College was the first college to allow fellows to marry without having to resign their fellowships. Hereford George of that college could lay claim to being the first married fellow in Oxford when he married in 1870.

See Buxton and Williams, *New College Oxford*, p. 245.
21 SJC, *Register*, 14 October 1880. Engel suggests the average range of fees for tutors and lecturers, including fellowships, was between £500 and £800, somewhat higher than at St John's.
22 *Ibid.*, 11 October 1905.
23 Harold Perkin, *Origins of Modern Society*, 1969, p. 420.
24 SJC, *Appeal to the Visitor*, 1887, Muniments LII, 173.
25 Georgina Max Muller ed., *The Life and Letters of the Right Honourable Friedrich Max Muller*, 1902, p. 335.
26 *Wills*, Principal Probate Registry, Somerset House.
27 Date of Dallin's marriage confirmed by the Archivist, Queens College, Oxford.
28 SJC, *Long Lease Ledger*, 1863–84.
29 *Ibid.*
30 Oona Howard Ball ed., *Sidney Ball, Memories and Impressions of 'an Ideal Don'*, 1923, p. 61.
31 *Ibid.*, p. 62.
32 *Census Enumerators' Returns*, 1861, RG 9 891–2.
33 *Census Enumerators' Returns*, 1871, RG 10 1439.
34 Undergraduates would not have been strictly regarded as part of University society, but neither did they belong to the town, and for the purpose of this analysis the very small number of undergraduate heads are classed along with members of the University.
35 *Census Returns*, 1871.
36 *Census Enumerators' Returns*, 1881, RG 11 1499.
37 See Chapter 2 above.
38 Creighton, *Life and Letters*, pp. 87–8.
39 See Harold Perkin, *The Rise of Professional Society, England since 1880*, 1989.
40 *The Oxford Chronicle*, 20 January 1883.
41 Creighton, *Life and Letters*, p. 78.
42 *Ibid.*, p. 128.
43 Mrs Humphrey Ward, *A Writer's Recollections*, 1918, p. 119.
44 Charles Oman, *Memoirs of a Victorian*, 1941, p. 137.
45 Ward, *A Writer's Recollections*.
46 Bertha J. Johnson, 'First Beginnings, 1873–90', *Lady Margaret Hall, a Short History*, 1923, p. 24.
47 *Ibid.*, p. 26.
48 Annie M.A.H. Rogers, *Degrees by Degrees*, 1938, p. 10.
49 Bertha J. Johnson, 'First Beginnings', p. 26.
50 VCH, *Oxon*, III, pp. 335–6.
51 *Ibid.*
52 Rogers, *Degrees by Degrees*, pp. 157–8.
53 *Jackson's Oxford Journal*, 16 October 1886.
54 SJC, *Long Lease Ledger*, 1863–1884. The chapel has since been demolished.
55 SJC, *Bursar's Incoming Letters*, 16 April 1886.
56 *Ibid.*, 19 April 1896.
57 Bodleian, *Lodging House Delegacy Papers*, LHD.
58 Bodleian, LHD/D/1.
59 Bodleian, LHD/RP/8/1–12.
60 Bodleian, LHD/SF/9/2; LHD/SF/9/24.
61 Max Muller, *Life and Letters*, p. 335.
62 *Census Returns*, 1871.
63 SJC, *Estates Committee*, 29 February 1884; 20 April 1894.
64 For 14 Norham Gardens see *The Oxford Chronicle*, 17 October 1874 and *Jackson's Oxford Journal*, 16 October 1875; Plan of Myres' extension, SJC, *Norham Gardens*, Muniments V.
65 K.M. Elizabeth Murray, *Caught in the Web of Words*, 1978, p. 244.
66 SJC, *Bursar's Letters*, 13 January 1885.
67 Murray, *Web of Words*, p. 244.
68 Harvey Cushing, *The Life of Sir William Osler*, 1925, II, p. 3.
69 SJC, *North Oxford Architectural Estate Drawings*, Muniments.
70 Peter Maurice, *The Ritualism of Oxford Popery, a Letter to Dr Macbride*, 1869, p. 150.
71 SJC, *Bursar's Incoming Letters*, October 1879.
72 Margaret Fletcher, *O, Call Back Yesterday*, 1939, pp. 45–6.
73 See C.H. Jacques, *A Dragon Century, 1877–1977*, 1977.
74 SJC, *Bursar's Incoming Letters*, 5 December 1894.
75 SJC, *Long Leases*, 1893; Louisa K. Haldane, *Friends and Kindred; Memoirs of Louisa Kathleen Haldane*, 1961, p. 168; Carola Oman, *An Oxford Childhood*, 1976, p. 92.
76 SJC, *Estates Committee*, 4 December 1909.
77 *Ibid.*, 1 February 1907.
78 William W. Craik, *The Central Labour College, 1909–29*, 1964, p.80.
79 SJC, *Bradmore Road*, Muniments V.
80 *Ibid.*
81 SJC, *Bursar's Letters*, 2 October 1909.
82 SJC, *Estates Committee*, 2 June 1911.
83 Christopher and Edward Hibbert eds., *The Encyclopaedia of Oxford*, 1988, p. 101.
84 Engel, *Clergyman to Don*, pp. 212–13.

CHAPTER EIGHT

1 SJC, *Estates Committee*, 18 June 1922.
2 *Ibid.*, 15 June 1923.
3 *Ibid.*, 10 February; 5 and 19 October 1932.
4 E.R. Barrow, RIBA Biography File.
5 SJC, *Estates Committee*, 19 January 1937.
6 Ministry of Health, *Interim Report of the Committee Appointed by the Minister of Health to Consider and Advise on the Principles to be Followed in Dealing with Unhealthy Areas*, 1920.
7 John Henry Newman, *Historical Sketches*, 1891, III, pp. 24–5.
8 Rev A.C. Headlam, 'Oxford', *The Burlington Magazine*, 1913–14, XXIV, p. 53.
9 It will be remembered that Oxford was described as 'Always a century behind other towns' in 1837 when the town was resisting the establishment of a railway terminal. See VCH, *Oxon*, IV, p. 186.
10 Thomas Sharp, *Oxford Replanned*, 1948, p. 53.
11 SJC, *Register*, 26 June 1938.

12 *The Building News*, 30 October 1925, p. 445.
13 Oxford City Council, *Reports*, 12 January 1925.
14 *The Builder*, 7 July 1936, CLI, p. 104.
15 T. Lawrence Dale, *Towards a Plan for Oxford City*, 1944, p. 20.
16 Sharp, *Oxford Replanned*, pp. 113–20.
17 Oxford City Council, *Redevelopment Plan*, 1955.
18 *Oxford Times*, Supplement, 30 November 1960.
19 *Official Architect*, 1969, XXXII, pp. 1389–93.
20 Goodhart-Rendel, 'North Oxford', pp. 254–5, 284–6, 316–17.
21 Dale, *Towards a Plan for Oxford*, pp. 20–1.
22 *Ibid.*, p. 21.
23 Sharp, *Oxford Replanned*, p. 176.
24 SJC, *Long Wittenham*, Muniments XII, 38.
25 SJC, *Estates Committee*, 28 January 1948.
26 *The Builder*, 1849, VII, 500; Dale, *Towards a Plan for Oxford*, p. 18.
27 SJC, *Estates Committee*, 16 April 1951.
28 *Ibid.*, 8 February 1950.
29 *Ibid.*
30 SJC, *Governing Body*, Muniments Box A, File 25a, 1953.
31 'Tagg's Gardens' was the name used to designate this area during the middle years of the nineteenth century and had long since dropped out of use by the 1950s. On the other hand the name 'Walton Manor' had referred to the area of Woodstock Road north of Tagg's Gardens when Seckham was undertaking the College's first attempts at development in the 1850s.
32 SJC, *Estates Committee*, 30 September 1954.
33 SJC, *Finance Committee*, 21 October 1959, Muniments Box A, File 26c.
34 SJC, *Estates Committee Memoranda*, 9 January 1960.
35 *Ibid.*
36 *Ibid.*, 22 November 1960.
37 SJC, *Finance Committee Minutes*, 1 December 1961.
38 SJC, *Estates Committee Memoranda*, 17 February 1961.
39 *Ibid.*, 20 November 1961.
40 *Ibid.*
41 *Ibid.*, 14 March 1962.
42 SJC, *Estates Committee*, 9 October 1962.
43 *Ibid.*, 6 May 1964.
44 Oxford City Council, Estates Committee, *Reports* 1960–1, 7 February 1961, 1217.
45 *Ibid.*, 1966, 300.
46 SJC, *Estates Committee*, 17 April 1962.
47 *Ibid.*, 4 October 1960.
48 Written communication from R.W.F. Barnes, Messrs Cluttons.
49 *Leasehold Reform Act*, 15–16 Eliz II c 88, 1967.
50 Michael O'Halloran, 'Leasehold Reform', *The Financial Times*, 16 December 1967.
51 SJC, Muniments Admin XVI/IV/I, 16 March 1966.
52 *Ibid.*
53 *The Times*, 3 January 1967.
54 SJC, *Governing Body*, Muniments, Box A, File 25n, 27 May 1966.
55 University of Oxford, Report of Commission of Inquiry, 1966, I, paras 112, 113, 303; SJC, *Register*, 5 June 1966.
56 Written communication from Harry Kidd, former bursar St John's College 1967–77.
57 SJC, Muniments, Admin XVI/IV/I, 28 December 1967.
58 SJC, Muniments, 1300.
59 *Ibid.*
60 In conversation with R.D. Hill.
61 SJC, *Register*, 7 October 1969; *Estates Committee*, 15 January 1971 and 13 June 1973.
62 SJC, *Register*, 31 January 1913.
63 SJC, *Estates Committee*, 7 February; 30 May 1934.
64 *The Builder*, 5 July 1957, CXCIII, p. 9.
65 SJC, *Governing Body*, 1 February 1966, Muniments, Box A, File 25n.
66 Oxford City Council, Planning Committee, *Reports*, 22 March 1966.
67 *Architects' Journal*, 27 March 1968, CXLVII, p. 642.
68 Colvin, *Unbuilt Oxford*, p. 187.
69 Oxford City Council, Planning Committee, *Reports*, 1966.
70 N. Pevsner, *Oxford, The Buildings of England*, 1974, p. 271.
71 *The Times*, 26 July 1966.
72 Summerson, 'The London Suburban Villa', pp. 63–74.
73 John Betjeman, *An Oxford University Chest*, 1938, pp. 161–2; see also *First and Last Loves*, 1952.
74 Oxford City Council, Planning Committee, *Reports*, 9 April 1968.
75 Oxford City Architect, *City of Oxford Conservation Areas*, 1975.

CONCLUSION

1 Cannadine, *Lords and Landlords*.
2 Donald Olsen, *Town Planning in London*, 1982, p. xx.
3 Barbara Baird, 'The Web of Economic Activities in Oxford', *Ekistics*, No 274, 1979, p. 42.
4 Goodhart-Rendel, 'North Oxford', pp. 284–5.
5 Oxford City Architect, *City of Oxford Conservation Areas*, 1968, 1974, 1975.
6 Peter Snow, 'Here Be Dragons', *Oxford Magazine*, No 23, 1987, p. 8.

GAZETTEER

1 Between 11 and 19 was William Shelton's carpet cleaning factory.
2 31 Banbury Road was not one of St John's houses, but it was one of the Oxford houses that William Wilkinson included in *English Country Houses*.
3 A house and shop had been built for John Gee at 61A Banbury Road by John C. Gray in 1882.
4 Between 61A and 81 Banbury Road is North

Parade, already developed by Richard Carr during the 1830s and 40s.

5   Between 66A and 72 Banbury Road was the Banbury Road end of Park Town.

6   Between 122 and 160 Banbury Road is the site of Cunliffe Close and Greycotes School.

7   1 to 31 Museum Road were built as Museum Terrace by Lincoln College on land owned by them.

8   2 to 8 Walton Well Road formed part of small-scale development related to shops in Kingston Road.

9   Between 10 and 21 is the west end of North Parade.

10   The property between 40 and 48 was owned by University College.

11   The property between 50 and 56 was owned by Lincoln College.

SELECTED BIBLIOGRAPHY

St John's College Oxford Muniments

Building Agreements
Building Proposals
Bursar's Incoming Letters
Bursar's Letters
College Leases
Computus Annuus
Estates Committee Memoranda
Estates Committee Minutes
Finance Committee Minutes
Governing Body Minutes
Lease Books and General Ledgers
Long Leases Ledgers
College Register
St Giles's Allotment Award

Bodleian Library

Galpin, Sydney, *The Oxford Branch of Galpins*, Top oxon d. 473.
Lodging House Delegacy Papers, LHD.
Minn, Henry, *North Oxford*, MS Top oxon d. 501.
Notes on Oxford Market, MS Top oxon e. 620.
Oxford Building and Investment Company, G.A. oxon c. 152.
Oxford Canal Navigation, MS Top oxon c. 752–3.
Park Town, MS Dep b. 217.
St Philip and St James, MS Top oxon a. 28.

Local Studies Library, Oxford Central Library

Howell, Peter and Andrew Saint, *Notes on Victorian Architecture in Oxford*, MS, 1970–6.
Oxford City Engineer's Office, *Register of Plans Deposited*, 1876–
Oxford Directories

Oxford Country Record Office
London and Midwestern Railway, PD 2 57.

Official Publications

Census Enumerators' Returns, 1841 HO 107 891; 1861 RG 9 891–2; 1871 RG 10 1439; 1881 RG 11 1499.
Ministry of Health, *Interim Report of the Committee Appointed by the Minister of Health to Consider and Advise on the Principles to be Followed in Dealing with Unhealthy Areas*, 1920.
Report of the Commissioners appointed to inquire into the property and income of the Universities of Oxford and Cambridge and of College Halls therein, 3 vols, 1874.

Journals

Architects' Journal
The Builder
Building News
The City Press
The Ecclesiologist
Jackson's Oxford Journal
Official Architect
Oxford Chronicle and Berks and Bucks Gazette
The Oxford Times
The Times

General Bibliography

Acworth, Rev William, *The Acts of Uniformity Set at Nought in the Diocese of Oxford*, Oxford, 1866.

Arnold, E.M., 'Social Life in Oxford', *Harper's Monthly Magazine*, July 1890, p. 248.

Arnold, Thomas, *Passages in a Wandering Life*, London, 1900.

Bailey, Gemma ed., *Lady Margaret Hall, A Short History*, London, 1923.

Baird Barbara, 'The Web of Economic Activities in Oxford', *Ekistics*, 274, 1979, pp. 36–44.

Ball, Oona Howard ed., *Sidney Ball, Memories and Impressions of 'an Ideal Don'*, Oxford, 1923.

Batey, Mavis, 'First of the Garden Suburbs', *Country Life*, 20 March 1980, pp. 888–9.

Battiscombe, G., *Reluctant Pioneer, The Life of Elizabeth Wordsworth*, London, 1978.

Bax, Anthony, *The English Parsonage*, London, 1964.

Bermingham, Ann, *Landscape and Ideology the English Rustic Tradition 1740–1860*, London, 1987.

Bertram, James, *Letters of Thomas Arnold the Younger 1850–1900*, Auckland, 1980.

Betjeman, John, *An Oxford University Chest*, London, 1938.

Betjeman, John, *First and Last Loves*, London, 1952.

Brooke, Christopher and Roger Highfield, *Oxford and Cambridge*, Cambridge, 1988.

Burrows, Stephen Montagu ed., *Autobiography of Montagu Burrows*, London, 1908.

Butler, C.V., *Social Conditions in Oxford*, London, 1912.

Cannadine, David, *Lords and Landlords: the Aristocracy and the Towns*, Leicester, 1980.

Catto, J.I. ed., *The Early Oxford Schools*, Oxford, 1984, vol 1 of *The History of the University of Oxford*, T.H. Aston, general editor.

Chadwick, George, *The Park and the Town*, London, 1966.

Chadwick, Owen, *The Victorian Church*, 2 vols, London, 1972.

Chalklin, C.W., *The Provincial Towns of Georgian England, A Study of the Building Process 1740–1820*, London, 1974.

Clode, C.M., *The Early History of the Guild of Merchant Taylors of the Fraternity of St John the Baptist*, 2 vols, London, 1888.

Colvin, Howard, *Unbuilt Oxford*, London, 1983.

Colvin, Howard, *The Canterbury Quadrangle*, Oxford, 1988.

Costin, W.C., *The History of St John's College Oxford 1598–1860*, Oxford, 1958.

Craik, William W., *The Central Labour College, 1909–29*, London, 1964.

Creighton, Louise, *Life and Letters of Mandell Creighton*, 2 vols, London, 1904.

Crossley, Alan, Chris Day and Janet Cooper, *Shopping in Oxford*, Oxford, 1983.

Crowther, Margaret A., *Church Embattled*, Newton Abbot, 1970.

Cushing, Harvey, *The Life of Sir William Osler*, 2 vols., Oxford, 1925.

Dale, T. Lawrence, *Towards a Plan for Oxford City*, London, 1944.

Davidoff, Leonore and Catherine Hall, *Family Fortunes: Men and Women of the English Middle Class 1780–1850*, London, 1987.

Dennis, Richard, *English Industrial Cities of the Nineteenth Century*, Cambridge, 1984.

Dick, Marcus and A.F. Kersting, *Portrait of Oxford*, London, 1956.

Dixon, Roger and Stefan Muthesius, *Victorian Architecture*, London, 1978.

Dodgson, E.O., 'Notes on Nos 56, 58, 60, 62, and 64 Banbury Road', *Oxoniensia*, 1967, XXXII, pp. 53–9.

Dunbabin, J.P.D., 'College Estates and Wealth 1660–1815' in L.S. Sutherland and L.G. Mitchell eds., *The Eighteenth Century*, 1986, vol v of *The History of the University of Oxford*, T.H. Aston general editor.

Dunbabin, J.P.D., 'Oxford and Cambridge College Finances, 1871–1913', *Economic History Review*, 2nd Series, 1975, XXVIII, pp. 631–47; 1978, XXXI, pp. 446–9.

Dyos, H.J., *Victorian Suburb. A Study of the Growth of Camberwell*, Leicester, 1961.

Edis, R.W., *Decoration and Furniture of Town Houses*, London, 1881.

Engel, A.J., 'Oxford College Finances, 1871–1913: a Comment', *Economic History Review*, 1978, 2nd Series, XXXI, pp. 437–5.

Engel, A.J., *From Clergyman to Don*, Oxford, 1983.

Fasnacht, Ruth, *Summertown Since 1820*, Oxford, 1977.

Fenby, C., *The Other Oxford*, London, 1970.

Fletcher, Margaret, *O, Call Back Yesterday*, Oxford, 1939.

Gamlen, Florence Mostyn, *My Memoirs, 1856–1952*, Oxford, 1952.

Gibbs, John, *Designs for Gothic Ornaments and Furniture*, London, 1853.

Gibbs, John, *English Gothic Architecture*, Manchester, London, 1855.

Gibbs, John, *The Old Parish Church: with the Ghost of the Merton Hall*, London, Oxford, 1861.

Gifford, Margaret Jeune ed., *Pages from the Diary of an Oxford Lady 1843–1862*, Oxford, 1932.

Girouard, Mark, *Sweetness and Light, the 'Queen Anne' Movement 1860–1900*, Oxford, 1977.

Goodhart-Rendel, H.S., 'North Oxford', *Architect and Building News*, 1936, CXLV, pp. 254–5; 284–6; 316–17.

Gordon, Barry, *Political Economy in Parliament 1819–1823*, London, 1976.

Graham, Malcolm, *The Suburbs of Victorian Oxford*, unpublished Phd thesis, University of Leicester, 1985.

Griffin, P., *St Hugh's: One Hundred Years of Women's Education in Oxford*, Basingstoke, 1986.

Haldane, Louisa K., *Friends and Kindred; Memoirs of Louisa Kathleen Haldane*, London, 1961.

Hargrave, Grace, *St Denys School Oxford, 1857–1957*, Oxford, 1957.

Hart, E.P. ed., *Merchant Taylors' School Register, 1851–1920*, London, 1923.

Harvey, A.D., *Britain in the Early Nineteenth Century*, London, 1978.

Headlam, Rev A.C., 'Oxford', *The Burlington Magazine*, 1913–14, XXIV, pp. 52–3.

Hibbert, Christopher and Edward eds., *The Encyclopaedia of Oxford*, London, 1988.

Hill, Christopher, *Economic Problems of the Church*, Oxford, 1956.

Hinchcliffe, T.F.M., 'Highbury New Park: a Nineteenth-Century Middle-Class Suburb', *The London Journal*, 1981, VII, no 1, pp. 29–44.

Hinton, David A., 'An Early Garden Suburb', *Country Life*, 26 September 1974, pp. 844–6.

Holcombe, Lee, 'Victorian Wives and Property: Reform of the Married Women's Property Law, 1857–1882', in Martha Vicinus ed., *A Widening Sphere*, London, 1977, pp. 3–28.

Holcombe, Lee, *Wives and Property: Reform of the Married Women's Property Law in Nineteenth-Century England*, Oxford, 1983.

Horn, Pamela, *The Rise and Fall of the Victorian Servant*, Dublin, 1975.

Howell, Peter, 'Samuel Lipscomb Seckham', *Oxoniensia*, 1976, XLI, pp. 337–47.

Jackson, T.G., *Modern Gothic Architecture*, London, 1873.

Jacques, C.H., *A Dragon Century, 1877–1977*, Oxford, 1977.

Johnson, James H. and Colin G. Pooley, *The Structure of Nineteenth Century Cities*, London, 1982.

Jones, Enid Huws, *Mrs Humphrey Ward*, London, 1973.

Jordan, W.K., *The Charities of London. The Aspirations and the Achievements of the Urban Society*, London, 1960.

Kellett, J.R., *The Impact of Railways on Victorian Cities*, London, 1969.

Kerr, Robert, *The Gentleman's House or How to Plan English Residences, from the Parsonage to the Palace*, London, 1864.

King, Georgiana Goddard, *George Edmund Street Unpublished Notes and Reprinted Papers*, New York, 1916.

Loudon, J.C., *An Encyclopaedia of Cottage, Farm and Villa Architecture and Furniture*, New Edition, London, 1836.

MacDermot, E.T., *History of the Great Western Railway*, 2 vols, Revised, London, 1964.

Mathias, Peter, *The First Industrial Nation*, London, 1983.

Maurice, Peter, *The Ritualism of Oxford Popery, a Letter to Dr Macbride*, London, 1868.

Mitford, Mary Russell, *Our Village, Sketches of Rural Character and Scenery*, 3 vols, London, 1824–32.

Morris, R.J., 'The Friars and Paradise: An Essay in the Building History of Oxford 1801–1861', *Oxoniensia*, 1971, xxxvi, pp. 72–98.

Morris, R.J., 'The Middle Class and the Industrial Revolution', Derek Fraser and Anthony Sutcliffe eds., *The Pursuit of Urban History*, London, 1983.

Morris, R.J., 'The Middle Class and the Property Cycle during the Industrial Revolution', T.C. Smout ed., *The Search for Wealth and Stability*: *Essays in Economic and Social History Presented to M.W. Flinn*, London, 1979.

Morris, R.J., 'Voluntary Societies and British Urban Elites, 1780–1850: An Analysis', *The Historical Journal*, 1983, xxvi, 1, pp. 95–118.

A.L. Morton ed., *Political Writings of William Morris*, London, 1979.

Muller, Georgina Max ed., *The Life and Letters of the Right Honourable Friedrich Max Muller*, 2 vols, London, 1902.

Murray, K.M. Elizabeth, *Caught in the Web of Words, James A.H. Murray and the Oxford English Dictionary*, New Haven, London, 1978.

Musgrove, Frank, 'Middle-Class Education and Employment in the Nineteenth Century', *Economic History Review*, 1959–1960, 2nd Series, xii, pp. 99–111.

Musgrove, Frank, *The Migratory Elite*, London, 1963.

Muthesius, Stefan, *The English Terraced House*, New Haven, London, 1982.

Muthesius, Stefan, *The High Victorian Movement in Architecture 1850–1870*, London, Boston, 1972.

Nettleship, R.L., *Memoirs of Thomas Hill Green*, London, 1906.

Newman, John Henry, 'Rise and Progress of Universities', *Historical Sketches*, iii, London, 1891.

Nicolls, Maj O.C.C., *A Register of the Alumni of Keble College Oxford from 1870 to 1925*, Oxford, 1927.

Offer, Avner, *Property and Politics 1870–1914*, Cambridge, 1981.

Olsen, Donald J., *The Growth of Victorian London*, London, 1976.

Olsen, Donald J., *Town Planning in London*, New Haven, London, 1964, 1982.

Oman, Carola, *An Oxford Childhood*, London, 1976.

Oman, Charles, *Memories of Victorian Oxford*, London, 1941.

Osmond, Anson, 'Building on the Beaumonts: An Example of Early 19th-Century Housing Development', *Oxoniensa*, 1984, xlix, pp. 301–25.

Oxford City Architect, *City of Oxford Conservation Areas*, 1968, 1974, 1975.

Oxford City Council, *Redevelopment Plan*, Oxford, 1955.

Oxford City Council, *Reports*.

Parker, J.H., *Introduction to the Study of Gothic Architecture*, Oxford, London, 1849.

Perkin, Harold, *Origins of Modern English Society*, London, 1969.

Perkin, Harold, *The Rise of Professional Society, England since 1880*, London, 1989.

Pevsner, Nikolaus and Jennifer Sherwood, *Oxfordshire, the Buildings of England*, Harmondsworth, 1974.

Pollins, Harold, *The History of Ruskin College*, Oxford, 1984.

Poulton, Edward Bagnall, *The Life of Ronald Poulton*, London, 1919.

Rait, Robert S. ed., *Memorials of Albert Venn Dicey*, London, 1925.

Reynolds, J.S., *The Evangelicals at Oxford 1735–1905*, Oxford, 1975.

Rodger, Richard, 'Rents and Ground Rents', James H. Johnson and Colin G. Pooley eds., *The*

Structure of Nineteenth Century Cities, London, 1982.

Rogers, Annie M.A.H., *Degrees by Degrees*, London, 1938.

Ryan, Alan, 'Transformation 1850–1914', in John Buxton and Penry Williams eds., *New College Oxford, 1379–1979*, Oxford, 1970.

Saint, Andrew, *Richard Norman Shaw*, New Haven, London, 1976.

Saint, Andrew and Michael Kaser, *St Anthony's College, Oxford*, Oxford, 1973.

Saint, Andrew, 'Three Oxford Architects', *Oxoniensia*, 1970, xxxv, pp. 53–102.

Salter, H.E. ed., *A Cartulary of the Hospital of St John the Baptist*, iii, Oxford, 1917, vol 69 of *Oxford Historical Society Publications*.

Scott, George Gilbert, *Remarks on Secular and Domestic Architecture*, London, 1857.

Sharp, Thomas, *Oxford Replanned*, London, 1948.

Simpson, M.A. and T.H. Lloyd eds., *Middle Class Housing in Britain*, Newton Abbot, 1977.

Smith, Goldwin, Arnold Haultain ed., *Reminiscences*, New York, 1910.

Snow, Peter, 'Here Be Dragons', *Oxford Magazine*, No 23, 1987, pp. 5–9.

Stevenson, J.J., *House Architecture*, 2 vols, London, 1880.

Stevenson, W.H. and H.E. Slater, *The Early History of St John's College, Oxford*, Oxford, 1939.

Stilgoe, John R., *Borderland: Origins of the American Suburb, 1820–1939*, New Haven, London, 1988.

Street, A.E., *Memoir of George Edmund Street, 1824–1881*, London, 1888 (Reissued 1972).

Summerson, Sir John, *Georgian London*, revised edition, Harmondsworth, 1969.

Summerson, Sir John, 'The Beginnings of Regents Park', *Architectural History*, 1977, xx, pp. 56–62.

Summerson, Sir John, 'The London Suburban villas', *The Architectural Review*, 1948, civ, pp. 63–74.

Sutherland, John, *Mrs Humphry Ward, Eminent Victorian, Pre-Eminent Edwardian*, Oxford, 1990.

Talbot, E.S., *Memories of Early Life*, London, 1924.

Thompson, F.M.L., *English Landed Society in the Nineteenth Century*, London, 1963.

Thompson, F.M.L., *Hampstead, Building a Borough, 1650–1964*, London, 1974.

Thompson, F.M.L. ed., *The Rise of Suburbia*, Leicester, 1982.

Thompson, Paul, *William Butterfield*, London, 1971.

Tillyard, A.I., *A History of University Reform from 1800 A.D. to the Present Time*, Cambridge, 1913.

University of Oxford, *Report of Commission of Enquiry*, 2 vols, Oxford, 1966.

Vicinus, Martha, *Independent Women*, London, 1985.

Victoria County History, *Oxfordshire*, vols iii and iv, London, Oxford, 1954, 1979.

Viollet-le-Duc, E., *Habitations Modernes*, 2 vols, Paris, 1874, 1875.

Ward, Mary Humphry, *A Writer's Recollections*, London, 1918.

Ward, W.R., *Victorian Oxford*, London, 1965.

Wilkinson, William, *English Country Houses*, London, Oxford, 1870, 1875.

Williams, Thomas Jay, *Priscilla Lydia Sellon*, London, 1965.

Wolff, Janet and John Seed eds., *The Culture of Capital: Art, Power, and the Nineteenth Century Middle Class*, Manchester, 1988.

Wordsworth, Elizabeth, *Glimpses of the Past*, New Edition, London, 1913.

Wright, Gwendolyn, *Building the Dream: a Social History of Housing in America*, New York, 1981.

INDEX